OFF THE CLIFF

ALSO BY BECKY AIKMAN

Saturday Night Widows

OFF THE CLIFF

HOW THE MAKING OF
THELMA & LOUISE
DROVE HOLLYWOOD
TO THE EDGE

Becky Aikman

PENGUIN PRESS
New York
2017

PENGUIN PRESS
An imprint of Penguin Random House LLC
375 Hudson Street
New York, New York 10014
penguin.com

Photograph credits:
Insert page 1 (top), 6 (top and middle), 7 (top right), 11 (top): From the MGM/UA photographs of the
Margaret Herrick Library, Academy of Motion Picture Arts and Sciences. Courtesy of MGM Media
Licensing. "Thelma & Louise" © 1991 Metro-Goldwyn-Mayer Studios Inc. All rights reserved.
1 (bottom left): Image from the Jim McGuire collection, courtesy of the Grand Ole Opry LLC
archives. For image licensing requests, contact opryphotos@opry.com.
1 (bottom right): Courtesy of Amanda Temple
2 (top): Photograph by Larry Bessel. Copyright © 1990 Los Angeles Times. Reprinted with permission.
2 (bottom left), 15 (bottom): Ron Galella / Ron Galella Collection / Getty Images
2 (bottom right): Courtesy of the photographer, Lauri Gaffin
3 (top left): TM & Copyright © 20th Century Fox Film Corp. All rights reserved. Courtesy Everett Collection.
3 (top right): Courtesy Everett Collection
3 (bottom): Courtesy of mptvimages.com
4, 5 (top and bottom), 8 (top), 9, 10, 11 (bottom), 13 (bottom), 14: Photo by Roland Neveu / mptvimages.com
6 (bottom), 16: © MGM / Courtesy Everett Collection
7 (top left, bottom): Courtesy of MGM Media Licensing. "Thelma & Louise" © 1991
Metro-Goldwyn-Mayer Studios Inc. All rights reserved.
9 (top): Mary Evans / Ronald Grant / Everett Collection. Courtesy Everett Collection.
12 (top and bottom): Courtesy of Ridley Scott
13 (top): Courtesy of Anne H. Ahrens
15 (top): Jean-Claude Deutsch / Jacques Lange / Paris Match Archive / Getty Images

ISBN 9781594206719 (Hardcover)
ISBN 9780698405639 (eBook)

Printed in the United States of America
1   3   5   7   9   10   8   6   4   2

DESIGNED BY MEIGHAN CAVANAUGH

For my mother,

Barbara Aikman

CONTENTS

OFF THE CLIFF

PROLOGUE

BEVERLY HILLS, JULY 24, 1989

The lights along the side of Diane Cairns's phone lit up, every last one of them, and it wasn't even nine o'clock on Monday morning. This was how any Hollywood story had to begin. For the characters to be made flesh, the flesh made celluloid, for the audience ultimately to embrace or detest them, a fast-rising young agent like Cairns, lunging in the first hour of the day to get her hands on the oversize console phone on her desk, had to see those lights.

Lights. Action. It was all on her to make the deal.

The screenplay she had hustled out to studios on Friday was so audacious, such a departure from anything else in the movies at the time—or at any time, for that matter—that it was anybody's guess what could happen when the studio executives plucked it from their stacks of weekend reading. Most likely? The script would blow past the couple dozen rejections it had racked up from studios, producers and other agents before Diane took it on.

After all, this was Hollywood in the 1980s. On its merits, Diane knew, the screenplay should have triggered one of those bidding wars that fueled the industry scuttlebutt over lunches at Le Dome. The writing was sharp, whipsawing from humor to deep-seated longing. The characters were complicated, vulnerable and flawed, careening through the sorts of hair-pin emotional turns that could win awards for the players who snagged the roles. The plot hurtled along from one brazen surprise to the next, yet it was simple, too: two outlaws lam it in a hot convertible after shooting a would-be rapist. The story fit safely within the cinema template of broken taboos, antiheroes and screw-the-system attitudes that Hollywood had championed since the breakup of the old-time studios.

But there was a catch, as they say in the movies, and it was a sticky one. The outlaws behind the wheel of that convertible were named Thelma and Louise, both of them women, recognizably ordinary as the story began. Yet along the way they drove fast, drank hard, picked up a one-night stand and shed their conformist skins to embrace intoxicating freedom against the landscape of the American West. With the law closing in, they realized they couldn't go back—*Something's crossed over in me*, one said—and rather than submit to convention, they chose a shocking fate, certain to polarize the audience. . . . But that's getting ahead of the story.

Thelma and Louise—the characters—didn't seem to realize at first what trouble they'd stumbled into, and maybe the filmmakers who hoped to bring them to life didn't fully grasp it, either. The woman who wrote the screenplay, Callie Khouri, had tapped out this first and only effort late at night after her soul-crushing, behind-the-scenes job making music videos. She was so green that she surely had no idea that out of the top-fifty movies at the box office the year before, only two had been written by women without male partners; that in the previous five years, only thirteen had been, and that no such woman had won an Oscar for an original screenplay since 1932.

Ridley Scott, an acclaimed director who still had something to prove at the box office, had decided he wouldn't feel comfortable directing such a women's story, but he had signed on to produce. Perhaps because he was a Brit, perhaps because he just didn't care, he seemed oblivious to the conventional wisdom that women protagonists ranked well below talking babies and pockmarked psycho killers in the hierarchy of the industry. Only seven of the top-fifty movies the year before showcased a woman as the main character, only five a year, on average, over the previous five years. And how many starred a couple of women together? Get ready for it: less than two a year.

When Diane first devoured the script during her own weekend reading, she had cycled through a menu of emotions. She identified with the characters, regular gals who spoke and behaved the way women really do when they are alone. She got a charge out of the way they reveled in rebellion once they broke the bounds of accepted behavior. As an agent, she wasn't necessarily supposed to think this way, but the story stirred up her juices, got under her skin, not so much as a viable Hollywood property, but—dare she say it?—as a labor of love.

Holy mackerel, Diane thought as she turned the final page, *it's one of the best screenplays I've ever read.*

But then Agent Brain kicked in and spit out a single word: *impossible.* The whole thing was such a departure from the norm, she didn't think it could ever get made. The only hope was to lure a couple of major actresses, then package them with this otherwise shaky venture. Luckily, Michelle Pfeiffer and Jodie Foster jumped on board without hesitation. The two exercised as much muscle as any female stars in the brawny era of Arnold Schwarzenegger, Sylvester Stallone and Tom Cruise, and with those two attached to the project, Diane knew that the bundles she sent out to studios that Friday would land with a red alert.

Some major studios had already passed—"I don't get it," one executive had said to Ridley Scott. "It's two bitches in a car." Now the strategy was to blitz the others all at once. This story was going to live or die off whatever happened that Monday.

BY ALL APPEARANCES, Diane had the town just where she wanted it when she hit the office, a boxy space that overlooked a nondescript stretch of Beverly Boulevard in a wing of the industry powerhouse ICM. An assistant, Bonnie Blackburn Hart, greeted Diane with a buzz of expectation. "The phone is ringing off the hook."

Diane took up her position behind the red industrial desk, snapped a headphone over her full head of blond eighties hair and squared her padded shoulders. Ready. Bonnie prepared to play blocking guard with a second phone on the credenza.

Universal, Fox 2000, Disney, Hollywood Pictures—the row of lights blinked like marquees on the Vegas Strip. This was the kind of breakout moment that made careers, when some crafty, or merely lucky, agent sat on the property of the moment, the one that made everyone want to claim, "I snagged it first." Bonnie fed the calls to Diane, and she picked them off one by one.

"You have a great movie here." Ah, the first caller was warm and positive, just as Diane had hoped. She fought to hold her adrenaline in check while Bonnie kept the others circling the landing strip. "I see what you see in it."

Uh . . . huh. Was there something *off* in the tone? "I knew you would," Diane said brightly. Perhaps too brightly.

A too-long pause. Then: "Female leads . . . Ridley's not directing the movie . . . that ending . . . a worthy submission . . ." Yes? Yes? Diane knew all this. "But we're going to pass."

Pass? Diane was flattened. No choice but to shake it off. Next call, and then the next: "We certainly talked about it at the morning meeting . . .

why won't Ridley direct?... female leads... risky... too risky... *way* too risky... they do *what* at the end? It's just not really for us."

No. No. No. No. She was horrified, *horrified*. Diane viewed her job on days like this as catching a tidal wave and finding a way to guide the surfboard to the beach. Now a real monster was cresting over her head and the board was spinning, spinning, losing any connection to gravity or reality in a sickening churn. She foresaw a terrible end to this morning, to this pipe dream—she, helpless under a crushing wave, and Michelle Pfeiffer and Jodie Foster and Ridley Scott and Callie Khouri and ICM and the beautiful script body-slammed into the pilings of a jetty, an unseemly pileup of talent, glamour and misdirected clout. Wipeout.

Diane considered plunging back in, fighting gravity and the tides, but the answers were definitive. If she begged reluctant studios to reconsider, she knew, something would be lost. They would bring in another writer to mangle the script, the dicey ending would give way to sunsets and butterflies, or dudes like Richard Gere or Mel Gibson would get roped in to rescue the ladies. Word was that Warner Bros. was interested but might want to alter the ending, and Diane's client, beginner that she was, wasn't willing to compromise. Only later did Diane consider: "If it was the male equivalent, with Richard Gere and Mel Gibson as the leads, would I have gotten all those passes? Every studio would have said yes."

Her boss, Jeff Berg, was on the line. Not only was he chairman of ICM, he was also Ridley Scott's personal agent, and he had been tasked with contacting perhaps the best hope, Orion Pictures. Orion was a rare studio, a tasteful studio, up for greenlighting smart adult fare based on nothing more substantial than the fact that the executives liked it, damn the latest fads. The company also had first-look deals with Jodie and Michelle, and where else would they find vehicles that offered them such delectable roles?

"I think you should know that Orion passed," Berg said.

God, what a disaster. Diane started framing what to say to the lineup of people who were hanging on the outcome.

There was a slim remaining course, she realized, to guide the surfboard to safety. Pathé Entertainment, an outlier, was nobody's first choice in those days. A sort of disadvantaged stepsibling of MGM, Pathé couldn't swing the budgets for blockbusters and certainly didn't have a track record for pulling them off. But the studio had made the submission list on the strength of two people. Alan Ladd Jr., the venerated chairman, was pure old-school Hollywood, son and namesake of a studio-era movie star and unabashed admirer of studio-era movies, including women's pictures with stars like Bette Davis and Joan Crawford. In previous posts at other, bigger studios, Laddie, as everyone called him, had backed some of the only women's stories in the modern era, critical darlings like *Julia* and *Norma Rae.* And he trusted a young, relatively untried lieutenant, Rebecca "Becky" Pollack, the daughter of director Sydney Pollack.

Becky had a Hollywood pedigree, too, but didn't conform. Soft-spoken, thoughtful, she was that rare executive who preferred reading, really reading, rather than endless rounds of lunches and drinks with what she called "the chop-chop people" in town. ICM's reasoning was that Becky, backed by Laddie, might recognize a great story when she read it and flout the accepted wisdom that women were box-office cyanide.

Now, in the middle of this slow-motion crash, Diane realized she hadn't heard yet from Becky, and there wasn't a moment to waste. In one stroke of a speed dial, word would get out, if it hadn't already, that no one else had the nerve to take on *Thelma & Louise.* Diane had to connect with Pathé before the grapevine did. It was perilous for her to pick up the phone instead of waiting for the call, usually a sure sign of panic, but delay could be riskier. Diane deployed her steely-confident voice, something she had mastered like a foreign language, to mask the fear.

"What can I say?" Becky answered the phone in her gentle, low-key way. Say? Diane could only imagine. She sucked in her breath—here it comes.

"Everybody loves it here."

Diane exhaled for what seemed like the first time that day. The angels sang. She thought: *I have about a nanosecond to get this right. Becky is truly the only person who gets this. She is the only person who is going to make this deal. And only I know this.*

To Becky, she said, "I'm really thrilled. I thought you would love it, and here's what I'm going to tell you: Get your business affairs people on the phone now. I want this to be with somebody like you who loves it. And I want to close this deal now." Now. As in: before anyone gets wiser. Get the contracts drawn up before Pathé hears the news or, God forbid, comes to its senses.

At that moment, sorry little Pathé was the only studio standing between this movie and oblivion. The people committed to making *Thelma & Louise* didn't know it, but they were hanging out there all on their own.

CHAPTER 1

ONCE IN TEN LIFETIMES

Less than two years earlier, Callie Khouri nudged her sage green Saab into a space in front of her house on a Santa Monica street scented with fig trees. It was four in the morning, a dangerous hour to be thinking and alone, especially for someone who knew, if she let her thoughts go there, that this wasn't the life she had in mind. Best not to catalog the ways. Turning thirty, she divvied up the rent on a ramshackle bungalow with two roommates. She had recently split with a kind and steady boyfriend. And most galling, she was utterly at a loss as to how to put her ambition to use, or even to understand what her ambition might be.

Since dropping out of Purdue just short of a degree, Callie had waited tables, parked herself behind a reception desk, studied acting and auditioned for an agent who offered just one observation after she performed an impassioned monologue in his office: she didn't wear enough makeup. Her current dispiriting job juggling logistics for music videos occupied the outer-planetary fringe of show business. Callie lined up equipment and hired strippers and would-be starlets to display their wares behind spandex hair bands like Alice Cooper and Winger spewing power chords up front. She swept the soundstage at the end of the day while better-paid, better-connected players spiraled off to parties pollinated with promise and cocaine.

"There were directors who used their powerful positions to get girls to do things," she would say later. "It was a skanky time. It would have been less objectionable if I had had any creative… oh, anything. But I was just a facilitator."

So no, Callie did not let her mind go there that night in 1987, to the painful subject of her squandered abilities, whatever they might be. Instead, in the solitary predawn clarity and fatigue of her car, she had an epiphany, born equally of frustration, chafing intelligence and throttled talent: two women go on a crime spree.

She would create a movie about outlaw women on the run, busting out of tedious, thwarted, humdrum lives—lives like hers—for freedom that let them finally become their true selves. She imagined it all: a movie unlike any she had ever seen, where women drove the story, maybe even got to drive the car. Written by a woman. Why not her?

What came to her seemed fully formed, not so much a plot as a feeling, that thing that would wallop people as they walked out of the theater, if by some outrageous turn of events the movie ever got made. "I saw, in a flash, where those women started and where they ended up," Callie said. "Through a series of accidents, they would go from being invisible to being too big for their world to contain, because they'd stopped cooperating with things that were absolutely preposterous and just became themselves."

All she had to do was figure out how to get these two normal women, living everyday lives, into this extraordinary place, this extraordinary mind-set. "We would get to see them in this full glory. And then they would have to leave, not kill themselves, because that's never how I thought of it. But literally, they would have to fly."

This couldn't be a book or a short story or a poem, Callie realized. It had to be a movie, because she saw it all visually. The Grand Canyon figured in there somewhere—she saw all of it in that flash. She would write this story. And perhaps in this act of creation, she might find her own true self.

Callie tuned out the reality that no one who worked in movies would care about her and her half-formed vision. Why should they? Callie was a Hollywood nobody who knew nobody outside her circle of relative nobody friends; she was a woman in a man's town; she had no credits, no bona fides, no cred, no hope. In a business full of boy wonders with film-making degrees, she was a college dropout who had never written anything more than a few unfinished short stories and a rejected TV script she had spitballed with a friend. She had this embryonic idea for a screenplay, but unlike every film school grad trying to peddle a high-concept action picture about two guys who... (fill in the blank), she had come up with the kind of movie that nobody actually made, that nobody had ever made. Two women in a car—so elementary it was groundbreaking.

Looking back years later, Diane Cairns calculated the odds that Callie's idea would ever reach completion: "Just to write it and get it made—astronomical. To get it made well—impossible. To go through what this movie went through—once in a lifetime. *Ten* lifetimes."

But Callie had only this one. Silence descended as she cut the ignition. She decided to tell no one. She would start writing dialogue on a legal pad after work.

NOTHING IN CALLIE'S BACKGROUND destined her to create anything of note, much less a breakthrough in the realm of cinema. She'd grown up in Paducah, Kentucky, far from the buzzy outposts of the East and West coasts, and the South in all its contradictions had molded her into a person sporting plenty of her own. It instilled in her a lifelong appetite for bluegrass music and chess pie, a selective capacity for both genteel manners and hell-raising defiance, and a southern eccentricity that she knew people everywhere else found colorful, even entertaining. Even so, Callie was attuned to the dark side of the region's special brand of crazy, one that fed an acute sense of injustice. "A lot of really bad things went down in the South," she once said in an interview. "There's a lot of rationalization that goes on there. I mean, it's known for hospitality and lynching."

Born in 1957, the third of four children, Carolyn, later nicknamed Callie, spent her childhood just outside Paducah, a sleepy town that had served as a vigorous hub for steamships and railroads back when steamships and railroads mattered. The family made its home in an 1890s log cabin shaded by pine, oak and magnolia trees that were ideal for climbing on summer days.

Her mother, Virginia Khouri, the model for Callie's gracious side, was artistic and pale as porcelain. She led the Paducah Art Guild and threw herself into church work—"All my family are much better Episcopalians than I am," Callie says—while her father, Eli Khouri, a first-generation Lebanese with an infectious laugh, kicked into overdrive as a chief of surgery at the local hospital and head of the regional medical association. Callie adored him and for many years considered their relationship the most significant of her life. "I don't think anyone has ever had a greater influence on me," she says. "He was an overachiever the likes of which I could never touch." He assured Callie that ultimately only her own high achievement would grant her meaningful satisfaction.

Segregation was still a glaring fact of life when Callie was a young girl in the sixties. Black customers had to mount an outdoor staircase to sit in the balcony of Paducah's Columbia movie theater, and schools weren't integrated until 1966. The Metropolitan Hotel on the South Side had long been a rousing stop on the chitlin circuit, hosting musicians like Louis Armstrong, B. B. King and Ike and Tina Turner, unwelcome elsewhere in town but endowing it with a soulful musical legacy.

Callie, a tall, rangy teenager with long blond ringlets and an intellectual bent, was alert to the hypocrisy. It was difficult for her to get one thousand percent behind her heritage, she says in retrospect, "and yet there are so many things I love about it—the crazy, wonderful, funny people set in their ways, their food, their rituals and music." She filled the cultural void of a backwater upbringing with reading: P. G. Wodehouse, Dorothy Parker and James Thurber, with generous helpings of Kurt Vonnegut and Joseph Heller.

The small-town languor fired up a rebellious side as well. Callie stole out of the house just about every night, boosting the car at the age of twelve to joyride with friends. The relatively privileged perch of the Khouris might have allowed her to become an oblivious party girl, but she lapped up adult conversation, and her critical mind wouldn't rest in the face of absurdities and unfairness. In the school library, she came across copies of *Ms.* magazine, which blew apart her perception of the place of women in Paducah, where the few who held jobs did so out of economic necessity and were looked down upon for it. She remembers thinking, *Oh my God, there's not anything they're going to let us do if we don't take it ourselves.*

This premature awareness of all kinds of bias rendered her opinionated, outspoken, sharply funny, sometimes angry, but also a bit vulnerable, because she took it all so personally. Then something happened that cranked up the vulnerability and left her foundering.

On an August weekend when Callie was sixteen, she stayed home while her parents attended a wedding in Louisville. In the middle of the night, Eli woke Virginia to complain of a headache. "It's my brain," he said. "Call an ambulance." He knew. Dr. Khouri died of a cerebral aneurysm within twenty-four hours, on Monday, August 19, 1974. He was forty-seven years old.

There had always been a lightness to the family, a sense of fun. It disappeared overnight, replaced by an absence that could never be filled. Virginia grew quiet, retreated, after that staggering early death, and as time went on she turned ever quieter.

Callie, who was about to enter her senior year of high school, engaged in her own sort of retreat. "For a good ten years after that, I don't remember being fully conscious about much of what I was doing or why," she says. During that lost and drifting decade, she struggled with depression, piercing enough for her to seek treatment, although she never sank so far as to consider suicide.

When she enrolled at Purdue University, for no particular reason except that it was a humongous place where she could get lost, Callie majored in landscape architecture, a pursuit with no particular appeal. "You could have said I would be a pinball major, and I would have said okay," she says. Later she switched to theater, remembering how high school productions served as a refuge from a sorrow-filled house. She never heard about opportunities for women to direct or write. Acting seemed like her only opening, but she was appalled that the parts open to women were limited, shallow and steeped in sexuality: hookers in *Hot l Baltimore,* courtesans in *A Funny Thing Happened on the Way to the Forum.* "College was a wasted experience," she says.

IN 1979, CALLIE LEFT SCHOOL and moved to Nashville, where every night promised a party at live venues that rocked to a mixed brew of southern roots rock, bluegrass, jazz, honky-tonk and rockabilly, but, surprisingly, not much country back then. The constant lineup of musical talent spoke to the twenty-one-year-old's ill-defined but powerful yearning for a creative life. Yet after picking up some work at a local theater, she wound up waiting tables at clubs like the Exit/In, lugging trays of boilermakers to drunken shitkickers who felt that their admission stamps entitled them to cup her ass as she threaded her way through close-packed tables. "You just feel hands on you," she says. One boss, who liked to flash photos from *Hustler* to the staff, fired Callie for not being "a good sport." The expected response to such affronts, maintaining a blank façade, felt obliterating to her.

One night a young country singer named Pam Tillis set up to play. "Could somebody bring me a Coke?" she asked. Callie stepped up onstage. The two women, both on the cusp of finding their way in their early twenties, sized up each other's sangfroid and intrinsic intelligence with a jolt of reciprocal recognition.

"Hi, who are you?" Pam said in a soft twang. "You're not just a waitress." Callie ricocheted back, "You're not just a singer."

They were tight as thieves from then on. "We kind of looked at each other and thought, *Yeah, I know you*, and then we just started hanging," Callie remembers.

This entailed double-teaming the after-hours party scene, holing up all night reading copies of the *New Yorker* and generally forging the kind of friendship that proves that while men might have their place, ladies still need their ladies. "We had more power as a team" was how Callie saw the relationship. "We were very different, but together, we were like a *third* thing." Stronger, surer and a lot more laughs.

They were also nicely balanced. Pam was messy and scattered; Callie, methodical. Pam was innocent, even naive; Callie, more jaded, with what Pam called a smart-ass mouth. "We were both ultimately ambitious for all our being goofballs," Pam says. They would remain friends for life, telling each other when they were crazy, when to trust their guts, when to move on. In all their differences, loyalty and affection, Pam and Callie were the precursors of Thelma and Louise.

————————

AFTER NEARLY FOUR YEARS IN NASHVILLE, Callie's gut told her it was time to hit the pike. She had befriended performers and songwriters, bucking them up as they won acclaim and record deals, but she couldn't kid herself that she was a musical talent herself. "I can play the radio," she liked to say. She had a spark that was not being lit. Maybe acting was the answer after all. An offer to crash at a songwriter's place led Callie to Los Angeles at the end of 1982. With her ever-marketable waitressing skills, she soon set herself up with an apartment in West Hollywood, acting classes with the renowned Peggy Feury at the Lee Strasberg Theatre & Film Institute and a job at the Improv, a comedy club in the heart of Hollywood that was the piping hot center for stand-ups angling to become stars.

Miracles could happen every night in that combustible room. The hand of a network might reach down and offer a $50,000 pilot deal to a comic who'd been working by day cleaning apartments, grateful to rake in a couple hundred dollars and two free-drink tickets for twenty minutes at the mike. Jerry Seinfeld hit early. So did Paul Reiser, Jay Leno and the Wayans Brothers. Robin Williams and *Saturday Night Live* headliners popped in often, while scouts from networks and films scrutinized the talent from the floor.

Callie was once again waiting tables in the orbit of other people's creative whirl. She hooked right into the social scene, where conversation was fierce, funny and competitive. "*He* always goes on last? *He* got a TV deal? *He* got on *Carson*?"

The atmosphere could be harsh, comics topping each other, zap-zap, with the meanest, most negative, most aggressive comeback always winning the biggest laugh. Everyone was fair game, but Callie could sling it with the best of them. "You had to have your sword ready at any time," she says. "Okay, motherfucker, you want to go? Let's go." Callie dated some of the Improv talent, but very few comics, especially voracious ones starting out, pulled off steady relationships. Sex was regarded as a perk of playing Indianapolis.

Callie didn't present herself as a person who could be taken advantage of. If she did, she knew, people would. But the late-night lifestyle entailed hazards. Two thugs with a sawed-off pump-action shotgun held up Callie and Larry David one night as he walked her to her car. Once when Pam visited, some men jumped the friends as they left a party, knocked Pam down and took her coat, while Callie, unwilling to let go of even a nickel she had worked so hard for, held tight to her purse. Pam, usually the ditzy one, transformed on the spot and took charge. "Callie! Quit your dog-headedness!" Pam yelled. *"Let! It! Go!"* Callie dropped the purse, and they ran.

Surrounded by comics, Callie never considered trying stand-up her-self—not that it was a field that would have welcomed her. Women weren't perceived as having the requisite aggression, and audiences weren't com-fortable with those who did. Only Roseanne Barr, able to own her hostil-ity and wield it with caustic self-possession, killed on *Carson*, the sole major female breakthrough since Joan Rivers.

If there was a smaller group than women stand-ups, it was women writers. Jim Vallely, a comic and friend who later wrote for television, admired Callie's clever smackdowns at all-night hangouts and asked her to collaborate on a spec script for Bill Maher, an Improv buddy. The ver-dict was crushing when they turned in their draft: "You guys write like a couple of actors."

Yet two years of lessons and auditions had given Callie no purchase on acting, either. Striking in thrift-shop clothes and cowboy boots, with long, wavy hair, she attracted attention, but not the kind she craved. She didn't enjoy being looked at, at least not the way prospective agents looked at actresses, and so she aspired to play character roles. "Debra Winger was having the career I would have wanted," Callie says, "because she was beautiful but not *that* kind of beautiful." What's more, Callie panicked that she might actually get a part, "and then there would be a permanent record, and it would be awful."

By 1985, she realized that acting wasn't going to happen for her. Still afflicted by the long malaise after her father's death, still smarting from his adage that only achievement would give meaning to her life, she hit a wall. She quit her job and moved out of Hollywood to the little shared house near the ocean in Santa Monica. The distance might help her think things over, recalibrate her breakneck pace, reconsider a career, perhaps find a foothold in the film business. To most of the comics, it was as if she had disappeared.

"Those early years in her twenties, being smarter than so many of the guys she was hanging around, and knowing it, I know she got hurt," says Vallely. "She took a big hunk of hurt and turned it into *Thelma & Louise*. I think she became a great writer because she lived some life."

Film was the art form of the moment, where the stakes were higher, the stars brighter and the visions grander, the principals—actors like Clint Eastwood, Harrison Ford, Eddie Murphy and directors like Spielberg, Coppola, Scorsese and Lucas—its reigning cultural gods. Callie started at the bottom of the bottom, again, landing a gig as a receptionist for a company that made music videos and commercials, the tawdry, slippery beginner's rung on the ladder to Mount Olympus. She was a long way from Paducah. The hazing rituals of comedy were nothing to what the movie business held in store.

CHAPTER 2

PROSTITUTES AND EMPTY-HEADED BLONDES

Oddly, someone like Callie might have found a warmer reception in the earliest days of cinema, when it was the bastard child of the arts in a new century. Filmmaking welcomed innovators, inventors, outsiders, immigrants—all the sorts of nervy geeks who latch onto a new technology in its semiamateur phase. This unexplored territory was wide open for women, too, like Lois Weber, a writer, director and performer from 1907 through the early twenties. More prolific than D. W. Griffith, Weber owned her own studio and scandalized audiences with stories that championed birth control and temperance and opposed abortion, poverty and religious hypocrisy. Dorothy Arzner, the first woman admitted to the Directors Guild, broke in as a writer and editor on such smoldering projects as 1922's *Blood and Sand* with Rudolph Valentino but threatened to leave Paramount in the late twenties unless she could direct, which she did, outfitted androgynously in pants and a coat.

Some of the foremost pioneer screenwriters were women as well.

Anita Loos applied her sharklike wit to well over a hundred scripts by 1915, more than a decade before she published the gal-pal novel *Gentlemen Prefer Blondes*. Frances Marion chalked up more than three hundred film credits, writing roles for no less than Mary Pickford, Greta Garbo, Jean Harlow, Marlene Dietrich and Myrna Loy. These women made boatloads of money, which was when the trouble started. Once filmmaking ceased to be a lark and turned into a business, studios modeled themselves after businesses everywhere else—hierarchical and run by men.

It's hard to believe that from the late 1920s to the mid-1960s, scholars identify only *two* women directors: Arzner, who quit in 1943, and Ida Lupino, who started six years later. Lupino was a former film noir trouper who had held her own on-screen with George Raft and Humphrey Bogart. Unable to get the juicy roles she craved, she formed her own production company in 1948 and went on to direct seven steely melodramas like the rape-themed *Outrage* in 1950 and *Hard, Fast and Beautiful* in 1951, all while pretending to know less than she did around the crew. Lupino professed, "You don't *tell* a man, you *suggest* to them, 'Let's try something crazy here. That is, if it's comfortable, love.'"

As for actresses, at the peak of the studio era the moguls recognized that stories about women filled seats, so stars like Joan Crawford, Barbara Stanwyck and Rosalind Russell shone clear and bright. "These women were the center of the universe in their films, and they *did stuff*," says film historian Jeanine Basinger. "They ran corporations, they flew airplanes, they edited newspapers, they were doctors, lawyers, judges. When you think about the great women stars of the thirties, forties and into the fifties, those women dominated the films they were in, and in order to do that, they had to *do* something."

A few women writers also still made the cut, like Leigh Brackett, first hired by Howard Hawks when he assumed from her name that she was a man, but kept on to contribute to features like *The Big Sleep* and *Rio*

Bravo. Yet somehow the idea took hold that directing was the province of men.

THE COLLAPSE OF THE STUDIO SYSTEM should have opened more doors for outsiders, but female luminaries got left on the other side. "Women just disappeared out of the business," says Basinger. By then, the all-male central command was so ingrained, it might as well have been inscribed on tablets handed down unto Moses, or at least Charlton Heston.

A complete shake-up of the industry in the sixties didn't help. No one seemed to be fully in charge anymore. The freedom could be intoxicating, an invitation to play for writers, directors and actors who, with a wave of a wand, morphed from hired help to free agents. But there were virtually no women writers or directors by then anyway, so none were in place to seize the new opportunities. And once studios stopped grooming their careers, even actresses lost what little stature they'd enjoyed. The remaining studio bosses, impressed by the success of subversive statements like *Bonnie and Clyde* and *The Graduate* in 1967 and *Easy Rider* in 1969, threw up their hands and ceded unprecedented power to their insurgent directors.

This new Hollywood glorified auteurs, writer-directors who abandoned stodgy concepts like old-school glamour and straightforward narrative in favor of personal expression, which, because all the auteurs were men, necessarily skewed far to the masculine, heterosexual point of view—dramas about moody outlaws or comedies about hapless, insecure nebishes befuddled by the sexual revolution. There was little regard for stories that didn't arise from the subterranean urges and priorities of the male psyche. Sexual-fantasy girls fleshed out the movies while the female aviators, journalists and lawyers of the old studio pictures got the hook.

"When women do get parts at all, they are usually cast as prostitutes, empty-headed blondes, sex kittens or neurotic housewives," the *New York Times* reported during a conference about the issue in 1974. Male speaking roles outnumbered female ones by twelve to one, and the only bankable female star was Barbra Streisand, who for four years in the early seventies was the *sole* actress on the top-ten list of box-office stars in polls of theater owners.

By the mid-seventies, the new generation of film school auteurs—Francis Ford Coppola, Martin Scorsese, Peter Bogdanovich, William Friedkin, Hal Ashby, Bob Rafelson, Robert Altman and Brian De Palma—set off so many pyrotechnics that roles for women devolved into an afterthought at best. Critical and commercial smashes like *The Godfather, The French Connection* and *M*A*S*H* shifted the balance of Hollywood power further into the camp of the young male countercultural renegades.

The social milieu that trailed in their wake didn't do women any favors. As filmmaking as an art form caught fire, with hedonism as the fuel and cocaine the accelerant, no behavior was off-limits, just as no artistic choice was out of bounds. "A lot of talented people came along and then got plied with gobs of money and drugs," says Martha Coolidge, who was spinning her wheels trying to gain traction as a director. "They lived in a bubble of indulgence that will probably never be seen again."

None of this engendered much respect for the women in town, many of whom, whether they aspired to act, direct or write, were treated more as sexual playthings than professional colleagues. "I was appalled at the men of my generation, my age, who went around with the hookers and dopey girls and had group sex and did a lot of coke," says Paula Weinstein, who arrived in Hollywood in 1973 as a script reader for Jane Fonda and by 1981 had made it as head of production at United Artists. "There was this essentially secret club of guys who all hung out and didn't take women seriously at all."

Few women gained admission to the club. Between 1966 and 1979, the number of women directing a studio-backed film was a whopping *one,*

Elaine May, the former comedy partner of Mike Nichols, director of *The Graduate*. May was a true auteur who wrote, directed and starred in the 1971 black comedy *A New Leaf*, a commercial and critical hit. She followed up the next year by directing the similarly successful *The Heartbreak Kid*, written by Neil Simon. Despite this double triumph, May ran over budget, filmed interminable retakes and dithered over the smallest decisions. When her third feature, *Mikey and Nicky*, tanked in 1976, she wasn't given another chance until the disastrous *Ishtar* ended her directing career eleven years later. The argument could be made that male wunderkinds indulged in similar feats of excess and turned out similar flops (see *Sorcerer* by William Friedkin), but May's former assistant Todd McCarthy acknowledged, "I do really believe that she set back the cause of women directors in Hollywood by ten years."

DURING THE SEVENTIES AND EARLY EIGHTIES, only two women in town had real clout, the kind that could get a movie made with a complex female at the center of the story. They were Barbra Streisand and Jane Fonda, leading actresses who leveraged their box-office power to develop their own projects.

Following a Best Actress Oscar for *Funny Girl*, Streisand was reduced to playing, yes, a prostitute in the middling comedy *The Owl and the Pussycat*. The experience spurred her to form her own production company as a means to seek out more up-to-date material. Her first effort, *Up the Sandbox*, a 1972 comedy about the liberating fantasies of a housewife, didn't catch fire, but her next, the 1976 rock 'n' roll remake of *A Star Is Born*, racked up $140 million, her biggest box-office take for several decades.

Still, she wanted more, namely to direct. Even though many actors had been given the nod—Paul Newman, Dennis Hopper, Warren Beatty, Marlon Brando and Clint Eastwood, to name a few—years passed as studios balked at backing Streisand, in spite of her box-office punch. When she secured a deal to direct *Yentl,* an adaptation of an Isaac Bashevis Singer story about a girl who poses as a boy to study the Talmud, Streisand had to swallow a deal that took away the routine powers and perks granted to her peers. "I had to eat shit, put it that way," she said in a magazine interview at the time. The studio trimmed Streisand's usual salary for acting, granted her only the guild minimum for directing and built in all sorts of hair-trigger penalties if she ran over time or budget. All that, *and* she had to give up casting approval, script approval and final cut.

"It was as if they had this very antiquated notion of an actress as this frivolous creature," she recalls. "How could she be financially responsible? How could she handle a movie crew? How could she make all the myriad decisions that go into making a film? It just didn't compute for them. It was a man's world."

Yentl earned a solid $40 million at the box office on its release in 1983, and five Oscar nominations, although none for Streisand. It satisfied her jones to direct, but her acting career faltered afterward. Following an unprecedented run as one of the top-ten bankable stars for ten out of twelve years, she disappeared from the list in 1981, never to return.

FOR A TIME, JANE FONDA wielded her own kind of authority, not by directing but by cannily producing projects that made gutsy statements and gave her central roles. At first, even a member of Hollywood royalty like Fonda had struggled to find her place. Despite an Oscar nomination for *They Shoot Horses, Don't They?* in 1970 and a win for *Klute* in 1972— as, yes, a prostitute—she kept fielding offers for witless sex comedies that featured the requisite empty-headed-blonde part.

She formed her own production company in 1973, vaguely aware that Mary Pickford and Streisand had done so, and assuming that others had, too. Fonda reasoned that because she was famous and a respectable box-office draw, she could get movies made by agreeing to star, and she was savvy enough to understand how to make projects commercial. "If you're going to do a story about Vietnam vets, make it sexy and make it a love story. If you're going to do a story on nuclear energy, make it a suspense thriller." Her first project, 1978's *Coming Home,* turned into a surprise hit in which Fonda, playing the wife of a gung-ho soldier, had an affair with a paraplegic veteran played by Jon Voight. Released ten months before *The Deer Hunter, Coming Home* was the first Hollywood production to take a serious look at the morality of the Vietnam War. The film scooped up eight Academy Award nominations and won three, including Fonda's second for Best Actress. The following year, she scored another Oscar nomination and another hit with the *The China Syndrome,* playing the part of a reporter who uncovers the dangers of nuclear power plants.

Producing her own movies launched Fonda to a new level of stardom. Starting in 1978, she landed among the top-ten box-office stars for five years in a row, one of only eight women to make the list throughout that stretch. She also fought to slip women onto the crews of her movies, but she didn't think about recruiting women to direct. "A movie about Vietnam, are you kidding?" she says. "These were hard enough movies to get made, let alone if I was insisting on a woman director who wasn't proven." Fonda didn't regard herself as a trailblazer for others. In fact, she was surprised when Sally Field asked her for advice on how to set up a company. *Why does she have to come to me?* Fonda thought. "I didn't consider myself an expert or particularly good at it." Like most other women trying to crack the industry, Fonda didn't realize how alone she was.

Nevertheless, as the eighties began to unfold, more women were angling to produce, direct, write—or at least try. But there wouldn't have seemed to be much chance for a former waitress from Paducah, Kentucky, who worked in the vaguely scuzzy world of comedy clubs and music videos. Not unless she came up with one hell of an idea.

CHAPTER 3

"NEXT! *NEXT!*"

The sound of desperate banging broke Callie's concentration. Heavy metal throbbed and wailed outside the thin walls of the production trailer where she had been toting up the budget for a music video. She cracked open the door. One of the backup dancers stood in the frame, chilled and trembling in little more than a Band-Aid.

"I'm really sorry." The dancer shuddered. "I have to leave. I was hired to dance, and people are putting their hands all over me. I feel like this whole experience is degrading."

Callie's heart bloomed with pleasure. Finally, someone speaking her language! It was the first time she'd heard anyone say, "What the fuck is going on here?" she recalls.

"It's terrible, because I really need the money," the dancer said.

"No, no," Callie said. "I'm paying you. I'm writing a check *right now.*"

Years later she still savors that moment, the one when she paid a modicum of reparations for all she had witnessed in the trenches of music video.

Degrading? Welcome to the rodeo.

For the most part, if a woman wanted to break into the movies in the 1980s, she put on blinders and plowed ahead, whatever she might think of the lame or skanky entertainment product she was called upon to enable. So it was when Callie Khouri worked her way through the ranks of video production. Stifle the outrage, avert the eyes and get the job done.

Those who weren't stars like Barbra Streisand and Jane Fonda could rarely attack the industry head-on. Video production was a viable flanking maneuver, a side entrance for somebody who could tolerate the drugs, the inanity and the groping of women who were hired to slink around behind the musicians while sparsely attired in a mockery of 1980s dress for success.

Around the time Callie left the comedy scene, she signed on as a receptionist at N. Lee Lacy, a tony commercial production outfit. To get the job she had to promise that she would never try to move out from behind the reception desk, swearing on her life that answering the phone was her highest ambition. The company had just launched a division to crank out music videos for the record industry, which was bankrolling attention-grabbing clips to break bands on MTV.

Callie started by greeting visitors in the serene white foyer at Lacy's on Melrose Place. The job was classy but dull, seemingly another dead end. "I was literally running out of ideas," she says. Eventually she did push her way into the fun part, working on commercials and videos, climbing the ladder through a jumble of titles—runner, production assistant, production coordinator and production manager. By 1987, she was freelancing as a line producer, which meant she delivered film to the lab, ordered the lighting, scouted locations, juggled schedules, arranged casting sessions—you name it—all in the service of the creative visions of the directors. "It was incredibly unsatisfying," Callie says, "but I learned a lot."

Young film school grads who worshipped at the altars of the auteurs jumped at the chance to direct those music videos, which could serve as a ticket in. With their flamboyance, visual flair and utter lack of restraint, the quick clips offered ripe canvases to showcase the talents of comers like David Fincher and Michael Bay. Yet while video production may have functioned as the minor leagues in Hollywood, the milieu matched or even exceeded feature films for lurid, outrageous behavior, on and off the set.

"Everyone was snorting through their days, coke everywhere, and everyone was just out of hand," says Amanda Temple, an English-born friend who produced a number of videos with Callie. "I have to say, we did have a lot of fun. We did laugh."

Directors basked in what there was of cachet in the genre. But production people, the women especially, felt conscripted into the coal mines of long hours, low pay and dismal taste. One night, when Callie was cleaning the soundstage as other PAs took off, one of the guys announced, "For a hundred a day, these people can go fuck themselves. I'm out of here." *A hundred?* Callie thought. *I'm making seventy-five.* Callie worked on clips for a lot of bands that went nowhere and a few others that did—Robert Cray, Brian Setzer, Iggy Pop, Billy Idol. Having never studied film, she soaked up the process of how to tell a story visually, how all that mattered was what happened when the shutter opened wide. But ultimately the work seemed trivial, just this side of artistic—and worse.

"There were really talented directors making beautiful images," Callie says, "but still nobody was saying anything. It wasn't *important*. Some of it was beautifully crafted. Some of it was cheaply crafted and culture destroying, which was the other side of it. I got exposed to the objectification of women in a whole new way."

She and Amanda often quarantined themselves in the production office, but still they could hear the male directors and crew routinely snickering and commenting on the bodies of the dancers who stripped down to underwear or less on the sets and in auditions. Directors bellowed: "Not big enough tits! Next! *Next!*"

"We were both mortified a lot of the time by the work we were doing," says Amanda. "It was Mötley Crüe, it was Whitesnake, it was all those spandex-pants and big-hair guys with girls in bikinis." Watching directors film women's asses shaking from a foot away, she and Callie cut glances at each other: *What the hell are we doing?* "What we were doing was, we were paying bills," Amanda says. "We needed to work, so we kept our heads down and we did it."

Those casting sessions got to Callie. Sometimes they enraged her. Sometimes she spoke up. "The thing that was so powerful about Callie was that she had a really strong sense that this was wrong, that it was time for a change," says Amanda. "She got up people's noses." Some of the guys complained that Callie had a mouth on her. Amanda stood up for her colleague, and they became tight as only allies become tight if they're trapped together behind enemy lines, surviving on nothing but camel jerky and gully water. Callie devised an expression that kept them going: "You get what you settle for."

"It was like having a warrior queen at your side," says Amanda. "I felt like I could fight every battle with this woman."

On balance, Callie was tactical enough to put the paycheck ahead of her opinions. "She could play pool with the boys," says David Warfield, who dated Callie at the time and often worked on shoots with her. "Her attitude was essentially professional. She's not so fragile that she can't be around dancing bimbos."

The relationship with David provided sweet relief and proof that not every guy working in show business was a cad. In a classic California interlude, he became smitten with her when they shared a hot tub at a party, where she torpedoed the customary mellow vibe to hold forth on all the sexist and patriarchal sins of society. "It made me fall in love," David says, "just because it was so smart, so deeply authentic, and because so few people are eloquent enough to express such a meaningful statement on the human condition that way. A couple of years later it manifested itself in *Thelma & Louise*."

Callie was pulling herself together. She was happy in her house near the beach, happy with David and not altogether miserable at work, where she had caught a serious case of the movie bug. In fact, she had acquired a profound sense of mastery from her job. If a crewmate got a motor home stuck in a ditch, Callie would say, "I got this," and drive it out. Despite the tedium of production work, the ridiculous inequality and lack of respect, she became fascinated by the craft or, in rare instances, the art of telling stories on film. The work she'd witnessed from the sidelines had all the substance of, let's face it, an MTV video, but it was enough of a taste that she fixed on this as something she might be able to do, and do well—telling stories, expressing something that *mattered* for a change, with images, words and music, creating a vision that was beautiful and true. Ever since the loss of her father, she'd been grasping for the accomplishment that could satisfy his ambitions for her. Filmmaking? There were crazier ideas.

One night she flew with a load of camera equipment to Monument Valley to work on an Estée Lauder commercial. All alone, Callie packed up a van and drove toward the motel where the crew awaited. A full moon lit the fabled rock formations. Stretching toward the horizon, they towered like silvery apparitions in absolute clarity and perfect silence as she guided the van down the empty highway. It was both hyperreal and otherworldly, a visual spectacle that sent her thoughts spinning.

Callie felt that she understood herself in a way that had evaded her for ten muzzy, cluttered—*frustrating*—years. She considered how glorious it would be to communicate that sensation in a movie, that feeling of facing who you are, perhaps for the first time, in a grand, impassive space that opened the mind to reflection. She had something to say, something that mattered, and she knew it belonged on film.

CHAPTER 4

WIELDING A GRACEFUL CLEAVER

By the mid- to late 1980s, when Callie chose to join the filmmaking fray, the romance of the movies had summoned a new batch of hopeful women writers, producers and directors to throw themselves against the well-guarded gates of the studios. The prospects for women had improved since the near shutout of the seventies, but still only a few found a way in. The latest contenders weren't so much celebrities like Barbra Streisand and Jane Fonda as people more like Callie, with nothing but experience in starter jobs or student films to recommend them. If a novice wanted to tap into the collective experience of these contemporaries to find out what to expect, it might sound something like this:

- Know that film schools and studio bosses will assure you that women do not write, produce or direct.
- Hold the champagne on ice if a studio decides to back you after

your first film wows the critic from the *Village Voice*. It is the second or third film you need to worry about.

- Channel the prom. When you are offered the opportunity to make a movie, it will be a comedy about horny teenagers.
- If that movie makes money, the press, the industry, your colleagues and possibly your mother will call it a "sleeper hit."
- Expect sexual overtures or assaults from guys dangling low-level job opportunities.
- And there will be crying, but preferably only in the ladies' room.

Such givens crop up throughout the stories of women from all corners of the industry, from art house obscurities to commercial triumphs, who rose to prominence during the years when Callie worked to leave videos behind by writing a movie of her own.

The first strike against Callie might have been that she had parked herself on the wrong coast. Often those who had wangled opportunities before her had done so through independent films in New York. Joan Micklin Silver, the first woman to make an independent movie with a more commercial bent, was pushing forty and shooting educational films there when she approached studios for directing work. Everywhere she went, she ran into the first industry given: women simply did not do this.

"Look, feature films are expensive to make and expensive to market," one executive told Silver. "Women directors are one more problem we don't need."

Her husband, Ray, a real estate investor, pulled together $375,000 so that his wife could write and direct *Hester Street,* about a woman who found emancipation when she immigrated to America. No studio or distributor would take on the film, and so the Silvers submitted it to the Cannes Film Festival, where they sold rights to three foreign countries, raising enough money to open the movie themselves in New York in 1975. Lines formed around the block in a rainstorm on opening day, and *Hester*

Street emerged as a critical favorite and widely touted sleeper hit. It earned an Oscar nomination for actress Carol Kane and sold $5 million in tickets, a spectacular return on a pea-sized investment.

Hollywood did not come calling. But Silver's next self-financed film, *Between the Lines,* about an alternative newspaper, prompted United Artists to underwrite her following effort, *Chilly Scenes of Winter,* based on an Ann Beattie novel. The company saddled the 1979 film with a slapstick title, *Head Over Heels,* dumped it on a double bill and wrote it off as a fast flop. A rerelease three years later restored the original title and Silver's smart reputation, but the experience established a persistent pattern for aspiring directors: promising indie debuts by women who then stumbled when graduating to full-scale studio productions.

THE "BEWARE THE FOLLOW-UP" CURSE proved persistent for other filmmakers throughout the seventies and eighties. "I cannot tell you the number of people who said, 'Don't hire her—she's indecisive,' or 'Don't hire her—she's difficult,'" says Paula Weinstein, a rising studio executive at the time. "Women, if they falter, get dismissed a lot faster than men."

It happened to the New York writer-director Claudia Weill, who landed a deal with Columbia following her 1978 independent sleeper, *Girlfriends,* an endearingly awkward friendship comedy that Lena Dunham later cited as an influence. When Weill's next picture tanked in 1980 amid studio second-guessing and interference, she retreated to theater and television.

The pattern repeated with Susan Seidelman, an NYU film school graduate, who caught the wave of New York's independent film surge with 1982's punk-infused *Smithereens,* which she pulled off with minuscule grant money. Studios sent her scripts, but she hesitated. "A lot of them were female teen comedies, and just very silly," she said. "I was very aware that because there were so few women directors to begin with, if a woman got some attention for making an independent film and landed a Hollywood movie—and it didn't succeed at the box office—you never heard from her again."

Two first-time producers, Midge Sanford and Sarah Pillsbury, approached Seidelman with the script for *Desperately Seeking Susan,* a singular romp by first-time screenwriter Leora Barish about a bored housewife who borrowed the identity of a punk free spirit, a character that served as the movie debut for Madonna. Barbara Boyle, an executive at Orion Pictures, persuaded her bosses to back the film if the budget stayed under $5 million.

Seidelman applied visual flair and a feel for the energy of downtown New York to whip *Desperately Seeking Susan* into a fizzy alternative screwball comedy, brimming with a cast of barely known performers like Rosanna Arquette, Aiden Quinn, Laurie Metcalf and John Turturro. The Orion marketing department didn't know what to make of this outlier, suggesting a poster that showed the face of the housewife reflected on the side of a toaster. But Sanford prevailed when she pushed for a cheeky photo of the two leads, defiantly punked up in thrift-shop threads, even though one of the marketing guys held the slides up to his office window and squinted with distaste. "You put two women on a poster," he said, "and people are going to think it's a lesbian movie."

Audiences showed they were eager for a fresh take. On its release in 1985, the movie grabbed $31 million in box office and designation within the industry as one of those unexpected sleeper hits. Seidelman landed four more studio gigs that didn't measure up before moving to television, eventually directing the pilot for *Sex and the City.*

THE PATH SEEMED EVEN MORE PUNISHING for those who tried their luck in Los Angeles. When Martha Coolidge headed west after she aced

NYU's film school with a trophy case full of awards, she ran smack into the third and fourth givens of the industry: unwanted sexual come-ons and offers that were nearly as distasteful to her—to direct nothing but teenage comedies.

Coolidge's agent, the powerful Bob Bookman at ICM, told her that an executive once warned him about another writer-director client, "Don't ever send a woman to me again that I wouldn't want to fuck." Once during a pitch, a studio chief locked the door to his office and chased Coolidge around the room, forcing his tongue into her mouth. Otherwise, women seemed invisible except at industry parties, where some tried to parlay their sexuality to associate with power and fame. "The girls were dressed up really sexy, and they'd all drop Ludes, which would make them completely helpless," Coolidge says. "The guys took them or left them. It was for the picking."

To her added despair, the only scripts that came her way were essentially soft-core porn with teenage characters. Desperate for a break, Coolidge finally agreed to take on one called *Valley Girl*. She thought she might be able to buff it up to respectability by adding a falling-in-love scene and a breaking-up scene to bracket the sex. At a meeting with two production executives who put up $350,000 to make the movie, one of them said, "We want you to promise that there will be nude breasts in four scenes in the picture. Is that a problem for you?"

They insisted that she shake on it while repeating a solemn vow: "Four naked breast scenes."

Valley Girl made $17 million in 1983, but the doors it opened led only to other teen comedies, the low-budget, low-prestige genre that was fast becoming a certified safe zone for women directors. "I kept trying to change my luck from these sleazy movies where the women didn't have names," Coolidge says. "I read more bad scripts than you can imagine."

WHATEVER IT TOOK, female aspirants sucked it up and moved on, each only vaguely aware of whoever else was doing what to whom to bring their movies to life. The film industry was a free-market free-for-all, a hive of creative killer bees striking their own deals and jump-starting their own projects with a fragmented dispersion of companies and producers. There was no central human resources department to monitor hiring and behavior, no coffee cart where workers could compare notes. All kinds of remarks and conditions that might lead to a lawsuit in a formal workplace went unchecked in the freewheeling, unscrutinized world of the movies as women chipped away at a ceiling that was more concrete than glass. Nevertheless, women began to break through.

The producer Lauren Shuler Donner produced her first movie, the hit comedy *Mr. Mom,* in 1983, moving on to some three dozen others, including the billion-plus-earning *X-Men* franchise in the 2000s. But when she was starting out earning a living as a camera operator, there was no recourse for a long series of human resources no-no's. At a job interview where she insisted she wanted to be a producer rather than a secretary, she was told, "Honey, either learn to type or get yourself a see-through blouse, because that's the only way you're going to get a job in Hollywood." The director Sam Peckinpah countered a request for employment with the question "Do you wear a bra?" And when she worked on television's *Soul Train,* she was off the show the day after she turned down an overture from the host, Don Cornelius.

Penelope Spheeris finally made it as a director after enduring similar offenses when she scrounged for work in the seventies and eighties. A UCLA film graduate, Spheeris eked out a living at first by making early music videos. Once, a music executive invited her to his hotel room to pitch a video for David Essex. She showed up in a satin jumpsuit—a little sparkly for the afternoon, but that was the scene. The guy reached over, grasped the neckline of the jumpsuit and ripped it open down to the waist, then tried to jump on top of her. Spheeris jerked away and ran out of the hotel, clutching her clothes to cover herself. Instead of slinking away, she found her way to the nearest phone and called the room.

"You've got three choices," she said when he answered. "You can let me do this video. You can get some sugar poured in the gas tank of your stupid-ass Porsche. Or I can talk to your wife." She got the job.

Eventually, wheedling some money from guys in the porn industry, Spheeris made a documentary about punk rock, *The Decline of Western Civilization,* which led to teen-movie features. When at the age of forty-five she eventually got a shot at a mainstream commercial comedy, 1992's *Wayne's World,* it took in $183 million worldwide.

By the late eighties, a few other female filmmakers had won respect with box-office winners of their own. Penny Marshall directed Tom Hanks in *Big,* the first movie by a woman to break the $100 million mark. And Amy Heckerling followed a trajectory from teen comedy to eventual blockbuster after she made the most of a small budget for her first feature, *Fast Times at Ridgemont High,* to win critical acclaim and sleeper-hit status. Not satisfied, she declared: "I wanted to have hits the way boys had hits, not like a 'girl hit' that made fifty million, but a boy hit that made hundreds of millions." She could afford just enough to hire Bruce Willis for voice-over work as a talking baby in *Look Who's Talking,* which she both wrote and directed. When it earned $140 million in the United States and another $157 million abroad—boy-hit territory for sure—it took sleeper hits to a whole new level.

ANOTHER FACTION MADE ARTISTIC STRIDES during the decade. Kathryn Bigelow, destined to become the first female winner of the Best Director Oscar for *The Hurt Locker* in 2010, began to make an impression in the eighties with somber, philosophical action movies that mostly centered on masculine codes of honor. It was therefore absurd that after her debut feature, a biker movie called *The Loveless* in 1981, studios pursued Bigelow with the same lame teen-comedy scripts that stalked other women directors like deranged ex-boyfriends. In a later interview, Bigelow diplomatically stated the obvious: "It was an intersection of absolutely inappropriate sensibilities."

An even more highly praised debut director at the time was Randa Haines, who got tapped from television for a first feature film, *Children of a Lesser God,* that earned five Academy Award nominations in 1987, including Best Picture, although Haines didn't make the cut for Best Director. A Best Actress statuette did go to the star, Marlee Matlin, a first-time actress, only twenty-one years old, playing a student in a school for the deaf. "I had a good period with the big boys," Haines says. "I didn't feel any kind of weird stuff was going on." But she left the business after two more features, frustrated by producers who undercut her decisions: "Strange behavior toward me, people lying to me—it didn't have any clear goal. It was the only time I thought this boys' club I was playing in doesn't like something about me."

SOME CRACKERJACK SCREENWRITERS blazed trails in the 1980s, too. Melissa Mathison wrote 1982's *E.T.* Nora Ephron spanned the decade with *Silkwood,* written with Alice Arlen, and her own *Heartburn* and *When Harry Met Sally.* Ephron would segue into directing in the nineties, as did Nancy Meyers, who started by writing neatly crafted hit romantic comedies for grown-ups, like *Private Benjamin* and *Baby Boom,* with her husband, Charles Shyer.

By this time, Hollywood women had been at it long enough to develop some winning strategies, deploying soft power to make the old guard comfortable with somebody in the mix who reminded them of a wife or girlfriend. "Being part of a team helped me so much," Meyers said. "I know the fact that there was a man in the room with me all those years made the medicine go down." Like others of her generation, she walked a delicate line, putting across her point of view while taking care not to offend. "She was the funny, smart girl in rooms full of men when I first met her," the director and producer James L. Brooks recalled. "She'll hit you with a cleaver, but gracefully."

Lauren Shuler Donner says she advanced her producing career by confining her crying to the ladies' room and cultivating an ability to let things slide. "I used to go in with my fists up," she says. "I'd go, 'I'm tough, I'm tough, I'm tough.' Eventually I had to learn that that is the worst thing; that is what men *really* hate. A lot of women fell by the wayside because they'd be so tough-ass in trying to prove themselves."

FOR ALL THE STRIVING WOMEN of the era, it was ever so easy to make the wrong tactical move—on anything from choice of material to choice of demeanor—and end up back as the script girl or, worse, the girl taking Quaaludes at the party. "When the stakes are high, when fame and extreme amounts of money and power are involved, it's a jungle out there," Penelope Spheeris once said. "It's brutal. How hard do you want to fight?"

Carrie Frazier, a casting director on many seminal eighties movies, advised director friends to treat meetings as auditions for roles, to dress in army boots and convey the impression they'd been soldiering through mud. "People want to hire a director who's a general, who has that kind of masculine energy," she warns. "She can't be 'I'm a nice girl, let me direct your movie.'"

Then again, she can't be too threatening, either.

Like women breaking into other tough jobs, as so many did back in the eighties in just about every line of work, women in Hollywood had to calibrate aggression with standards of femininity, ambition with diplo-

macy, and that didn't even factor in talent or skill. Most likely, any attempt to cull advice for women in the business at the time would have
yielded a ludicrous muddle of contradictions:

Wear combat boots, or a see-through blouse.

Put down your fists, or act like a general.

Hold fast to your position, or let things slide.

Hit them with a cleaver, but do it gracefully.

Get a studio deal, but don't trust the studio.

It's no wonder so few women made it all the way to the closing credits,
like the last girl standing in a slasher movie. The rules were as ruthless
and arbitrary as a chain-saw massacre.

Many who succeeded tried to bend the rules to their will, carefully,
strategically plotting their campaigns. So did many who failed. Then
again, there was the naive option, the one with virtually no record of
success, the one that would defy most of the givens and much of the advice that Hollywood had come to sanction. That was the option Callie
Khouri chose: create a story from the heart, a story about grown-up
women, not teenagers, where what's at stake is bigger than who gets to
sleep with whom, and hope that the strength of that story will somehow
allow it to live.

CHAPTER 5

TITS AND BULLETS

Perhaps the screenplay for *Thelma & Louise* came so easily to Callie because, after all the years of pining for something meaningful to accomplish, years of self-doubt, vexation and disrespect, she knew, finally, at the age of thirty, exactly what she wanted to say.

"I was the product of a lot of wasted years and bad relationships and ennui and the frustration of not really knowing what I wanted to do," she wrote later. "And I just wanted out of that." So she dreamed up two women who broke free of the conventions that governed their lives, just as she wanted to break free of hers. For about four months after the idea struck, the characters lived in her head, and the details coalesced. She began to write in the off-hours from the music video grind, finishing the whole thing about six months later, in the summer of 1988.

She'd never enjoyed herself so much as when she was scrawling the script longhand in notebooks and on legal pads on the glassed-in porch of the bungalow in Santa Monica. Sometimes she took the pages to the beach to write in the sun. When she could, after hours, she let herself into the office of one of her employers to type up the drafts on a clunky word processor. She and David had broken up by then, and she withdrew from the rest of the social scene. Finally, her father's prognostication came to be: that she would find true happiness through accomplishment.

"I had never done anything like it, and there was no expectation," she says. "I didn't have to deliver anything to anybody. It was as pure as the process can be."

The characters, a couple of smart, funny, authentic southern gals, fast friends like Callie and Pam, seemed to know what to do. Callie established why the cheerfully scattered housewife Thelma Dickinson might want a break from her domineering doofus of a husband, Darryl, the philandering manager of a carpet store. Louise Sawyer, a tightly wound coffee-shop waitress, had frustrations of her own, including her boyfriend, Jimmy, an itinerant musician with commitment issues. Callie gave the women a breather, letting them head out on a weekend escape at a borrowed fishing camp, gleefully tearing out of town in Louise's convertible, a bright red 1966 Impala in the script. If you stopped right there, you'd have the premise for a Tina Fey–Amy Poehler vehicle, a screwball comedy stocked with the wisecracking rapport of longtime friends.

Are you at work? the script had Thelma ask Louise on the phone in a typical exchange.

No, I'm callin' from the Playboy Mansion.

And when Thelma maintained that she didn't know how to fish, Louise countered, *Neither do I, Thelma, but Darryl does it; how hard can it be?*

The good-time vibe rolled on when they stopped to eat at a roadside honky-tonk, with Wild Turkey and margaritas on the side. Callie had read a few screenplays and skimmed a couple of how-to books to get a sense of format and structure, but once her story arrived at the saloon, she bolted off any conventional course, flipping the comic tone she'd established and taking the rest of the film someplace completely unexpected, someplace wilder and weighted with conflicting impulses toward emancipation and dread.

The flashpoint occurred when a slick charmer named Harlan steered Thelma out to the parking lot and tried to rape her. Louise cut him short by jabbing a pistol into his neck. But even as he backed off from the rape, Harlan taunted Louise with some crude, ill-advised lip, and, impulsively, she blew him away. A crime of passion? Indefensible? Either way, it turned a lighthearted girlfriend romp—okay, a chick flick—into something else entirely.

It got crazier when the women made a rash call to run rather than face a probable murder charge. Louise was dead certain no one would believe their story, and Callie elliptically signaled why throughout the rest of the script. Something had happened to Louise in Texas, something she vehemently refused to discuss, but she made enough unguarded slips to indicate that she had been raped herself, and the law had left her undefended.

The rest of the script unspooled as a gonzo road movie, two women on the run toward the Mexican border, the cops in pursuit. Once Thelma and Louise turned desperado, Callie let them revel in becoming freer, wilder, more tuned in to themselves and not caring what anybody thought, as she cut them loose to play out high-spirited fantasies of rebellion. She treated Thelma to an ecstatic night in the sack with a sexy drifter they picked up on the road. She gave Louise the chance for a bittersweet breakup with Jimmy. Strapped for cash, Thelma tried her hand at holding up a convenience store, and when a truck driver heckled the friends with obscenities, they didn't cower or cringe; they blew up the truck. All of this was far enough out there for female characters in a movie, but it wasn't until the very end that Callie unleashed them completely, letting them take flight, literally, into a cinematic stratosphere exceptional for its audacity. With the law at their backs, Callie had them gun the engine of the car and hurtle it right off a cliff into the Grand Canyon. Just as she had envisioned it from the beginning.

The novice screenwriter didn't see that final flourish as the characters killing themselves. She thought it carried to the extreme an irrepressible impetus to bust out of an untenable life. "They flew away, out of this world and into the mass unconscious," Callie wrote afterward. "Women who are completely free from all the shackles that restrain them have no place in this world. The world is not big enough to support them."

For Callie, the journey was about seeking justice in a society where there was no justice. "It required a certain somnambulism to get through a world that thought so little of you," she says. She shook those characters fully awake.

THE TARGET LENGTH for most screenplays was 120 pages. Callie's clocked in closely enough at 135, but she didn't realize how unusual it was in other respects. Despite the tragic ending, her script felt buoyant and liberating. Lord knows, it was funny. And not only were the main characters female, they weren't anything like any other women in the movies—the randy teenagers or the wives or girlfriends or moms of *somebody else* who drove the plot. Thelma and Louise were working-class women, not glamorous in any traditional sense. What's more, they weren't kids who were first learning the possibilities of life, but adults, disillusioned by its limits but capable of willing themselves to an astonishing place.

The men matched them in movie-character peculiarity, all of them flawed versions of the sorts of everyday guys we encounter in real life, but miles away from the big-screen Rambos, Indiana Joneses and *Star Wars* heroes of the day. The script captured the absurdly narcissistic Darryl in two stage directions: "Polyester was made for this man," and "He is making imperceptible adjustments to his overmoussed hair." Jimmy, a musician of indeterminate means, was a feckless lover doomed to realize what he had in Louise only when she was lost to him. Hal, the cop hot on the ladies' tail, was torn between duty and sympathy for their plight. The sexy drifter personified that ultimate rarity, the sex object as a man.

"YOU CAN WRITE A TRUE STORY that never really happened," Callie would say about the screenplay for *Thelma & Louise*. It wasn't *about* Callie Khouri, but it was unmistakably *her*. She had never been raped or perpetrated a crime spree, but the frustration, the rage over constant disrespect, the yearning for self-expression—she had seen enough of that in her years of low-wage work to make a church lady want to blow something up. Anyone who knew Callie could spot elements of her personality in the wary, jaded Louise, with her cutting wit and what her Nashville friend Pam called "a pretty good bullshit meter." Pam, on the other hand, was all over Thelma, from the lovable ditziness to the chaotic packing technique, suitcase spilling over with frilly excess. Their friendship, in which two individuals bound together become a third, bigger thing, was the heart of the story. And a sudden plot shift, when Thelma took charge in a crisis, mirrored the robbery years before when Callie lost her cool and the usually scattered Pam kept a level head.

Other touches from Callie's life made it in there, too. There was the introspective ride through Monument Valley. The time she was walking down a street and a man in a car said something so vile that the thought flashed through her head, *If I'd only had a gun* . . . And Louise's catchphrase, the same one Callie often employed herself: "You get what you settle for."

Although she still worked in video production, Callie was so far removed from the power centers of Hollywood that she nurtured her creation in chaste obliviousness to the norms. She didn't see anything universal in the story; it felt too personal to her. And she didn't see anything especially commercial, either. She wasn't writing the kind of movie that got made, she says. "I was writing the movie I wanted to see."

AS FOR WHAT WAS LIGHTING UP the movie industry at the time, *Thelma & Louise* couldn't have been more out of sync. It might have been seen as the female version of the countercultural road movies of the sixties and seventies. But their defiance of the mainstream had lost favor with the studios by the eighties, replaced by a quest for surefire blockbusters, products of the Reagan years, all bluster, muscle and triumphant endings.

Early eighties popcorn movies like the Indiana Jones series charmed audiences with the old-fashioned storytelling of studio B pictures, but by the mid- to late eighties, the byword was *action,* and action meant large men with large guns. They appeared in ever-splashier versions of the same movie, sequel ready, featuring a guy—better, two guys—battling flamboyant evildoers to the accompaniment of fast-cutting MTV-style visuals, pounding scores, gunshots, explosions, car crashes and a landfill's worth of slow-motion shattering glass. Walking briskets like Sylvester Stallone and Arnold Schwarzenegger emerged as stars, and women were relegated to set dressing, decorative and provocative.

These features earned the label "high-concept," because they could be summed up in a few words, a simple poster and a punchy television commercial, which became critical for roping in opening-weekend crowds as movies released wider and wider. Marketing budgets soared, scaring off anyone inclined to tell a smaller, more emotional story, which was pretty much how Hollywood defined the Women's Picture.

In 1985, the cartoonist Alison Bechdel devised what became known as the Bechdel Test to call attention to the disparity. To pass the test, a movie had to meet a spectacularly minimal standard: it had to include at least two female characters with actual names, they had to have at least one conversation with each other and that conversation had to be about something besides a man. From 1985 to 1989, only a little more than a third of movies passed the test.

From what Callie could see, all this represented a missed opportunity for the film industry to draw ideas for stories from the culture at large. Outside of movie theaters, the eighties were a decade marked by epic change for women, a tangle of firsts and frustrations in the emerging struggle over women's rights. There were new benchmarks set by Sandra Day O'Connor, Sally Ride and Geraldine Ferraro, offset by the failure of the Equal Rights Amendment and reports that women made only sixty-eight cents for every man's dollar. Growing pains played out in the workplace and at home, as the women's movement challenged the very nature of work and family life.

Such a profound cultural disruption would seem to offer fertile material for either comedy or drama. Women and men alike might have wanted to let off steam by seeing the turmoil play out on-screen. But studios shied away, just as they had shied away from depicting the Vietnam War for its duration. In 1981, Jane Fonda managed to push through a project that once again served up issues disguised as pop entertainment. The movie *9 to 5*, a comedy about secretaries who took revenge on a sexist boss, earned more than $100 million to rank as the number two movie that year. But no one rushed to follow up such a solid blockbuster with copycats about secretaries blowing up their typewriters or flinging them through shattering glass, or any other women objecting to anything else.

An industry truism emerged, soon to be set in stone: women's stories belonged on television. When a couple went out on a date, the thinking was, the men chose the movies. Women could watch *Dynasty* or *The Love Boat* at home.

CALLIE KHOURI LIKED going out to the movies, but she hated most of the movies she saw. The year before she wrote *Thelma & Louise*, she was horrified by *Beverly Hills Cop II,* directed by Tony Scott, the younger, less cerebral brother of Ridley. Especially galling was the climactic shootout, when a cop blew away the movie's glamazon secondary villain, played by Brigitte Nielsen. After her body flew through the air to land with a shuddering thump, the shooter punctuated the moment by turning to Eddie Murphy and declaring with a grin, *Women!* Murphy cut loose with his trademark braying laugh. In the theater where she saw the film, Callie remembered, "the audience went crazy." It didn't merely offend her; it scared her.

Beyond such outright hostility, she was fed up with the "bimbos, whores and nagging wives" of most movies and hungry to see a woman as a complete human being, someone she might want to know. There was a handful of women, at most, who made Callie want to proclaim, "Right on, man, she is a righteous chick."

Callie could get behind 1984's *The Terminator,* which saw Linda Hamilton battling a cyborg played by Arnold Schwarzenegger. Her character wasn't cowering or shrieking; she fought for her life. Callie also approved of *Raiders of the Lost Ark,* from 1981, because Karen Allen held her own as Harrison Ford's droll sidekick. But her replacement in the 1984 sequel, a high-maintenance showgirl played by Kate Capshaw, exasperated Callie by squealing helplessly and fussing about breaking a nail, while Indiana Jones grumbled dismissively: *The biggest trouble with her is the noise.*

Yet the traditional notion of a women's film, all weepy and profound, didn't appeal to Callie, either. She hankered to be entertained, to enjoy a little fantasy, to take a ride with characters who were identifiable but still larger-than-life.

In the summer of 1988, when she completed that draft of *Thelma & Louise,* she felt like she'd nailed it. Callie showed it to a few friends. Amanda Temple, Callie's video production buddy, called as soon as she finished reading, too thrilled at first to exclaim much beyond "Oh my God!"

"It's ready to go," Amanda finally insisted. "You need to get an agent, and you need to get this off the ground."

David Warfield read it, too. In the year after their breakup, he and Callie kept running into each other at stoplights, to the point where it seemed absurd not to stop and chat. They reconciled, this time deciding to live together. In the meantime, this screenplay had somehow appeared. David had been trying to get his own movies set up as a producer, so he'd been around a bit. As far as *Thelma & Louise* went, he doubted that the moneymen would underwrite that ending, but he also said this: "It's *9 to 5* meets *Easy Rider*." And he added: "You are going to win the Oscar for this."

Please! It was just as plausible that she'd be cast as the next *Die Hard* supervillain. Nevertheless, Callie nursed a more realistic fantasy. She thought someone who didn't know any better might invest some money— $5 million would be nice—so Amanda could produce and Callie could direct. If she had her druthers, she would cast the rising indie favorites Holly Hunter as Thelma and Frances McDormand as Louise.

Callie wasn't so naive that she couldn't foresee pitfalls. She was savvy enough to know that in the male-driven, violence-tinged world of movies of the time, where women were sex objects at best, *Thelma & Louise* would have to blast through barriers as diverse as the old-boy network, the star system and the creaky, dated inertia of a company town. *If this script ever makes it to the big screen*, she thought, *it would be a miracle if they haven't changed the title to* Tits and Bullets.

CHAPTER 6

UNLIKABLE

Amanda Temple didn't waste a minute getting *Thelma & Louise* into the hands of anybody who could help, delivering the pages on three-hole-punched paper held together with little brass fasteners. During the fall of 1988, she sent out ten, then twenty, thirty, maybe even forty copies. Usually she delivered them in person, the better to plead, and kept up the pressure with a demoralizing burden of daily phone calls. Sometimes Callie dropped the script off herself. Most of the time, the response was no response. First, they solicited agents in hopes that one would represent Callie as a screenwriter. No one would. Then they tried to find some tony little art-film producer to put up some money. No one did.

"It drove me mad," Amanda says. "We were these two blond girls walking around with a script. It was like we were invisible or a joke."

Callie couldn't have asked for a more fiercely determined ally. Amanda's belief in the screenplay was unshakable, and she enjoyed some helpful film-biz cachet. Besides her music video production credits, she was married to Julien Temple, a young English director who had made the British feature film *Absolute Beginners*. Amanda and Julien touched down in Hollywood during the mid-eighties, when Warner Bros. put them up at the Sunset Marquis, a hotel near the clubs along the Sunset Strip. The place attracted a mongrel mix of rock 'n' rollers and other entertainers who lounged by the courtyard pool. After Julien left for the studio on their first morning there, Amanda faced the question of where she, a production secretary back in London, could secure a place for herself in this tantalizing town.

She peeked out the window. "There were these girls by the pool in micro-bikinis with these enormous breasts," she says. "I was twenty-five years old, and I had never seen breasts like that, all pumped up. There were guys with big hair and chains and the whole thing, and they thought it was just so funny to push these girls into the pool. The girls would giggle and get out of the pool, and the guys would do it again and again and again. I was like, 'Where have I landed?'"

One of her first outings was a dinner where she was seated next to Joan Rivers. "She was hilarious," Amanda says. "I was the youngest at the table, and she took one look at me and saw raw meat." "You've moved to LA?" Rivers asked. "Well, first thing, we've got to give you some tits. And look at that little button nose, it's just off-kilter. Yeah, we're going to do that, too."

Amanda played along, but she was shaking by the end of the meal. "Everything was so surface, so about the way you look," she says. "My God, I had to toughen up, I really did."

But she also perceived that in contrast to England, where people regarded her as "a little blonde behind a typewriter," Los Angeles was a city where someone could reinvent herself, given enough energy and conviction. Hollywood appeared so wide open, so thrumming with enterprising zeal, that it seemed possible to turn herself into something more, a little blond *producer*. It was heartening that men and women there were unashamedly passionate about everything to do with film and fearless about seizing opportunity. They galvanized her to muscle her way into music video production, eventually starting her own company.

Until she and Callie started working together, Amanda felt like an alien in Southern California, set apart by her self-deprecating British humor and her refusal to take everything seriously, but the two clicked right away. "Her being from the South, we really connected," Amanda says. "We were both refugees, able to poke fun and see through a different lens. We could see that this place was... ridiculous."

HER HUSBAND'S CONNECTIONS and Amanda's own resourcefulness got her nowhere with *Thelma & Louise* as fall and winter rolled by. She walked the script into the office of Julien's agent, Jim Crabbe at William Morris, but he told her later that he didn't remember it crossing his desk. Harvey Weinstein's office got a copy, but she never heard back. The same with Amy Pascal, a new production executive at Columbia. Amanda theorized that the bolder tastemakers in town might get what she was peddling, but she couldn't slip it past their minions who didn't have the authority to challenge the standard molds.

A British producer, Stephen Woolley, a partner of the writer-director Neil Jordan, assigned one of his development executives to take a meeting, the first of three that Amanda and Callie snagged at small-time indie companies. Each time the objections were firm and always the same: no one would take a liking to women who committed violence, and no one wanted to watch them drive off a cliff. "Can't they just shoot the guy in the leg?" posed one executive. Another asked, "Don't you think you should have a *guy* shoot the guy and the women should just run?"

The absolute deal breaker was always the ending. "Maybe the Grand Canyon should be more like a ditch," someone said, "and they floor it and land on the other side."

Callie wouldn't entertain suggestions; she wouldn't play the game. "I wasn't interested in telling anybody else's story," she says. The goal wasn't fame or riches—she wanted to make *Thelma & Louise*.

"Let's go, we're out of here," Callie would say to Amanda before turning to address the executives in a flat, dismissive tone. "We've got nothing to talk about. You're not going to talk me into anything, and I'm not going to talk you into anything. So we're done."

The first couple of times, the two friends broke into laughter as they headed out the door, vowing, "We're not going to change a thing." But after their third and final impasse, at a company called Palace Productions on Third Street, dejection trailed them as they trudged home along the wide, flat Santa Monica beach. It seemed increasingly farfetched that anyone would be willing to make *Thelma & Louise* the way it was written. No one saw what Callie and Amanda saw.

"This whole issue of the women being unsympathetic—come on!" Amanda railed, her voice rising with exasperation. "Guys can be unsympathetic and violent and unpleasant and abusive, and they get away with it. But you put trousers on the women and *they're* outrageous?"

The disappointment made her frantic. By now it was the spring of 1989. Months had passed on their fruitless quest, and a clock was ticking. Amanda was heavily pregnant and would soon return to England for the birth, with Callie stuck behind, still churning out godforsaken music videos.

Callie stopped short. "We were sure there would be plenty of people who don't understand this and say no," she assured her partner. "We only need one yes." If they tapped out all their resources in Los Angeles, maybe they could find some foreigner who hadn't wised up to the ways of Hollywood to put up the cash.

"I was savvy enough, as was Callie," Amanda says, "to know that as soon as you start diluting something you are passionate about, it will dissolve into nothing. I've seen what happens when people get stuck in the Hollywood machine and their movies morph into something they don't recognize. If you stick to your vision, you can at least sleep at night. You may not be the biggest hotshot, but at least your conscience is clear."

AMANDA SOUGHT ADVICE FROM SOMEONE she had met through friends: Mimi Polk, a thirty-year-old American who ran the Los Angeles production company of Ridley Scott, the British director best known for the science fiction features *Alien* and *Blade Runner*. They sometimes worked with foreign investors, Amanda had heard.

"Mimi," she said as she turned over the precious bound pages, "am I going mad? Why do I think this is such a brilliant thing? Why doesn't anybody get it?"

Six weeks passed without a word. When Callie said good-bye to Amanda just before she left to have the baby, the mood was glum. "I can't believe it," Amanda said. "Not even Mimi is getting back."

But when Callie picked up the phone a few weeks later, Mimi Polk was on the line. Callie heard a crisp, professional voice cut through all the layers of rejection and indifference and say the magic words: "I loved your script."

You... *what*?

"I love the characters. I think they would be accessible to a lot of people."

Callie absorbed this news with as much outward composure as she could muster. Finally... the kind of reaction she had been expecting all along. Finally... a believer, a believer with some connection to people with clout. But she froze at Mimi's follow-up. "Is it all right if I let Ridley see it? Not to direct, but maybe he would be willing to produce."

"It had all gone so well," Callie says. "The momentum had started with the idea and then kept up through the writing, and now I was coming to the moment when a *real* director was going to read it." *Oh my God,* she thought. *Is this where the whole thing ends?*

She consented, then steeled herself for more rejection and delay, but Mimi called back about a week later. "Ridley loves it, too," she said. "He'd like to meet with you." Callie froze again. "The only difficulty is that you would be a first-time director," Mimi continued. "You are going to have to make a choice. Do you want to take a shot at directing it yourself? Or do you want this first movie to be with bigger stars and a bigger-name director, which would really put you on the map?" Ridley had no interest in directing this script, she said, but he might produce it for another director.

Callie rang Amanda straightaway. The news stirred up a monsoon of emotions—justification, joy, relief and, for Amanda, irritation that Mimi had cut her out of the picture by contacting Callie directly, but Amanda didn't flinch. She knew that she could speak up for a producer credit, but she also felt the most righteous action she could take for her friend, for the script, was to let it go and walk away.

"Callie," Amanda said, "this could be a magic wand. They can wave it and make the movie happen. You're an idiot if you don't do this with them. *It's going to get made.*"

Perhaps, but in what form? "Oh my God, the Scott brothers," Amanda says later, conflating Ridley with his brother Tony, the hotshot behind *Beverly Hills Cop II.* "Yes, of course, you think, *Tits and Bullets*—perfect!"

Ridley's work had more taste, the two friends agreed, but could he understand this profoundly female story? His movies were overwhelmingly commercial sci-fi epics, strong on action, light on character, *guy* movies, except for his casting of Sigourney Weaver in the lead of *Alien,* a part originally written for a man. Callie knew the gamble she'd be taking by relinquishing this exquisitely balanced script.

Take this opportunity, Amanda advised, and the story would benefit from the kind of clout they couldn't hope to summon on their own. "Callie, it's now going to be a Ridley Scott movie," she cautioned, "which is a completely different animal than what we envisioned. It's going to get a lot of attention. It's going to be a movie that everyone is talking about."

They couldn't be sure what else it would be. Back and forth, they tried to parse just who Ridley Scott was and what his intentions were, little considering that Hollywood had been working the same puzzle for the previous ten years.

CHAPTER 7

THE EPIC IN RIDLEY SCOTT'S HEAD

It was customary in the movie business to read scripts late at night, propped on a pillow in bed. Ridley Scott never worked at night. "You think you're winning," he says. "You're not."

The director approached the script for *Thelma & Louise* the way he read any new material, at seven in the morning, at his sharpest. He sat on a hard chair with good light in the study overlooking the formal garden at his eighteenth-century home in the affluent Hampstead area of London, a cup of strong, hot coffee at his side. No one was permitted to enter the room until he finished.

Mimi Polk had pitched the script as a possible project for him to produce and told him something about the writer being a friend or a friend of a friend who had been a receptionist at a place that made videos or commercials. He couldn't quite remember. Ridley was skeptical of any amateur who claimed to have written a screenplay. Nevertheless, right away, he started laughing. By nine o'clock, he reached the last page, where the car leaped off the cliff. *Wow*, he thought. "The script flew," he says. "It was very well written. I started to see faces. I started to think, *Damn! This could be this, this could be that. This is good enough to get any actress.*"

After seven years at art school, Ridley benefited from what he considered his greatest gift—his mind saw everything in picture form. "I could see the film almost immediately as I was reading," he says. "I thought, *This is epic.* The landscape should be epic. The ending would be epic. But, unusually, it was a comedy. I mean, it was *funny.*"

He knew this wasn't for him. It was too much from a woman's point of view, full of womanly banter and a wrath he couldn't quite grasp. But he knew there had to be some director who could carry it off.

On that morning in the early spring of 1989, Ridley formed a firm opinion about *Thelma & Louise.* It was an epic comedy about how women act when guys aren't around, and it would end not with tragedy—he didn't see the ending as tragic—but with the right decision. *As long as a studio doesn't try to make it better by not having them go off the cliff,* he thought. "They *have* to," he insists. "I saw it more as them continuing their journey. It was what they were intended to do."

He asked Mimi to set up a meeting with this Callie Khouri person as soon as he returned to LA.

WHEREVER DIVERSITY IN THE WORKPLACE is an issue, as it certainly was and is in the movie industry, it's essential that some white guy stick his neck out to start to set things right. That guy doesn't have to be a flaming activist, but he has to be able to empathize with the group that lacks a voice, to listen to the people who've been deprived of power up to now, to be willing to give over some responsibility, to trust their judgment, to stand up for their point of view. Could Ridley Scott be that guy? Aside from the casting coup with Sigourney Weaver in *Alien*, his oeuvre was largely devoted to guys waging battles with robots or monsters or other guys. His agent, Jeff Berg, called him Mr. Macho, and he wasn't alone. "He hadn't been any kind of a woman's director," says Susan Sarandon, summing up the industry consensus. "He was seen as a very male, very macho action director."

Yet for all the typically eighties subject matter of his movies, they lacked the formulaic simplicity of the typical eighties blockbuster. Ridley Scott's films possessed a sumptuous visual splendor, an elegant pace and a dark moral ambiguity that tipped in the direction of art. Hans Zimmer, the film composer who often collaborated with Ridley, says, "The bottom line is that Ridley just wants to make a really good movie, and it never occurs to him to be patronizing about the characters, or sexist, or whatever words you want to pick."

It would strike many in Hollywood as odd that a European man like Ridley Scott could become a champion for a movie that tapped a powder keg of outrage about American women and their place in American society, but he didn't think about that on the morning he read the script. He liked it. It made him laugh. It made him see pictures.

RIDLEY HAD MADE FIVE MOVIES by this time, and yet as a personality he was something of an unknown on the Hollywood scene. Pale, freckled, with the short, stocky stature of a Celtic Briton, he rarely socialized in Los Angeles, preferring his home in London and often filming and editing abroad. In a town built on faux friendships, Ridley Scott didn't do chitchat; he worked. People in the business knew his work, certainly, and his perfectionism had earned him a reputation for being somewhat crusty, if not outright difficult, but few would have known him well enough to be aware that at least one formidable woman had figured prominently in his life.

"My mom was four foot eleven and insisted she was five feet tall," says

Ridley. She ruled a pack of three sons through an itinerant boyhood set mostly in Northumberland, an industrial county wedged hard against the Scottish border and the coast of the North Sea. Ridley was born in 1937, following his older brother, Frank, who grew up to serve in the merchant navy, and six years before the youngest, Tony. Their father, Francis, served in the Royal Engineers during World War II, rising to acting brigadier general, while his wife, Elizabeth, imposed discipline on the home front and continued her rigid reign when the family reunited after the war.

"By the standards of mothers today, she must sound pretty tough," Ridley concedes. "If I broke my arm, it was my fault. If I fell in the sea, it was my fault. You were not allowed to be ill." Her favorite expression was "Pull yourself together."

Ridley got the belt and he got the stick. "To me, it was a medal of honor," he recalled later. "If I got a bruise on my ass from a cane? It was normal."

Yet the family was tight, according to Tony. "Dad was a very gentle and sweet man," he said. "Mum was the matriarch and the patriarch of the family. She ran the roost with a steel fist, but at the same time there was respect and love for her. The driving force Ridley and I have comes from Mum, but they were chalk and cheese."

Ridley stumbled and brooded through a bewildering array of ten or eleven schools as the family followed his father's career, first to Germany during the rebuilding after the war, then back to Northern England. "I hated school," Ridley says. His performance reflected his disdain. Years later he framed a report card and hung it in his London office. It showed him ranked 29 out of 29 in his class—no half measures.

But he could do one thing inordinately well—he could draw and paint. He and his father sat quietly together making watercolors on a balcony in Bavaria, and he gave Ridley books for his birthdays: *How to Draw Boats, How to Draw Horses.* It was his mother who first took Ridley to the cinema—*The Black Swan* with Tyrone Power was the first; *Great Expectations* and *Citizen Kane* made big impressions. Soon he started to go alone, nursing a secret ambition to work on a film someday, maybe as an art director, a promising job title that he spotted in the credits. This was an absurd ambition for a shy, underachieving, working-class boy from the North. "It was just too silly for words," he told himself. "I wouldn't dare." The film industry was the far side of the moon.

When a teacher suggested he switch to art school, Ridley jumped headfirst, and "the world began for me—I adored it." He thrived at the local West Hartlepool College of Art for four years, followed by three more earning a degree in design at the Royal College of Art in London. There was no course of study for film, but he borrowed a Bolex camera to make a short, *Boy and Bicycle*, on a budget of £65, drafting Tony to perform as star and chief equipment carrier. After graduation in 1961, Ridley scored a job as a set decorator at the BBC, where he talked his way into a quickie directors' training course. That catapulted him into overseeing episodes of hits like *Z Cars*, a police drama shot with social realism.

Ridley thought like an artist but was sharp to the ways of business, too. He bit when Gerber, the baby food company, offered him a chance to moonlight by making his first commercial. The young star spent the shoot spitting the product into the director's lens, but at the end of a day Ridley was handed more cash than he earned in a month at the BBC, and he savored a budget that allowed him to create a tight visual gem on a short turnaround. A company that he formed, Ridley Scott Associates, soon emerged as one of the most successful and innovative makers of commercials through the seventies and eighties, many of them directed by Ridley or others on his roster, including Tony, who had followed him from art school into the field.

Ridley seized the opportunity to experiment with the charged emotional and marketing possibilities of moving images. Each Ridley Scott commercial got the mini-masterpiece treatment, storyboarded, designed, lit with perfection and shot by Ridley himself. A sentimental, nostalgic 1973 ad for Hovis bread, featuring a boy with a bicycle in a picturesque village, was voted Britain's all-time favorite commercial. It was nothing like his 1979 "Share the Fantasy" ad for Chanel No. 5, an erotic reverie intent on a woman lounging by a swimming pool and the brazenly phallic figure of a man who rose from the water between her legs. That one turned heads with a glossy hint of kink.

Advertising made Ridley very rich and very busy—he sometimes made two commercials a week, completing more than a thousand commercials in little more than a decade. "You know how when you get hot you can do anything?" he says. "I loved the work and the pressure. There was a bit of stress, but there's positive stress and negative stress. Negative stress is sitting around when you're doing nothing, and *I don't like relaxing.* Positive stress is where you feel elevated and usually you are in the face of some bloody huge quandary. I kind of like that. My work is my pleasure."

But it drove him crazy as he approached his forties and other British ad directors made the leap to feature films before he did. He used his sizable stash of money to hire screenwriters to develop a property for him, settling on *The Duellists,* based on a Joseph Conrad story, a period piece about two French army officers who obsessively, even absurdly, fought each other for twenty years. It won the best first work award at the Cannes Film Festival in 1977, when Ridley was thirty-nine. He started prepping another art house project, a nonoperatic version of *Tristan and Isolde.*

That's when he took a sharp turn and went Hollywood, never to pivot back. On a visit there in the spring of 1977, Ridley took in a movie that had opened that week, *Star Wars.* He flipped over the clever use of the landscape of Morocco, which he knew from commercials, over the mix of animals and human beings in the characters, over the technology of the spaceships. It stirred his competitive juices to the point of anguish. "My biggest compliment when I see a film is if I'm in a fit of total depression," he says. "I walked out—*damn!*"

He set aside the beautiful hand-drawn storyboards for *Tristan and Isolde,* determined to take a new direction. Other directors had already turned down an outer-space project called *Alien*, a seemingly standard monster movie set on a spaceship. But when the script came Ridley's way, it lit up his design imagination. He envisioned chilly, sinister imagery drawn from French heavy-metal comics and commissioned the Swiss artist H. R. Giger to create a monster that shunned the sci-fi cliché of dragonlike creatures.

Long after its release in 1979, what people remembered most about *Alien*, aside from the ravishing look of the thing and the hideous monster that pursued the crew of the doomed ship, was the lead role, named Ripley. Alan Ladd Jr., then the head of 20th Century Fox, said to Ridley during preproduction, "What do you think if Ripley is a woman?"

"It was not for any reason," Laddie recollects. "I wasn't trying to make it a women's picture. It was just a different way to go about it."

Ridley, heedless that Laddie was one of the only executives at the time who entertained the idea of movies with prominent female roles, and pretty much unaware that women rarely played the leads in anybody else's Hollywood movies, didn't see a problem with that. "Great idea," he said. "Why *not* make the hero female?"

"I never thought about it," he says. "I only think about the film. Every film is like a painting. I only think of the painting." His mind shifted immediately to the look of the star. "We need to find somebody who is physically powerful"—a tall order in a field of actresses prized for their passivity and delicate physiques.

The casting process lasted until just three weeks before the start of principal photography. When he heard about an imposing actress named Sigourney Weaver, who had never done anything of note outside of off-Broadway, he requested a meeting over sushi in New York.

"This giant walked in," he says, his face lighting up at the memory. "She had an Afro in those days. It made her a foot and a half taller. I thought she was about seven foot three." Ridley was convinced.

But Laddie wasn't, even after a screen test. As he hesitated, one of his production executives, the British-born Gareth Wigan, invited a dozen secretaries into the room to watch. "Who likes her?" Wigan asked, and all the hands went up. They told him they admired Weaver's strength. It reminded them of Jane Fonda.

The role of Ripley is often cited as a milestone for women in film, although the intention was mostly to ratchet up the shock value by placing a woman in jeopardy, as schlockier horror movies did. "I always felt that the decision to make Ripley the survivor was not made out of any great feminist sentiment," Sigourney Weaver said. "It was, 'No one will ever guess that this girl will end up being the survivor.' It wasn't a statement of any kind, but he really made it work."

Reviews for *Alien* were mixed, but its critical stature grew over time as viewers came to appreciate Ridley's visual artistry. With $79 million at the box office, the film was considered a hit, just not on the level of the Lucas-Spielberg blockbusters that then roamed the earth. And its novel look was hugely influential. All that gave Ridley enough cachet to land his next film, the futuristic thriller *Blade Runner,* released in 1982, which allowed his design sensibility to run wild. The story of a Philip Marlowe–like bounty hunter on the trail of rebel androids granted Ridley license to create an original world of dense, murky layers, centered in a decayed megalopolis with elements drawn from Hong Kong, Los Angeles and the north of England—industrial noir. Smoke, grime and rain added even more depth and dimension, a stark contrast to the art direction for typical movie versions of the future—so antiseptic that one could only assume that most of the androids were Roombas.

Blade Runner wielded influence over the look of every futuristic movie that followed—it put the *dys* in *dystopia*—and eventually surpassed even

Alien to be regarded as a landmark of cinema. But it was considered a cult obsession at the time. The *New York Times* review captured the critical consensus by calling *Blade Runner* "muddled yet mesmerizing," and the movie was a flop. "*Blade Runner* was a disaster," Ridley says. "When it was made, no one saw it. No one understood it, except some diehards. It was not a good result."

Yet Ridley wasn't humbled. To Hollywood players, he was a newcomer, but as he saw it, he had run more film through cameras in commercials than most anyone in the industry. He was forty-three on that set of *Blade Runner*, and he damn well knew what he was about. "They would never take into account that I'd been in business since I was twenty-seven, in New York, London and LA. I simply stood my ground because I knew I was right. I wasn't a twenty-five-year-old to get beaten up." He took particular heat for not communicating well with Harrison Ford, who played the lead, and later Ridley acknowledged that he paid most of his attention to the visuals at Ford's expense.

Given all the fuss over special effects and production issues, the women in *Blade Runner* didn't attract much notice. The star was a man, yet three female characters were commanding figures—Sean Young portrayed a somewhat typical love interest, but Daryl Hannah and Joanna Cassidy played androids that were fierce and physically robust. Whatever Ridley might say about his attitudes toward women, it's clear from his choices that he admired strapping ones, not simpering helpmates. He didn't mind showing them in their underwear, like the white cotton skivvies Sigourney Weaver wore at the climax of *Alien*, or in nothing but sequins and body paint, which barely covered Joanna Cassidy in *Blade Runner*. He liked to look at attractive women, but he invested them with personalities like his own, or his mum's—people who got stuff done and made their marks on the world.

Witness one of his most renowned sixty seconds of footage, the 1984 Apple television ad. An Orwellian pageant that famously omitted any shot of the Macintosh computer that the ad was promoting, it ran just once, during the Super Bowl. Ridley cast actual skinheads from the National Front to play automatons listening to a ranting leader on a giant TV, interrupted when a female athlete in red running shorts heaved a sledgehammer through the screen, a powerful blow against the man. Yet once again Ridley insists that any feminist message was inadvertent.

When asked if there was any significance that the athlete was female, Ridley replies with a mischievous smile: "No—she had a great ass. "

CHAPTER 8

D-GIRLS

Diane Cairns sent her assistant to drag a desk chair from the office next door when Mimi Polk showed up in the spring of 1989 with the new, unknown screenwriter. Callie Khouri cut an unusual figure in jeans and a pair of red Tony Lama cowboy boots with butterflies tooled on the sides. The agent, always outfitted in a uniform of three-inch pumps with a tailored dress or skirt and jacket, had never seen cowboy boots before in a professional setting. She masked any reaction with a proper game face.

As an agent for writers, not top directors or stars, Diane didn't command one of the offices with commodious seating areas belonging to ICM colleagues like Joe Funicello, who represented Jodie Foster, or Ed Limato, who handled Mel Gibson and Michelle Pfeiffer. It was Diane's strategy to slip these sorts of luminaries the script for *Thelma & Louise*. From there, it was a question of maneuvering it around the Hollywood game board, into the sight lines of people at the studios and, God willing, onto the screen.

Like everyone else who'd heard about the script, Diane had a far-from-promising introduction to it. She'd gotten the tip when she was on the phone about something else with Sue Williams, a development assistant at Ridley Scott's company. "The writer is looking for an agent," Williams said. She didn't mention that Mimi had run it by others who had already passed. "Do you want to read it?"

For Diane, the answer to that question was always yes. She read ten or twelve scripts every weekend, lying in the sun on the Santa Monica beach. Sometimes she set her alarm for 5 a.m. to bulldoze through a couple more before she headed to the gym and office. Other times she read scripts while she brushed her teeth. Diane's job was to represent screenwriters, but more important, she sought out material that kept work flowing for the rest of the agency, wading through a slag heap of available scripts and plucking the jewels that might make magic for the directors and stars and studio bosses on high.

She read *Thelma & Louise* reclining in bed before sunup in her Westwood condo, her mind fresh but half asleep. It jolted her awake as nothing had in years, although she had enough experience to understand the hurdles. "At the time, everything was all-male, action-driven," she says. "Even if you had a male-female script, it was the kiss of death." On the other hand, "I had youthful ignorance on my side," she says. "I liked it because I liked it."

Diane surmised that Mimi had tagged along to the meeting because she wasn't willing to let her discovery out of her sight. If all went well, this would be Ridley's first time producing for another director, and Mimi's first as a coproducer, but Callie needed an agent to sell the script to a studio that was willing to foot the bill.

Diane opened by praising the writer's work. Callie let the welcome words wash over her but didn't allow them to breach her defenses. She quickly laid down her ground rules, and they were cocky for a rank beginner: guarantees that the ending wouldn't be changed, that she would have the opportunity to direct and that when a studio signed on, it would pay half a million dollars for the screenplay, an aggressive figure during a time when only a few scripts reached such heights. "I remember thinking how distinctive Callie was," Diane says. "At a time when most women had been conditioned to be more reserved, she had no problem plowing right in there. She didn't even know how long the odds were. Mimi knew a little bit."

Diane said she'd try, but Callie would have to get real about her ambition to direct. Only two women the year before had made top-fifty movies, including Penny Marshall, as the director of *Big*, and none the year before that. "It was a no-brainer," Diane recollects. "At that time, women weren't directing movies. It was stacking the deck too much on top of the two female leads."

CALLIE SWALLOWED HARD and gave it a couple days before she signed on. From there the task of getting *Thelma & Louise* out of the starting gate would fall to Diane and Mimi, two women who had landed jobs on the business side of movies, most of them serving others by vetting stacks of raw material, one of the few Hollywood jobs that gave women a way in.

"You're never going to be an agent here," Diane had been assured in 1980, when she started as a xerox girl at a smaller agency. "I was this cupcake," she says looking back. "It made sense to me." Growing up in the sixties and seventies, she hadn't expected doors to be open to her, despite her business degree from USC. "You could be a teacher, a nurse or a housewife," she says. "We were still in the shadows of the big revolutions—the drugs, the Pill, Vietnam. I was the only woman in my college business classes. I sound like an old codger, but it didn't start to change until the mid-eighties."

When one of her first bosses told her she was too pretty to be taken seriously, her comeback was to laugh and say, "I'll scar my face."

In 1985, she traded up to the literary department of the industry giant ICM. Female agents there were still fairly rare, prized as nurturers, able to coddle and keep the clients happy, although there were exceptions, like Sue Mengers, a fireball who'd won a preeminent place in the seventies on pure bravado. Diane walked a middle line, rigorously competent, speaking in a kind of business staccato. "Everybody thinks they should be wearing white gloves when they walk into your office," a colleague told her. She scored some important victories before *Thelma & Louise* crossed her path, partly by exercising judgment that ran against the grain. Diane had sniffed out the script for the sexual thriller *Fatal Attraction* for the director Adrian Lyne, an important ICM client. She also played a part in placing the period drama *Dangerous Liaisons* with a studio and getting the script to Michelle Pfeiffer.

Diane didn't wind up on the right side of every call. Back when she was a pup agent at her first job, she read the script for what would become 1983's multiple-Oscar winner *Terms of Endearment*. "Honestly," Diane told her boss, "I don't know who wants to see a movie with two women bitching at each other for two hours."

"It was a complete whiff," she says. The next time she was handed a script about two fully formed difficult but funny women, she vowed to take off the white gloves.

FOR MIMI POLK, Callie's script represented a chance to break into a higher echelon. Mimi had worked primarily as a D-girl, short for development girl, the accepted industry term for the mostly female workforce in the bottom tier of studio or production jobs. Most D-girls had graduated from good colleges, often with literature degrees. If asked, they could probably parse the meager parallels between *The Count of Monte Cristo* and *Rambo*, but mostly they read piles of submissions so they could pass the best contenders along to higher-ups. For years, D-girl was by far the most common and, outside of secretarial work, often the only job for women at studios, recognition that they were smart enough to identify good material but not to greenlight pictures or manage their production. A few, including Sherry Lansing and Paula Weinstein, had parlayed the role into more-responsible jobs.

Mimi, whose father had been president and CEO of MGM in New York briefly in the 1960s, had apprenticed in theater and made in-house corporate films before looking for work in London. In one memorable interview for a D-girl job, a movie executive she already knew asked if she would be interested in auditioning for the mermaid role in *Splash*.

"You mean as a topless mermaid?" Mimi answered, masking her incredulity. "I'm not an actress. I want to be a producer."

No job was forthcoming, and when she got up and turned her narrow frame toward the door, the executive said, "Have you gained weight?"

"No," she replied.

"Because your ass got really big."

It was a relief to meet Ridley, who often put women in charge of his administrative dealings. "I found the best man for the job, and it turned out to be a woman," he was fond of saying. "I treat women like one of the guys. They treat me like one of the girls. I've never had a problem, and I never understand that bullshit." After five years in Ridley's employ, Mimi moved to LA in 1988 to run his office there. She hired a D-girl of her own.

Fair-haired, with pale blue eyes and fine, close-set features, Mimi invariably looked well turned out in flat shoes, with not a scrap of makeup. She could be secretive around the office to protect her interests, excluding her D-girl from meetings, and deployed a strictly composed personality and clipped way of speaking that made her emotions hard to read. "One of the best ways for a woman to succeed as a producer or anything else," she says, "is to be a defuser of drama."

Mimi calculated that producing the improbable screenplay by Callie

Khouri, such a departure from her boss's usual métier, would show off his range and enhance his career as well as her own. "Not many scripts came his way, because everyone thought of him as a big-action sci-fi director," says Mimi. "For drama, there were maybe thirty or forty directors in front of him in line. That's why it was a real gem to find *Thelma & Louise.*"

IT HAD TO COMPETE for her boss's attention with other pressing priorities. By the time Ridley read the script in the spring of 1989, he had taken some punches. His 1985 release, *Legend,* a dark fantasy with goblins and unicorns, had tanked despite ravishing visuals and the casting of a fledgling Tom Cruise. *Someone to Watch Over Me,* a 1987 romance about a cop who falls for a woman he is assigned to protect, met a similar fate. In 1989, he was wrapping up *Black Rain,* a cop melodrama starring Michael Douglas and set primarily in a rain-slicked, neon-lit Japan, but Fox had snubbed him for the sequel to *Alien,* turning to James Cameron instead. The producer Joel Silver was courting Ridley to make an elaborate special-effects action film called *Isobar* that Mimi nicknamed *Alien on a Train,* but it went without saying that another futuristic mayhem-in-transit project would hardly have represented a creative leap forward.

Meanwhile, by some measures Ridley's younger brother was eclipsing him. Tony had also moved from commercials to movies and shot to the top of the A-list with his second film, 1986's *Top Gun,* the Tom Cruise fighter-jet action extravaganza, which earned an astounding $357 million worldwide. He had caught the attention of the movie's producers, the action impresarios Don Simpson and Jerry Bruckheimer, with a fast-cutting commercial that pitted a Saab 900 against a jet, both of them sleek, fast and turbocharged under the camera's besotted caress. *Beverly Hills Cop II,* another huge hit for Simpson-Bruckheimer, kept the team soaring into another collaboration, the Tom Cruise NASCAR spectacle,

Days of Thunder. In all three, a few sexy women ceded the center of attention to the relationships that really counted among competitive men.

People in the business started to define the brothers in opposition to each other: Tony, the embodiment of the decade with his flair for high-concept action movies, the critics be damned; Ridley, the master of moody artistry, bent on success but steering clear of obvious commercial choices.

Coworkers warmed to Tony's sociability in contrast to Ridley's restraint. "Ridley is like a wizard—kind of mysterious and a little rough and a little more difficult, a little less accessible in some ways," says Susan Sarandon, who worked with Tony on his first film, the stylish vampire chiller *The Hunger.* "Ridley is more solemn, a man of few, very specific words, compared to Tony, who was bubbly, exuberant, very chatty and not particularly mysterious at all."

Their opposing personal styles led to very different pictures. While Tony's appeals to the masses didn't pretend to aim for gravitas, Ridley's delved deeper. He always seemed to strive for something more that he might not be able to put into words, at risk of leaving the masses scratching their heads. Ridley often resisted studio pressure for happy endings, while Tony delivered them in slow-motion showers of triumph. Yet Ridley's wealth and success in the advertising sphere, which continued in tandem with his movies, granted him a kind of superpower strength in insecure Hollywood—he didn't much care what people thought of him.

"He's a bull, and I am, too," Tony once told the *Hollywood Reporter.* "Nothing takes him down. We have enormous pain resistance."

HOWEVER MUCH HE NEEDED A CHANGE, Ridley still couldn't see himself directing Callie's story. "It was very much not my thing," he admits. "I tend to do action-driven things. I love period. This was about women talking about guys and what assholes guys can be."

Fortunately, he did know the perfect man for the job, someone with box-office clout and a flair for action tempered with comedy. "He was very good with women," Ridley says. "He could make them really sexy, because he had that kind of rapport with them. And he was hot then, so it would have been made easily."

Ridley hadn't yet met with Callie, who so abhorred the treatment of women in eighties blockbusters, but when he did, he planned to tell her that he would offer the job of directing *Thelma & Louise* to the man responsible for one of the films that offended her most, *Beverly Hills Cop II*. His hotshot brother Tony Scott.

CHAPTER 9

PLAYING A DIFFERENT GAME

Geena Davis was a star on the rise who had just collected a Best Supporting Actress Oscar for *The Accidental Tourist*, but she wasn't about to wait around for the rare good role to amble her way. There were three or four meaty, three-dimensional parts for women up for grabs in any given year. The competition was way too fierce for proud passivity.

Then she heard about not one, but—could it be?—two such elusive roles in a script that was beginning to float around in the summer of 1989. Someone slipped Geena an early copy of *Thelma & Louise*. "I was just mad for it," she'd decided. "Absolutely obsessed in love with it."

"These were two completely filled-out characters who were absolutely equal, who had so many colors and moments," she says. "And they had to transform themselves in four days into killing themselves, and it had to make sense!" So desperately did she want in that she cold-called Callie and went over to her house to comb through the script together, the better to make a case.

Geena wasn't an obvious choice for a female-driven action movie. Even though she landed sizable parts with enviable regularity, the word *quirky* had become attached to her, trailing her like a devoted mutt, which was strange, because with her lanky, dynamic six-foot frame and unconventional beauty, she radiated dazzling star power. She wasn't the obvious choice for typical docile-girlfriend roles, either, nor did she want to play them. Geena knew she was capable of more, if only the opportunity presented itself.

Her agent, David Eidenberg, who shared her fervor for *Thelma & Louise*, phoned Ridley to make the case. It was too late, Ridley said. ICM's marquee names, Jodie Foster and Michelle Pfeiffer, had already snapped up the roles.

In case someone fell out, Eidenberg called to badger Mimi Polk every week. "Has anything changed? Because Geena's still interested." But with parts that rare and that good, an unconventional midlevel star like Geena Davis didn't stand a chance.

LANDING JODIE AND MICHELLE WAS A COUP. It happened right away once Diane and Mimi locked in a deal for Ridley to produce Callie's script. Diane zigzagged through the halls of the agency to put the script in the hands of the actresses' reps, Mimi double-teamed with phone calls and the two blond superstars had enlisted by June of 1989. The only question left was who should play which role.

In terms of star power, those two were no Tom Cruises or Harrison Fords—no women were—yet both were critically respected and popular with audiences. Jodie was only twenty-six years old, but she had started earning her place as an industry fixture as far back as she could remember. Cast in her first commercial—wearing a swimsuit bottom in a Coppertone ad—at the age of three, she was firmly established as a working actor by the time she turned ten. Even then, she was self-possessed and precocious, with a firm handshake and a firm point of view. At twelve, she kicked off a series of provocative choices by playing, yes, a prostitute, one her own age, in Martin Scorsese's *Taxi Driver*. When the film played at Cannes in 1977, Jodie wowed a press conference when she translated her cast mates' comments into perfect French.

A Best Actress Oscar for *The Accused* a couple months before she saw the script for *Thelma & Louise* capped a slate of eighties films that met with mixed success but generally positive reviews for Jodie's performances. Her role as the victim of a gang rape in that film perfectly showcased her talent. With watchful, piercing blue eyes, delicate features, a husky voice and obvious intelligence, she often portrayed young women who were worldly beyond their years, their taut reserve masking barely visible insecurities.

But even with her notable gifts, Jodie found it difficult to land meaningful roles. Before *The Accused*, she considered quitting the profession. "I couldn't see spending my life working with bad material," she said. The director Jonathan Kaplan had to lobby to cast her in the movie over objections from studio executives who called her "not rapeable enough," he says. They worried that she was too "chubby" and "tough." Jodie won the role only after Kaplan asked her to film a second audition where she dressed and acted softer than he knew was right for the character. Once she got the part, she did it her way. With $32 million at the box office, the movie became one of those female-driven surprise hits.

Michelle Pfeiffer had followed a more conventional path, eased by a stunning Southern California beauty that left the entertainment media groveling with superlatives. BEING DROP-DEAD GORGEOUS NEARLY DOOMED MICHELLE PFEIFFER TO BIMBO LIMBO, said a headline in the *Philadelphia Inquirer*. The story went on to chronicle *People*'s description of her "turquoise eyes in a flawless blond setting" and "fragile, yet all-American voluptuousness" and to repeat the *St. Petersburg Times*'s paean to her "hair finer than corn silk, eyes clearer than the sky and skin smooth as porcelain." She broke records for winning slots on "Most Beautiful" lists.

It's true that the former Miss Orange County 1978 did land mostly bimbo roles at first, including a recurring character named only "the Bombshell" on a TV show called *Delta House*. She won praise mostly for her icy looks in her breakthrough film, *Scarface*, in 1983. But she proved to have real acting range when she played a Long Island mob wife in Jonathan Demme's comic *Married to the Mob*. She topped that with an Oscar nomination for her period turn as a French aristocrat in *Dangerous Liaisons* in 1988.

If any actress was hotter than Jodie Foster just then, it was Michelle Pfeiffer, and vice versa. ICM couldn't believe its luck at finding a vehicle to showcase them. "It was lightning in a bottle," says Diane Cairns. "That we got one to commit, much less *both*, much less in a nanosecond—I loved both of those actresses and thought, *I really want to see this movie.*"

The only problem was, they both wanted to play Thelma, the one who set the plot in motion by stumbling into trouble, and the one who followed the more exaggerated arc from flighty housewife to convenience-store bandit and hard-core desperado. Both were professional enough to get on the phone and work it out between themselves: Jodie would be Thelma. Michelle would be Louise. And the starriest female package since *Julia* in 1977 would test its luck with the studio bosses who could greenlight *Thelma & Louise*.

Only Callie was less than thrilled. She envisioned her characters as women you wouldn't notice if you spotted them in the grocery store. If Michelle Pfeiffer returned to the Vons supermarket where she had worked as a teenage checkout girl, she would set off a run in aisle 3.

———

DESPITE SUCH A POTENT COMBO, the package did not trigger a stampede at the studios. Columbia Pictures and Paramount both passed as soon as Mimi and Ridley approached. "Two girls commit murder and then suicide" was the consensus in the coverage. "For guys—no problem!" Mimi says. "But with chicks doing it, it was not so acceptable."

She got a better reception at Warner Bros. "It was brilliantly written," says Bill Gerber, Warner's vice president of development. "It was a great relationship movie, and just the conceit that there were two women in 1989 was original in and of itself." But other executives there expressed doubts about the ending. Gerber thought Warner would have insisted on filming two options and preferred a cast from its roster of in-house stars, with Goldie Hawn almost certainly one of the principals. And besides, Warner wasn't prepared to fork over Callie's asking price.

After hearing what was going on, Callie called her new agent in a panic: "You've got to get in there." All that work—it was slipping away. Diane got cracking before the stigma of rejection spread, calling the contacts that she, Jeff Berg and the agents for Jodie and Michelle considered most receptive. Two days later, on Friday, July 21, the messengers from the ICM mailroom fanned out across town bearing packets with a cover letter and Callie's script in hand.

BECKY POLLACK NEVER FORGOT that Friday night, July 21, 1989, even though she spent it exactly the way she spent every Friday night, in bed in her condo in Westwood, reading through a pile of scripts. She had read so many screenplays, treatments, books, articles and other possible source materials for movies since she'd started as a D-girl at Pathé Entertainment that her eyesight had degenerated from needing only distance glasses for driving at night to blind as a bat up close.

That particular evening fixed in her memory, though, because once she climbed into bed and perched her glasses on her nose, she never settled in. She never even leaned back. She read *Thelma & Louise* from beginning to end, all the while sitting straight up. She saw the same problems everyone else did, but she didn't think about the business end of the equation. She was purely entertained. "*Thelma & Louise* was a magical confluence of events," she says. "It was like the Big Bang. The right things happened, all at the right time." All the things that weren't supposed to happen.

One of which was Becky's employer, Pathé, with its sketchy recent history, getting a chance at a hot property. Owned by a mysterious Italian financier, Giancarlo Parretti, who also bought the more storied MGM, Pathé was seen as being perpetually on the verge of going bankrupt or being sold, so few would entrust it with a pet project. The company, housed in a rental office building on San Vincente, often couldn't afford blue-chip scripts or top-tier talent, couldn't pay for special effects or exotic locations. Once, Pathé took a meeting with the people from Marvel Comics, which was absurd—absent the existence of actual superheroes, Pathé didn't have the budget to make anybody fly. It could barely afford the spandex suit.

"Some days we had money to buy scripts, some days we didn't," says Becky. "Some days we had money to finance movies, some days we didn't."

The company's only chance at survival was to play a different game. "The other studios were the Yankees, and we were the Tampa Bay Rays," says Greg Foster, a young employee—most of Pathé's workers were young—in the marketing department.

At most studios, says Becky, "the goal was to make execution-proof movies," presold, with simple premises backed by proven stars—Tom Cruise drives a racecar, Eddie Murphy busts the bad guys. Character-driven, script-driven movies that required explanations and trafficked in nuance broke the rules. Female-driven stories broke the rules. Downer endings broke the rules.

Pathé's game, on the other hand, was ludicrously old-fashioned. Because they couldn't afford to play in the high-concept league, Pathé people had to fall back on the ancient ritual of unearthing great material and trusting their instincts to carry it through, rules or no. *Material*, company executives liked to say, was the great equalizer.

Becky herself played a different game, too, which suited her fine. She wanted nothing to do with the business of business as usual. It didn't suit her personality, which was reflective, studious, introspective. "Some people are great movers and shakers," she says. "They can go to lunch and breakfast and wheel and deal with agents. Some people do it by having a real imprimatur of their own, like 'this is the guy who does all the Marvel movies.' I was more comfortable doing it a much slower way. I loved to read. Reading was not only what I liked but what worked for me."

Despite her connections, Becky hadn't aspired to working in the industry. She'd planned to go to graduate school after earning a degree in history at UCLA but had some months to fill first. No one wanted to hire such a self-effacing intellectual until Paula Weinstein, who knew Becky's father, Sydney, advised her to talk to Alan Ladd Jr. At the time, in the mid-eighties, women executives were so unusual that there were few templates for them to follow. One of them was to work for Laddie. He hired women, Weinstein said, and he listened to their advice.

He placed Becky on the D-girl track to read material for him personally. After a couple years, he promoted her to director of creative affairs, then, by her late twenties, to executive vice president of production. "He cut me loose and let me start finding scripts and put together projects on my own," she says. "Laddie would really let you fly."

Becky had seen enough arrogant behavior in Hollywood that she was careful to conduct herself respectfully. Understated, with a round face and blond hair often tied back in a ponytail, she didn't want to be associated with the baby moguls who were common at the time: guys in their twenties who alienated the creative community with their power games and vainglorious poses. She had seen how they made her father cringe. Her pleasure was to nurture writers, like Randall Wallace, with whom she spent years working one-on-one while he wrestled with the script for *Braveheart.* "The next thing I knew, I was having breakfast at the Four Seasons with Mel Gibson, and I thought, *Okay, message to self, just work on the script. Just create the material and let that be your calling card.*"

Becky didn't see herself in the other women who had broken through as executives, either. "When I watched the women who had blazed a trail, they had a real mettle to them that I'm not sure I had," Becky says. "I didn't have the hunger to swim upstream like that. The thing that drove me was being able to work on writer-driven material that attracted really interesting filmmakers. I could hide behind that."

Becky's sympathetic style meshed with her boss's unassuming personality. Laddie, who shared his father's small stature and all-American features, was so intensely reserved that it was the first thing most people said about him, or at least the second. "Laddie is very, very astute," says Ridley. "I did five films with him. It took four for him to even speak to me."

Laddie's reticence, in fact, was legendary in the business—his junior executives mainlined coffee before joining him for lunch so they'd get a jolt of energy to keep up the one-sided conversation. They often called him on the phone, even though his office was steps away, to avoid the awkward silences in person.

But he had earned a right to swagger with a string of unusual hits. At 20th Century Fox, where he rose to president in the seventies, he risked ridicule by greenlighting the nutty, out-of-the-mainstream *Star Wars.* Between stints at Fox, his own production company and later as chairman of MGM/UA, he had a hand in films like Ridley's *Alien* and *Blade Runner,* as well as *Chariots of Fire* and *The Omen.* He was also willing to gamble on movies about women when no one else would: *The Turning Point* (1977), *Julia* (1977), *An Unmarried Woman* (1978), *Norma Rae*

(1979), *9 to 5* (1980) and *Moonstruck* (1987). Time after time, Laddie trumped the conventional wisdom all the way to the bank—and the Oscar podium—as the women's films others eschewed scooped up ticket sales, acclaim and awards.

Like Ridley, Laddie didn't see himself as championing women, but he had conducted his life surrounded by them—as the son of a single mother and father of four daughters, not to mention the women he hired for responsible jobs. "I didn't think of them as women," he says. "They were just smart people. They could have been men instead."

His explanation for making movies with female leads was equally simple. Among the studio pictures he appreciated as a child, he says, "There were women's pictures, and they were very important, and they did very well." People could say he was locked in a time warp, oblivious to trends, but Laddie saw the women's audience as an opportunity he had nearly to himself. He was so old-school, he'd become practically revolutionary.

Becky Pollack called Laddie and her other Pathé colleagues first thing Saturday morning and told them to drop what they were doing to read *Thelma & Louise* so they could all form an opinion by Monday. Pathé, the dark horse, knew it had to break fast out of the gate. Laddie, naturally, kept his response brief. He told Becky on the phone Saturday afternoon: "It's one of the few scripts that I've read that I can remember saying it's a perfect script. Let's go make the movie."

At the Monday-morning meeting on July 24, arguments flared over the screenplay, especially the ending, but that's what the staff of young iconoclasts at the studio liked about the script—it fired them up. Becky got the go-ahead to bid. She had tied herself into a knot expecting that Pathé wouldn't be able to keep pace with the richer studios. Her best chance, Becky thought, was to declare an absolute embrace of the story, right down to that ending. It helped that this was something she really meant. The finish felt organic to her, and it gave her an adrenaline rush to think that her studio might be the one to get everyone from the audience to the Hollywood establishment talking.

"What can I say?" Becky told Diane Cairns on the phone. "Everybody loves it here."

Becky backed up her praise with everything Callie wanted: $100,000 up front and $400,000 on commencement of filming, a top-dollar deal for a writer of any gender and a landmark for a woman, especially a beginner. Perhaps even more important for Callie, she got a guarantee that her ending would at least be shot, although everyone recognized that an alternative might slip in there someday, too. Becky and Laddie stepped up with such complete conviction that their business affairs department signed and sealed the deal within a day.

Over at ICM on Tuesday morning, the strangest thing happened. Orion called to feel it out: Was the movie still available? Other studios were on the line, too, hinting that they couldn't believe they had passed. It seems the script had scared them too much to commit until they saw someone else do it. But Diane didn't budge—Callie had got her deal, at a studio that was a true believer. *Thelma & Louise* needed a home where it could be appreciated for what it was.

CHAPTER 10

THE RIGHT MAN FOR THE JOB

The world would never know whether Tony Scott would have turned *Thelma & Louise* into *Tits and Bullets*.

"I like it," Tony told his brother, "but it's not really for me. I've got problems with women."

"But that's the whole point, dude!" Ridley said.

Tracking down a director without such problems, Ridley realized, might prove harder than he thought. Precisely because this material lived so far outside his own area of comfort, he scheduled a meeting with Callie, so he'd be ready to answer the inevitable questions from the directors or actors he tried to recruit.

At the first encounter, Ridley felt as if he were auditioning for the writer, attempting to convince her that he was worthy of producing her story. From there, they met repeatedly, combing through the script page by page and line by line, Ridley exploring Callie's intent and point of view, her opinions about the characters, about men and women. "It was like a sponge going into every crevice of my brain," Callie recalls.

Ridley's office consisted of a couple of rooms and a reception area on the Columbia lot, but he preferred to spend his days at the Four Seasons Hotel in Beverly Hills, where he lodged when he was in town. He enjoyed working outside, the staff shouting across the pool to ask what he wanted for lunch, and he held meetings in the bar when the crowds cleared out at two in the afternoon. Callie and Ridley split their conclaves between the office and the hotel.

Ridley searches for the right word to describe Callie Khouri. *Vociferous? Outspoken?* He wryly called the sessions "daily lectures," as she led him through a litany of reasons not to touch this, not to touch that. He questioned whether men really behaved the way the guys in the screenplay did, whether the women's anger was justified. Had any of this ever happened to her?

"Are you kidding me?" Callie exclaimed. "I walk down the street and I get all kinds of catcalls. It's disgusting."

Ridley thought to himself, *A little humor, dear.* He recalled an actress who once told him, "Shit, if I walk by a building site and there are no comments, I figure it's all over."

But he listened respectfully, and Callie hammered her point home. The events in the script hadn't happened to her, she said, except for the truck driver's lewd overtures. "*That* happens to everybody," she said. "The point is, it doesn't matter if it happened to me. These things happen *all the time*, and it could have been me and it could be any of the women you have ever come into contact with."

"I took it mainly because she's right," Ridley said later. "She's absolutely right." They went on to discuss questions of tone. Ridley worried that the story could tilt toward a crusading drama, and he argued for emphasis on the comedy. Movies aren't a cheap medium, he asserted, and part of the director's job was to pay for them by putting as many bums in the seats as possible. "If you make this serious, about two hard, tough women in a car, you will rule out fifty percent of your audience," Ridley said. "Guys are going to get irritated. The funnier it is, the more people it will reach." He thought the men in the audience should eat some crow, but he wanted them to enjoy the taste.

Callie was all for it. "If it's devoid of humor," she said, "then something has gone terribly wrong."

Ridley rarely shared his visual ideas with writers, but Callie, given her ambition to direct, was eager to engage. He asked what films had influenced her, and she said *Lonely Are the Brave* and *Out of the Past*— daytime noir in the West. "It should start out looking like a Sears and Roebuck catalog," she said, "and end up looking like a cross between a Maxfield Parrish painting and some kind of photorealist painting of the West." As for the two stars, Callie wanted "to see them become more and more natural but more and more beautiful as the movie goes on."

Mimi sometimes broke into the meetings to implore: "You're supposed to be cutting the script." "We are," Ridley said, although you wouldn't know it from the detours they'd taken about, say, the Westerns of John Ford. "Callie really cared about the integrity of the script, that the women were portrayed as real and multilayered," recalls Mimi. "She didn't want it to be too glossy or overproduced. Then it wouldn't have the depth she wanted."

A genuine collaboration developed, and a genuine regard. Callie found Ridley reserved but with a droll sense of humor. "I liked him a lot," she says. "I really did."

The feeling was mutual. "I respected the fact that she wrote it," he says. "I wanted it from a woman's point of view, and I *got* it from a woman's point of view."

In the end, they agreed not to change much of anything, just to cut a bit so it wouldn't feel overly long. The script got a little bit tighter, a little

more intensely what it already was. Whatever his initial feelings about
the relative outrageousness of men making catcalls and vulgar gestures
toward women, Ridley intended to subsume his point of view to Callie's.
A smooth start, except that Ridley still didn't want to direct the film, and
Callie still did.

RIDLEY SPENT MUCH OF THE SUMMER of 1989 searching for the right
man for that job. He headed straight toward what he knew: exciting visual stylists who had made their bones in commercials. Guys like him.
He probably shouldn't have been surprised when some of them weren't
feeling it, either.

Joe Pytka, for example, was something of a Ridley clone. A former art
student, Pytka had directed thousands of commercials, punchy Super
Bowl ads for Nike, Budweiser and the public service message "Your Brain
on Drugs." His first feature, *Let It Ride,* about a gambler at the track, was
about to debut to little fanfare. His background touting beer and sports
didn't equip him with much affinity for Callie's script. "He didn't really
get it," Ridley says.

Jeremiah Chechik, another commercial director, did. Ridley visited
the cutting room where Chechik was editing his first feature, *National
Lampoon's Christmas Vacation.* The newbie director admired the portrayal of Thelma and Louise in contrast to other scripts he'd seen, where
female characters were cartoonish, shallow and too young to be interesting. But at that point Ridley was having trouble getting the female-centric story past the studio gatekeepers, so Chechik moved on.

Not all of the candidates were white men who had made commercials,
but they were white men all the same, often with résumés that were similar to Ridley's in other ways. He danced for a while with Chris Menges, a
Brit who had worked on Tony's first student film and started as a cinematographer, going on to make *The Mission,* about Jesuit priests in South

America. And with Kevin Reynolds, who had made *Fandango*, a male-buddy road comedy with Kevin Costner. A number of the directors Ridley approached expressed interest, but Ridley fretted they wouldn't capture the humor he saw in the story, or the grandeur. "Tony could deliver an odyssey," Ridley says, "but I was worried about the others reading the script as too small."

Or the tone might not be as balanced as he envisioned. He and Mimi thought that Tim Hunter, who had directed the bleak indie drama *River's Edge*, had terrific ideas, but they worried he might go too dark.

Most of the candidates had made virtually all-male movies, as befit the times. Jonathan Kaplan, an anomaly, was coming off *The Accused*. But in a conversation with Ridley, Kaplan said he didn't want to become typecast as the rape director, and he expressed doubts about the final scene. "I was totally behind the relationship of the women," he remembers. "But it was an ending where they'd placed themselves in a corner."

A few other directors lodged more-heated objections to the script. Phillip Noyce, an Australian who'd struck gold with the thriller *Dead Calm*, "was irritated by it," Ridley says. Harry Hook, a Brit who had just delivered *Lord of the Flies*, claimed to have trouble getting the point.

Becky and Laddie urged Ridley to consider more-renowned directors. He and Mimi met with Bob Rafelson but doubted his feel for the characters. "I'm not sure it would have been as kind or as funny, as amusing, as I saw it," says Ridley. By now he had grown protective of Thelma and Louise. He balked when other directors wanted to fix them. He didn't think they needed fixing.

Becky sent memos listing dozens of possibilities, including Joan Micklin Silver, Susan Seidelman and Amy Heckerling, all masters of character and comedy, but no women made Mimi and Ridley's short list for meetings. Kathryn Bigelow was known to be on another project, not that she seemed to be in the running anyway. "She would have been a good idea," Ridley says in retrospect, admitting he hadn't thought of her back then.

"Ridley is very fair-minded as far as women making it in the work-place," says Sue Williams, the development assistant in his office. "But at the same time, he's got the attitude of 'I'll get my buddy to do it.' He's three-quarters of the way toward feminism."

Later Ridley told a British film magazine that he deliberately shied away from considering women, making it clear he didn't trust them to be objective about the subject matter. "Because the focus is two women look-ing at men," he said, "then the logic is that a man should direct it, if you can find the right guy, because if a woman directs it she might go into overkill and, you know, get into some kind of a vendetta. I think it's a film that you should come out of and recognize a little bit of yourself in there somewhere, and maybe agree with it. A man can get that perspective." He didn't seem to consider that men addressed matters of manhood in movies all the time without anyone fretting about bias.

"Why not me?" Callie kept asking Mimi. Many of the names she'd heard bandied about ranked well below the Hollywood stratosphere. Mimi escorted the screenwriter to make her case with Laddie, who lis-tened quietly and then assured her, "We're going to get the biggest A-list director and the biggest stars we can find for this movie. I'm sorry." He was taking enough risk with this half-million-dollar investment in the script; he wasn't about to risk more.

In the fall of 1989, it looked as if a solution might be at hand when Laddie put forward one of his favorite colleagues and friends, Richard Donner. Donner made big, successful movies, teeming with action and humor. His first feature, *The Omen*, launched him in 1976, and he went on to direct *Superman*, the first of the major comic book movies, and *Lethal Weapon*, one of the most influential eighties male-buddy block-busters. *Lethal Weapon* was the kind of large-scale, fast-paced but funny entertainment that Ridley had in mind for *Thelma & Louise*.

Donner found the script so rare as to be "historic." "It was a tough time for women in Hollywood," he says, "but Callie had written such a great piece of material that somewhere somebody was going to say *go*." He even approved of the ending, suggesting a way to make it more palatable to the audience. As the car charged toward the edge of the cliff, he told Mimi, the tires might kick up so much dust that it would obscure the scene. The characters would simply disappear in the cloud. "It would be up to the audience how it wanted them to conclude their lives," he says.

Ridley backed away, though, when Donner proposed that his wife, Lauren Shuler Donner, produce the film. Ridley didn't want to share producing tasks. And there were other signs that Ridley wasn't enthusiastic. He resisted scheduling places and times to meet, and when he did, he didn't show up. Eventually, Donner stopped hearing back.

"There was always a reason why so-and-so wasn't right," says Laddie. "Ridley kept rejecting everybody who wanted to do it, and they were all top directors. They were not secondary no-talent bums."

Turning the project over to another master was proving an anguishing proposition. "If you're a producer," Ridley said, "it's like being a great antique dealer. You've got to be prepared to sell your favorite table." The more he talked to Callie about adjustments and tightening and underlying ideas, and the more he talked to directors about look and feel and tone, the more clearly Ridley saw the movie in his head. The movie playing there was more elevated than two women taking a trip in a car. The trip was their last journey, a meaningful one, and as such it evolved into something more romantic, more majestic, more memorable in his mind. It should make a grand statement as the two figures moved through the American landscape to their inevitable demise. *Thelma & Louise* had transmogrified into more than a script that had made him laugh. It had become Ridley's favorite table, and he couldn't bring himself to sell it.

CHAPTER 11

THE CURSE OF KATHERINE

Stars like Michelle Pfeiffer and Jodie Foster weren't going to wait forever for Ridley Scott to get off the dime. They had careers to cultivate and other offers to consider. Jonathan Demme, who had directed Michelle in *Married to the Mob,* was wooing her for the plum part of Clarice Starling in the serial-killer thriller *The Silence of the Lambs.* Jodie was leaning toward joining *Love Field,* a melodrama with her *Accused* director, Jonathan Kaplan, about an interracial relationship. But when Michelle balked at *Silence* because she thought the violence was too grotesque, the opportunities flipped. Jodie signed on for the *Silence* part, and Michelle took *Love Field. Thelma & Louise* had lost its stars.

No stars, no director, no mojo—the production seemed stalled before it could begin. But, defying all logic, this latest turn transformed the project into something of a sensation. Not that long ago Callie and Amanda couldn't get arrested with the script. Now the vacancy at the top of the cast set off a flat-out scramble by some of Hollywood's biggest names to win the most substantial roles they had seen in years. It seemed as if every agent who represented anyone with a vagina and a pulse besieged Pathé and Ridley's company for a shot. "Every day, you'd hear different women who were attached to it," says Kaplan.

"It was a free-for-all," says Diane. Once, no top star would have lowered herself to openly pursue a part. She wouldn't meet for so much as a friendly drink without an offer on the table first. But by 1989 that taboo had yielded to a new reality. If actresses or their agents didn't jump on the phone to ask for a prime opportunity, they were out of the game. Agents told their clients: "The only way you are going to get this role is to fight for it." That went double for the two roles in Callie's once-neglected script.

Producers and studios might have shied away from it, but actresses were desperate for the meaty, flawed, fully loaded roles it provided, with character arcs that would put the players' skills to the test. "You would have to be a complete idiot to read that spectacular script and not respond to the material if you're an actor," says David Eidenberg, Geena Davis's agent at the time. "It was overwhelming." He continued to call Mimi or Becky on behalf of Geena once or twice a week, every week, trying to outflank the competition, but it didn't look promising. On weekly lists that Pathé drew up of dozens of potential stars, his client appeared only twice, each time misspelled as "Gina."

Script aside, you'd also have to be an idiot not to see another reason for the stampede. Good actresses wanted to *work*, in the broadest sense of pushing themselves to the limits of their abilities and being well paid to do it. But women captured only 29 percent of movie roles in 1989, and male actors were paid 60 percent more on average. Speaking at a Screen Actors Guild conference in 1990, Meryl Streep drily noted, "If the trend continues, by the year 2000 women will represent thirteen percent of all roles. And in twenty years, we will have been eliminated from movies entirely." Her prediction proved overly grim: twenty-five years later, the percentage of roles for female actors remained exactly where it was in 1989.

With the ongoing rise of action movies and the fading of seventies icons like Fonda and Streisand, the new generation of actresses could barely crack the annual top-ten lists of movie stars in the mid- to late eighties, and none could sustain that stature as Tom Cruise, Eddie Murphy and Michael Douglas did year after year. Meryl Streep managed to make it in 1984 and 1985, Bette Midler in 1986 and 1988 and Kathleen Turner in 1986 and 1989, but Cher, Whoopi Goldberg and Glenn Close each secured a spot just once and then disappeared. No one else made the cut. Susan Sarandon, who first broke into movies as a seventies ingenue, says, "There were very few women who started with me who survived."

Many men couldn't get a break in action blockbusters, either, if they weren't physically imposing enough, and those who did found their conservatory training wasted on the tasks of running, jumping, ducking and grunting. But at least there were plenty of minor roles and character parts for men—the guy who ran the deli, the boss at the office, the cop caught in the shootout, the third soldier from the left.

An actress often found herself the only woman on the set, a young, inexperienced girl whose only job was to be seductive. "By the time an actor was being given an opportunity to helm a project, he may have had fifteen to twenty little roles—the best-friend roles," says Carrie Frazier, a prominent casting director in the eighties. "He kind of knew how things worked. The actresses at seventeen or eighteen were being given leads and told to get naked. Oh my God, how did they survive? How did they manage the craftsmanship of it, the comfort level of it?"

While actors could explore a wide variety of human shadings, the female lead was so similar in every movie that Frazier had a name for her: Katherine. As in "Oh, here comes Katherine again." Katherine was attractive, of course, or "fuckable," as she was so often labeled behind the scenes. But the leading lady in an eighties movie had to be classy, too, to be a worthy girlfriend of the star. "Katherine is sexy, but not a slut," says Frazier. "She is smart, because the guy has to have an interesting woman, but not one that would surmount him in any way. She works in an art gallery—an art gallery is perfect. She can be a veterinarian but not a surgeon, a photographer but not an editor. She's a little more refined than the girl with the orange hair who is her best friend. The best friend is funny, and she gets the funny lines, because it shows that our girl has a sense of humor, but not too much, because that's not really feminine. Katherine can't be even a little crass or laugh too much."

It fell to men to shout orders and save the world from terrorists and maniacs. Actresses found their hopes for rounded and fulfilling careers stifled. The funny best friend offered an opening for someone like Bette Midler, who carried a couple movies as a lead but then later appeared in ensemble pieces. That left just about everyone else in the straitjacket of the Katherine role. Unless they landed Thelma or Louise.

ONCE JODIE AND MICHELLE DROPPED OUT, Becky Pollack could have made a full-time job out of fielding calls from actresses' agents. They told her Cybill Shepherd was interested. So were Daryl Hannah, Kelly Lynch, Rebecca De Mornay, Ellen Barkin, Theresa Russell, Nancy Travis and Madeline Stowe. Michelle Pfeiffer would become available again if the production could wait until the following July. Meg Ryan would do it in June. Kim Basinger, Kathleen Turner and Andie MacDowell would open up in August. So would Julia Roberts, who would outshine them all the next year as the lead in the enormous hit *Pretty Woman*, inhabiting Hollywood's favorite female character, once again a prostitute. Most of the actresses coveted the arguably showier Thelma role. Oh . . . and "Gina Davis." Files from Pathé note that her agent insisted she would play either part whenever, wherever. If all this happened in a movie, it would be called a catfight.

"Instead, it created a firestorm," Becky Pollack says. And it generated a lot of drama around town as agents tried to poach clients from other agencies by slipping them the script, as in "*He* didn't get you a hearing on *Thelma & Louise*, but *I* did."

Laddie yearned for Ridley to cast Cher, who was also interested. She had scored an Oscar and box-office success by playing a shy bookkeeper who found love in *Moonstruck*. "Cher could have been quite good, I think," Laddie says. "She could have played either part." But Ridley didn't think she would bring the humor he saw in the script. He kept dragging his feet, just as he did with choosing directors.

Then Laddie got a call that trumped them all. Meryl Streep and Goldie Hawn invited themselves to Pathé, together, to pitch themselves for Thelma and Louise. They didn't have their agents make the call; they did it themselves. No one would have expected the two friends, box-office champs and Oscar winners, to campaign for parts, but they showed up prepared to kill. "To sit in a meeting with Meryl Streep and Goldie Hawn was spectacular," says Becky. "They were enthusiastic and adorable and smart."

The discussion was vigorous, especially when it came to the ending, which gave the stars some trepidation. They didn't lobby to change it, necessarily, but they toyed with alternatives, like an escape to Mexico, for instance. Streep suggested it might work if her character, Louise, pushed Thelma out of the car at the last moment, saving at least the life of the one friend who hadn't committed murder.

Laddie was smitten, eager to capitalize on the oomph of such A-plus-plus-list stars. "I think that Meryl could do anything," he says. As for Goldie, "it would have been more of a comedic turn. When you think about it, it's a very dark movie, it's not a happy piece of fluff, which was how Goldie was thought of at the time. But I had worked with her on a number of pictures, and I did dramas with her, too." He was concerned that with Goldie as a lead, the audience would come in with false expectations of lighter material, but still he suggested that Ridley set up meetings with them both.

That two such prominent stars were willing to get out there and hustle for the parts spoke volumes about the state of their careers. Meryl had dazzled Hollywood with her technical mastery since she'd made the leap from Shakespearean roles on the stage to Oscar wins for *Kramer vs. Kramer* in 1980 and *Sophie's Choice* in 1983. She had the classy Katherine thing down, although some directors groused that her off-center beauty and all those proficient accents in her early roles limited her sex appeal. (Remember, Katherine can't surmount the man in any way.) *Silkwood* (1983) and *Out of Africa* (1985) burnished her sterling reputation, but by age forty in 1989, she was reaching a difficult phase. She'd taken on some middling comedies like *She-Devil,* and she said, "Every actress will tell you they have maybe two things per year that they can possibly stand to put themselves into."

Goldie had pulled off a loopier but still stellar course. She'd won a supporting Oscar in 1970 for her first movie role as a giggly girlfriend in *Cactus Flower.* In 1981, she made the list of top-ten box-office stars on the strength of the lead in *Private Benjamin* and went on to headline other popular comedies with infectious, giddy charm. At age forty-four, though, she could no longer count on ingenue roles, and what else was there? *Thelma & Louise* represented a career-making (or career-saving) opportunity for any actress at the time, from beginner to the most acclaimed.

WITH THIS EMBARRASSMENT OF RICHES and high-profile stars awaiting answers, the movie needed a director more than ever. After Ridley left Richard Donner hanging, Laddie called. "You just keep rejecting people," he said to Ridley. "You keep finding reasons why everybody is wrong. Why don't you do it yourself?"

Mimi kept up the pressure, too. The script for *Isobar* wasn't coming together as Ridley had hoped. *Black Rain* had hit theaters with underwhelming force that September, generating another so-so reception for one of Ridley's films. The critic Roger Ebert accused the crime thriller of being "all look and no heart," and wrote, "the screenplay seems to have been manufactured out of those Xeroxed outlines they pass out in film school."

"I needed to step off, step out of the perception of what I was as a director," Ridley said, "because I was really becoming pigeonholed. I felt I needed to emphasize that I could do a film really about people."

Ridley was pleased when Michelle Pfeiffer asked to sit down to talk about *Thelma & Louise* again at the Four Seasons. "I'm busy and can't do it now," she told him. "But I thought it was so good, I have to ask: Why don't you come to your senses and do it yourself?"

She's bloody right, Ridley thought. *I'm going to do it. This is ridiculous.*

At that moment, the best script in his quiver was the one that made him the most uncomfortable, the one that most got under his skin—but the one he couldn't let go.

Thelma & Louise was going to be a Ridley Scott film after all. With his usual workaholic precision, he threw himself into finding its stars.

CHAPTER 12

WHO'S PLAYING WHOM?

The wider community was puzzled by this odd choice of subject matter for the persnickety action director. Even Jeff Berg admits, "Ridley's not known for humor. Then again, Sydney Pollack was a very powerful director who was never known for humor, and he wound up directing *Tootsie*. The great directors—Billy Wilder, Howard Hawks—knew how to master three or four different idioms."

"I knew with Ridley that it was a deal with the devil," says Callie. "I figured it was going to have some grandeur to it, if nothing else."

The director's first order of business was to sit down with Goldie Hawn and Meryl Streep one at a time. Goldie cracked Ridley up when she sashayed into the Four Seasons insisting she wanted a part so badly she would buy him breakfast. She was effervescent—and funny as hell. "But she was maybe a tad old at the time," Ridley says. "I wanted to keep it below a certain age." With Goldie, rewrites would have been necessary. He decided to move on.

Meryl Streep was slighter in person than he expected, and she bombarded him with thoughtful queries over the course of two meetings. Why would a man want to make a film like this? she pushed. Was the role right for her? All good questions. The character had to be working-class, he thought, whereas Meryl had a different air, a different pedigree about her. "Not that she was posh," he says, "but the character needed to be tough." He wasn't sure that was the quality she conveyed. Besides, she hoped to spend the summer at home with her children while they were off from school, and Ridley wanted to get filming by then. Someday, he thought, he'd love to work with her, but with regret he let her slip away this time.

He also considered the double-edged bargain with the dominion of stars. Laddie was eager to harness it to sell the picture, but for Ridley, stars held less allure. To him, the power of stars—their CinemaScope dimensions, the vapor of well-known characters that wafted behind them from previous roles—was the very quality that worked against the most prominent candidates. He had plucked stars out of obscurity in the course of his work, helped to launch their careers, but once they were launched, he was leery of the reality-distortion effect they imposed on a film. With Ridley Scott, the film was the star, the look was the star. He cast his pictures with painstaking care; the actors had to fit within the scheme. He and Callie envisioned Thelma and Louise as regular gals. The sheen of stardom would muddle their function in the story.

Geena Davis's agent had kept working the phone for months, despite rumors that megawatt stars had already sewn up the roles. "She's still here," David Eidenberg parroted, day in, day out. "Can she meet you?"

Ridley had heard about those incessant pleas. He made a point of screening *The Accidental Tourist* to see what the fuss was about. "I was attracted to Geena because she was ditzy, or seemed to be ditzy, but she wasn't. She was very intelligent," Ridley says. "I thought there was something in there that was Thelma."

He saw Louise as what he called "the mum character," the older, wiser, maternal figure. Thelma, on the other hand, had to appear childlike at first but also possess a hint of steel, allowing the story to twist partway through to let her take charge. Ditziness alone wouldn't be enough. He wasn't sure whether Geena could flesh out the other side of the role, but he was curious. Ridley skipped over many of the bigger names on the studio list and invited her to tea at the Four Seasons.

He hadn't anticipated her... *scale,* for want of a better word, when she loped into the Windows Lounge. Towering, a magnificent creature, with legs and presence that went on from here to there. And that vivacious, demonstrative face—it was a director's dream.

He knew she'd be gunning hard for a role when she slid in opposite him at the table, and she didn't disappoint. Geena was an instinctive actress, loose on the set and averse to overrehearsing, but she plotted her career with the drive of an A student cramming for finals. By the time she met with Ridley, after spending the better part of a year begging, she was up to the test. "I had read the script *one million times,*" she says with typical enthusiasm, the italics audible in her voice. She had strategized with an acting coach over why playing Louise would be the better tactic for her as she closed in on the age of thirty-four. The more mature, responsible character, she concluded, would shift her career in a much-needed direction. She faced Ridley with a clutch of notes that spelled out the reasons why she was right for Louise.

Geena pitched her heart out for a good twenty minutes, bringing all her outré gifts to the effort—animated expressions, high-beam eyes, a voice that swooped two octaves with operatic zeal. "I need you to understand how *passionate* I am about this," she insisted.

Ridley let her go on, taking in her gooney-bird glamour, her robust physicality, all the while envisioning her not as Louise, but Thelma. "Geena's a tall girl, and I'd never seen that character as being that tall, but there it is, six feet," Ridley says. "Very attractive. I thought her quirkiness was great, enough that I wanted it for the film. In talking with her, I realized she was it."

Geena stopped long enough to take a breath.

"Soooo," Ridley said quietly, "in other words, you wouldn't play Thelma?"

To Geena's credit, she blinked only for an instant, recalibrating the entire spiel: "You know, I've been listening to myself talk, giving you all these reasons why I should be Louise, and I'm thinking... it's not a very convincing argument," she backpedaled. "Now that I think of it . . . I should play Thelma."

After a couple hours of frantic ad-libbing on her part, as far as Ridley was concerned, Geena Davis was Thelma Dickinson. From that moment on, he never considered anyone else. The next day her agent got the call: Ridley wanted Geena in the movie, depending on whether the actress he found for the other lead seemed compatible.

Weeks passed as she waited in agony for word. "We will both die if you end up not being in this movie," her agent said. "But there is only so long you can wait and not get on with your life." They delivered an ultimatum. Ridley had until five o'clock that Friday afternoon to commit to Geena, or she'd be forced to walk.

An unorthodox offer arrived as the final minutes ticked down. Geena would play one of the leads—or the other. It all depended who else signed on. "Getting *Thelma & Louise* was such an ordeal and such a long, drawn-out process that when I finally actually got it," Geena says, "it was just a *miracle*." Geena Davis was the first name up on the board. She would be Thelma. Or maybe Louise.

RIDLEY EXTENDED THE SEARCH FOR LOUISE, once again blithely by-passing the long list of stars the studio had dutifully compiled over the previous months. He had a certain ideal in mind, one that stood in contrast to the sugarcoated femininity embodied in the long line of Katherines gracing most of the movies at the time. In running his company and directing his films, Ridley had always viewed women without sentimentality or condescension, and he wasn't about to start now that he was directing a bona fide women's film.

He sought guidance from an unlikely source, Lou DiGiaimo, a New York–based casting director known for dead-on, deglamorized movies like *The Godfather* and *The French Connection,* populated with real-looking working stiffs and thugs, guys with scars. Lou brought up an actress no one had thought to mention before: the take-no-prisoners Susan Sarandon.

Bulbs lit up for Ridley when Lou suggested the name. They had met briefly when she worked with Tony on his first feature, the sexy vampire movie *The Hunger.* "Susan has always been a great actress," Ridley says. "She would be the mum figure of the two, so it was good that she was older"—forty-four, almost ten years older than Geena. And Susan could nail the working-class persona, as she did playing a casino worker in *Atlantic City.* Stunning on-screen but without vanity, she invariably grounded her characters in reality.

Visually, which was how Ridley guided most decisions, he was intrigued by how the appearance of the two actresses might evoke the differences in the characters. Susan's faint traces of crow's-feet and cool, assessing eyes would distinguish her from Geena's wide-open expression and butter-smooth skin. "The contrast in what their faces say to the camera—that visual image—would do so much of the work," says Brett Goldstein, an assistant casting agent who worked with Ridley and Lou. "Their features and the quality of their skin showed who they were and where they each were in life."

Jodie Foster and Michelle Pfeiffer both projected an almost glacial mien, whereas Geena and Susan, with their limpid brown eyes and wavy auburn hair, conveyed a warmth that could help stir audience sympathy for Callie's antiheroines. Despite the similarity in hair color, says Goldstein, "Geena and Susan are so *not* interchangeable."

Susan's career up to then signaled other qualities that were right for the self-reliant Louise. In movies ranging from *The Rocky Horror Picture Show* to *Bull Durham,* she had chosen such uncompromising roles that it was impossible to imagine her as a robotically supportive girlfriend or wife. She declined to think in terms of commercial appeal, which may explain why her name had been omitted from the studio wish list of box-office favorites. Ridley called her personally and offered to send the script.

Susan may have been one of the only actresses in America who hadn't lobbied for one of the parts. She hadn't even heard of them, most likely because she was based in Hollywood Siberia: New York City. "I've always made it a point," she says with pride, "not to care or watch or be involved with the corporate entity of show business."

When she finally got a look at the screenplay, turns out she wasn't all that impressed. There were some aspects she liked right away. "I thought it would be wonderful to be in a film with a woman," she says, "because you don't get more than one woman in a film, and if you do, they hate each other for some assumed reason that's not even in the script." Plus it would be a hoot to play bad girls and chuck the rules that governed women in the movies.

Like others involved in making this one, Susan didn't perceive it as making a larger statement about women. "I never saw it as a feminist film," she says. "I saw it in the genre of a cowboy film—except with women and trucks instead of guys and horses." In that light, Ridley Scott didn't strike her as such a peculiar choice to direct. They set up a meeting in New York.

If Ridley thought he'd gotten an earful from Callie, it was useful preparation for his encounter with the woman who'd been labeled "the outspoken Susan Sarandon" so many times that it might be considered her legal name.

"There are a lot of questions that need to be ironed out," she told him before he barely had a chance to say hello. It wasn't completely clear where the characters came from, she said, so she wouldn't know what accent to use.

The British director didn't know what she meant. "Just use the accent you have," he said.

Susan laughed and explained that there were serious regional differences. She went on to knock the script for not making it clear how many days passed during the course of the story. It was crucial, she thought, for the time to be compressed so it would be credible for two women to take the emotional plunge toward suicide, or whatever they wanted to call it. The same concern led her to object to a romantic scene between Louise and her boyfriend halfway through the story. It would only serve to defuse the tension.

"I hear you," Ridley said. The same issue had bothered Meryl Streep. "These are all things we can work out."

Then she really got down to business. "Promise me that I will die," she insisted. "Promise me we're not gonna shoot this, then you test it and we end up at Club Med."

"Oh, you will die," he assured her. He wasn't sure about Thelma, but Louise would make the plunge.

They spent even more time addressing her concern about the violence in the film. Susan's progressive politics informed all her important decisions. She recoiled at accepting the role of someone who shot a man, rapist or not. "It's a huge thing to take another life," Susan said. "I am not interested in doing a revenge film. I'm not interested in being Charles Bronson or Arnold Schwarzenegger. I'm interested in the fact that taking a life has consequences, that she has to pay for that." She said it bothered her that the script called for Louise to shoot the rapist "execution style," a term Callie didn't actually use. But the draft Susan saw did call for Louise to aim deliberately and shoot the guy in the face.

Ridley thought they could sort it out in rehearsal. Mostly he was struck by Susan's innate intelligence and challenging nature, the way she goaded him to sharpen his focus. He knew she had the authority, the competence and the cheek to portray Louise. It wouldn't be a quiet set; Susan wouldn't pull punches. She would make sure her voice was heard. That didn't faze Ridley the way it might have some directors. "For a guy's guy, Ridley doesn't think like a dumb-ass chauvinist," says Goldstein, the assistant casting director. "Most producers, directors or studio heads are scared to death of a strong woman, because, basically, they're all weak-kneed inside. Ridley wasn't scared." He offered Susan the part of Louise Sawyer, pending approval from the studio.

Unlike many of her peers, Susan relished the intellectual challenge of playing the more buttoned-up Louise rather than Thelma. "Even though Louise is not the flashiest or the most fun," she says, "it interested me more, the demands of trying to keep the movie together and on track and literally and figuratively driving the movie."

Even today, she admits she had no idea she was signing on to a project with any lasting significance or cultural merit. "It fit into my needs as a mom," she says matter-of-factly. Filming was scheduled for the summer of 1990, a perfect opportunity to take her kids on location after school let out.

RIDLEY'S CASTING DIDN'T SIT WELL with everyone. Geena and Susan were respected well enough, but respect didn't sell tickets. The two hadn't reached the level of celebrity and box-office sway wielded by other candidates. They couldn't open a film.

That suited Callie. She was content that these relatively underexposed actresses wouldn't outshine the story, although she wasn't exactly wild about Susan being in her forties. In Callie's backstory, the characters were the same age, friends from high school. This could have been one of the few examples of a Hollywood director casting actresses who were *older* than written.

The actresses were even harder for Laddie to accept. "Those were Ridley's choices, not mine," he says. "I didn't feel they were wrong for it, but these were very good parts, and most women in town would want to do it. I felt it lent itself to two well-known people."

The studio could have fought the decision, but Laddie was unique in stepping back and allowing offbeat ideas and talent to prevail. His diffident manner was a godsend for directors in that he kept his nose out of their business, and those times when he did stick it in, ever so gently, his instincts were often correct.

"He tended to have the most successful, groundbreaking movies, movies that were the first of their kind," says Becky Pollack. "They could also go out with a blaze of glory." That was the risk.

A risk he decided to take in this case. You are the director, he told Ridley. "If those are the actresses you want, it's fine with me."

Industry onlookers who'd been following the casting maneuvers buzzed at the news. "Given the star power that people like Meryl and Goldie or Cher would have brought to bear," says Diane Cairns, "probably no other studio executive would have backed the director on that play."

But the play was classic Laddie: Pick the script. Pick the filmmaker. Now let the movie be what it's supposed to be.

CHAPTER 13

"GOOD LUCK, HONEY!"

Geena Davis and Susan Sarandon—the matchup wasn't as improbable as everyone thought. Geena, gangly, goofy, a skyscraper next to most leading men, was extraordinary to behold, no one's image of the girl next door, but always eager to please. Susan, smaller in stature, more than made up for it with her no-bullshit manner. Geena conveyed an innocent quality and was unafraid to stand out. Susan Sarandon was a paragon of mature sexuality, her commonsense style lending a lived-in ease to the women she played. They never saw themselves as the chicks in the background. They played the leads in their own lives.

GEENA, WHO RARELY SAW GENDER as a drawback in the early days of her career, can't remember being exposed to the idea of a woman as mere appendage until her senior year in high school, when she overheard her uncle counsel her mother, "You don't send *girls* to college—it's a waste of money. They're just going to get married anyway." It shocked her, because her father, a civil engineer, and her mother, a teacher's assistant, treated Geena and her older brother as equals when she was growing up in Wareham, Massachusetts, a small, working-class town on the road approaching Cape Cod.

Her drive switched on early. She didn't merely deliver newspapers as a kid, she knocked herself out by handing over each one personally at the customer's door. Geena didn't merely study piano, she took up flute, too, and played the organ at the Congregational Protestant Church for the early-morning youth service. "Youth," she notes drily, "*love* to get up early." She bounded over high jumps and hurdles for the track team. She made the honor society and later joined Mensa, the organization for people with lofty IQs.

She and her best friend, Lucyann, acted out their own versions of television shows like *The Rifleman* in the backyard. "It never occurred to us that there were no female characters we wanted to perform," Geena says. "There was *Bewitched* and *I Dream of Jeannie,* where the women had superpowers, but every episode was about them having to sit on their powers so the man in their life wouldn't get upset or feel emasculated."

Up until tenth grade, she was the tallest student, boy or girl, in every class, where kids could be cruel. Rather than stoop over and withdraw, Geena presented herself as a bit of a kook, making her own clothes in crazy patterns and colors. Her dating roster numbered a grand total of one until senior year, which she spent as an exchange student among the blessedly colossal citizens of Sweden.

In New York after graduating from Boston University, Geena signed on with a modeling agency, hoping it would lead to acting roles. In the meantime, her only performances took place at the Ann Taylor boutique on Fifty-seventh Street, where, working as a sales clerk, she hopped into the window one day and froze while onlookers gathered to figure out whether she was a mannequin or real. Later, willing herself not to blink, she wore a cheesy wig or ran an electrical cord from her foot to look like a robot. She took pleasure in freaking out the ever-shifting audience, waiting until the perfect moment to move, just when she was about to lose them, and then delighting in their gasps. Geena worked her way up: Bendel's hired her for its Christmas window.

After one of her first auditions, she could blink all she wanted. The casting people had liked her reading, but it was her body that landed the job. They forgot to ask for the typical strip-down-turn-around to see the bikini she'd worn underneath her outfit, so they perused photos she'd taken for the Victoria's Secret catalog before making an offer. Member of Mensa or not, she was now in a profession where looks went a long way toward making a career. The small role in *Tootsie*, the 1982 Sydney Pollack movie, became her very first credit. She hijacked the screen, bending and stretching in a teeny underwire bra and panties while a discombobulated Dustin Hoffman in drag wriggled into the room. The setup treated her cartoony presence as a visual joke.

She began to develop comic timing, as when she warned Hoffman's character about a lecherous cast member at the soap opera where they worked. *Doctor Brewster kisses all the women on the show,* she said with uninhibited cheer. *We call him The Tongue.* She let the word coil out of her mouth like a snake and got a solid laugh.

A major part followed in the short-lived sitcom *Buffalo Bill,* as did roles as a secondary character in *Fletch* with Chevy Chase and a sultry vampire in *Transylvania 6-5000.* Watching dailies on that film, she attracted the attention of Jeff Goldblum, whom she married in 1987 after they costarred in *The Fly.*

Geena's was not a classic movie-star face. Her jaw was wide and strong, her eyes rather small, but she had cheekbones out to there, luscious lips and a smile that could light up a billboard. The parts she landed benefited from her uninhibited willingness to appear absurd. Even though none of the films would be mistaken for *Masterpiece Theater*, she did her best to invest the most wackadoo circumstances in supernatural movies like *The Fly* and *Beetlejuice* with straight-ahead feeling. When she won the Best Supporting Actress Oscar for *The Accidental Tourist* in 1989, it was considered a come-from-behind surprise.

Quirky and *kooky*—"I got a little tired of seeing those words all the time," she sighs, "but I don't think they limited what I was offered." There was a clear upside. The labels steered her to an arcane subcategory of roles that kept Geena from having to consider the female characters who stood by while others had the adventures, what she called the "Good luck, honey!" parts. "I didn't know how to be interesting if I wasn't doing something unusual," she says. If directors approached her with boring parts in hopes she would give them that special Geena Davis eccentricity, she balked. "Somebody has to *write* it that way," she explained, "and *then* I do it. I can't make something out of nothing."

The actress knew good roles were scarce, but by setting herself apart with unusual selections, she worked, if not frenetically, at least steadily. The only danger seemed to be of sliding from costar to the lesser slot of red-haired, funny sidekick. Geena was keen for a distinctive lead. *Thelma & Louise* couldn't have come at a better time.

SUSAN SARANDON LEFT HER CAREER more to chance, which is not the same thing as not taking it seriously. She took parts as they came along, but she turned them down, too, if they didn't satisfy her exacting standards. She declined the female lead in Clint Eastwood's 1984 *Tightrope*, for example, because it dressed up the murders of women to make them seem like glamorous turn-ons—the victims were raped and strangled in beds or Jacuzzis. She chose parts with substance over those that positioned her on bankable lists. "Not that I was the go-to gal for those anyway," she says with a half-proud, half-resentful shrug. "I was never offered

The Godfather or any of the big, iconic films." At times, she was jilted for honors that critics felt she deserved, and she engaged in political activism regardless of its impact on her career.

Her upbringing instilled in Susan Sarandon a strong moral center, if not the one intended by her parochial school education. The eldest of nine in a devout Catholic family, she grew up in Metuchen, New Jersey, where her parents needed any help she could spare looking after all those younger siblings. She was responsible, sheltered and serious.

Acting came to her almost by accident. She studied theater at Catholic University, but in a literary more than a practical way. After she entered a twelve-year marriage with a fellow student, the aspiring actor Chris Sarandon, she went along on an audition and landed an agent herself. Five days later, she won her first role, in the 1970 movie *Joe,* as a hippie whose father murdered her druggie boyfriend. Susan rewrote her lines and took charge of her own costumes and makeup. "I didn't know actresses weren't *supposed* to do that," she told an interviewer. It established a pattern: Susan Sarandon, troublemaker or a fully committed collaborator, depending on how much her input was welcome.

For ten years, she took haphazard roles, mostly just to learn and earn. Like Geena Davis, she found her appearance had much to do with her winning parts—Susan had those wide Bette Davis eyes, a good figure and a natural presence. The job itself seemed silly to her. "Acting is a profession where mediocrity is constantly rewarded," she says. "Anybody can act. It's surviving as an actor that takes more talent."

Among her contemporaries, ingenue after ingenue eventually disappeared, while Susan persevered by holding out for more-intriguing options. *The Rocky Horror Picture Show* granted her midnight-movie camp immortality as the naive Janet, who got seduced by a transvestite alien from outer space. Working with director Louis Malle as a prostitute in *Pretty Baby* in 1978 and as a waitress in *Atlantic City* in 1980, she staked claim to the persona of a sensual but forthright sex symbol, but hardly a pliant one. With the rise of sexual explicitness on film, Susan, like every actress, had to take a stance. She struck a balance. She was perfectly willing to be provocative but insisted on rooting scenes within the bounds of the story and character, so her work wouldn't edge toward exploitation. Susan Sarandon's characters never just got screwed.

The approach worked in one of her most iconic scenes, in *Atlantic City*, when Susan's clam-bar worker massaged her breasts with the juice of fresh-squeezed lemons. Keeping a straight face should have been challenge enough—"Anyone who would rub lemons on her chest is completely insane," she says now. But she rescued what could have been trashy by keeping it matter-of-fact. She told Malle, "This scene should be shown as ordinary. It should be done only because she wants to get the smell of fish off her body." It was the kind of pragmatic thinking that boosted her racy renown without entangling her in the meaningless sex scenes that dumbed down so many other eighties movies.

Viewers had no difficulty finding the scene erotic. For years, fans sent her lemons in the mail, and *Playboy* named hers the "Celebrity Breasts of the Summer" for 1981. When the columnist George Will named her as one of the things he'd like to take on a long space voyage, Susan said, "I am very stunned and flattered and glad to learn that the rest of Mr. Will's body is not as conservative as his brain."

Like many actresses whose job was to seduce on-screen, Susan found that people could make the wrong assumptions in reality. A director once dismissed the crew from a costume fitting in a motel room so he could proposition her. "I said something dumb like 'I really have to get back to my room,'" she says. "The rest of the shoot, he made sure I was very uncomfortable."

But for the most part, she devised a way of carrying herself that set boundaries and kept the work on track. Lucinda Jenney, who played a waitress in *Thelma & Louise*, studied Sarandon's ability to walk that line. "She's the kind of person who can laugh about these things," Jenney says.

"She's got a twinkle in her eye and a lightness to her spirit in the way she handles that stuff, which is liquid gold."

"I don't think I had many problems necessarily because I was a woman," Susan says. "Maybe there were instances where problems could have been solved more easily if I'd had more clout, which male stars seem to have. Directors are conditioned to see male stars as the power source." Men were more often invited to watch dailies, consulted on what was coming up next and included in the overall process, man-to-man, while she cooled her heels in her trailer.

Probably her most infuriating experience was on 1987's *The Witches of Eastwick*. She was cast above the title with Cher and Michelle Pfeiffer, but the producers kowtowed to Jack Nicholson while lumping the women together as one interchangeable supporting character. At the eleventh hour, Cher got swapped into Susan's part, which gave her only three days to learn to play a cello. Throughout the tense shoot, the women were referred to as "girls," which was hardly unusual. Even as feminism made inroads into what to call women in society at large, most movie sets clung to the "girl" moniker, even for the most established stars.

Sarandon pined for better parts and greater meaning in her work. In 1991, she told a magazine, "I'm just trying to find roles to hold on to that are frightening because you're not sure you'll do them justice, rather than frightening because they're so empty you have to fill them up."

Motherhood gave her satisfaction that was lacking in her career after a daughter was born in 1985. Later, she and the actor Tim Robbins had two sons, in 1989 and 1992. Meanwhile, she doubled down on her commitment to the Equal Rights Amendment, abortion rights, nuclear disarmament and opposition to arming the Nicaraguan Contras, priding herself on doing everything wrong in terms of courting the industry. "The thing about having a career in this business is that you might as well live the way you want," she says, "because there are no tried-and-true rules that actually work."

One of her best roles came her way when she broke the rules. All the actresses ahead of her refused to read opposite Kevin Costner for Ron Shelton, the writer-director of *Bull Durham*, but the part of a brainy baseball fan who was every bit the equal of her lover was so well written that Susan paid her own airfare from Italy to land the role. She appreciated that the character was sexually free and wasn't punished for it. Shelton included her in planning and brainstorming as much as he did Costner.

Her peers snubbed her for an Oscar nomination, but the role was the kind of mainstream-avoidant portrayal that endeared her to Ridley Scott. "She's always had a very strong selection of material," he said. "It nearly always has some kind of strong subtext to it, so it's not necessarily overtly commercial. Which means she's a ballsy lady, really."

If he didn't understand that before he chose her, he didn't have long to wait.

SUSAN SARANDON AND GEENA DAVIS came face-to-face for the first time in a conference room in the spring of 1990. Ridley had summoned the stars to the production's temporary offices on the second floor of an undistinguished building on Melrose Avenue in Hollywood, where the action was picking up in hopes of shooting starting in June. The meeting was called a rehearsal, but it wasn't like a rehearsal in the theater, with chalk lines on the floor to block out the action. This was more of an in-depth discussion of what felt right and what didn't in the script.

Geena bound into the room thoroughly prepared to play the flaky Thelma but still thinking she could have been right for Louise. She thought the script was so first rate that there were only a few adjustments she wanted to suggest, a slight rewording of a sentence here or there, and she had a game plan in her notes for presenting each of them indirectly, so as not to offend. One she decided to postpone and bring up later on the set. Another she would toss off as a kind of throwaway joke. "I had all these girly ways," she says. "I would disguise each one and make it as non-threatening as possible."

Susan blew Geena's approach out of the water. The New York actress strode into the meeting, sat down at the conference table, opened her copy of the script and said, "On page one, I don't think I would do that." Boom... no nonsense, just like that. And "Maybe we could take out this line or move it to a later scene." Pleasantly, but with authority, Susan dissected the entire script and made pointed suggestions while Ridley listened agreeably.

Geena's jaw was on the ground. She would never forget the way her first female costar handled herself. *People can be like her?* Geena gaped. *God, what a way to be.* "There is nothing calculated about the way Susan is in the world," Geena says now. "She just... *is.* She's not going to equivocate or be coy. She just says what she wants, and people go... oh, okay."

"Yeah, I have a problem with being very direct, which isn't necessarily the best way," Susan admits. "But there's not much time to resolve these things." She felt responsible for making sure each scene served a purpose, either in telling the story or developing the characters. If not, she wanted it changed or cut.

The romantic scene between Louise and her feckless boyfriend, Jimmy, for example, still grated. It called for Jimmy to offer Louise an engagement ring at a motel where the couple would perform a mock wedding ceremony while Thelma, in another room, got it on with the hitchhiker they'd picked up. The next morning Louise would lose it when she discovered that the hitchhiker had stolen her life savings. The first draft of the script didn't explicitly call for a sex scene for Louise and Jimmy, but it did say: "Louise has an engagement ring on her finger. It's really beautiful. Louise is practically in tears, she's so happy. They are in bed, having just made love."

Susan explained why the sequence didn't fly with her. "Here's a woman who had a memory of something that led her to pulling a trigger and killing someone," she explained to Ridley and Geena. "I don't mind having a sex scene, but I think after everything that's happened, Louise would come unraveled. She couldn't surrender to orgasm without falling apart. Which I'm happy to do, but then the problem becomes that she has to unravel again in the morning."

"I see your point," Ridley agreed, "but we can't eliminate this completely. I need something to cut to from Geena's scene."

Susan considered for a moment. "It'd be an interesting sex scene to have an orgasm that turned into hysteria or something. It would be different," she said with just a hint of a playful smile. "If you want, I can give it a try."

Ridley was on the money about Susan being ballsy. They put off a decision on whether to push the limits of cinema with an orgasm-slash-breakdown scene, but the rehearsal did settle one point.

It hit Geena like the beam of a klieg light from the moment she and Susan met: *Are you kidding that I could play Louise*? Susan was so self-possessed, so mature and centered. She was Louise and then some.

CHAPTER 14

A FRESH EYE ON AMERICA

The two actresses tackled the prep work with gusto, all the down-and-dirty stuff guys usually got to do. They took stunt driving lessons in the parking lot of the Hollywood Bowl, where they pulled squealing 180s with the emergency brake. Ridley sat in the backseat while they ran lines until driving and talking at the same time became second nature. They got the hang of pistol shooting at a target range, smudging their fingers and faces with gunpowder residue. It was freewheeling fun, certainly more fun than faking proficiency on the cello. A dialogue coach schooled them in an appropriate accent, with a drawl but not too syrupy, so the characters would seem sharp.

Geena realized she *became* Thelma in Susan's presence, slavishly admiring her maternal competence. And Susan found Geena funny and loopy in a way that only someone intelligent can pull off. "She was game and brave and smart and certainly more diplomatic than I am," Susan says. "That's the basis for a love story, really."

Ridley turned his attention to what many considered the real star of all his movies: the look of the thing. Callie's screenplay guaranteed that *Thelma & Louise* wouldn't take on the appearance of a typical women's picture, all weepy close-ups under flattering key lights. Ridley already had a clear scheme in his head, planted there the morning he first read the script, when his painterly brain elevated the seemingly simple road movie to an odyssey, an epic—a women's picture by Ridley Scott. He was convinced that in order to sell the ending, the film had to convey the kind of mythic grandeur he had in mind, to make a statement that befit the fate of two main characters flying off the known world to become the stuff of legend.

Whereas some of the directors he vetted had seen the story as visually ordinary, Ridley came at it with the fresh eye of a foreigner. He imagined a romantic vision of Americana, the notion of the old Route 66, the light and space, all of it the greatest possible contrast to his upbringing in the north of England. "European filmmakers get to look at America in a way that Americans can't, because they are in the eye of the hurricane," says Hans Zimmer. "We can hold up a mirror and make America look at itself, marvel at itself, be critical of itself or celebrate itself—not take it for granted. There's the whole thing about guns, for example, the accessibility of guns. It's culturally specific. There are these things you have in America that we don't have in Europe, that sense of endlessness, vastness."

Ridley saw his job as providing a proscenium for the actors that enhanced and multiplied the power of the story. In *Thelma & Louise* that proscenium would be America, for better and for worse.

The director didn't have the luxury of constructing a detailed imaginary world on an expensive set, as he had in *Alien* and *Blade Runner*. Instead he would rely heavily on landscape, or three different landscapes, to frame what he saw as the three acts of the story. Act I: the green hills and commonplace hominess of the starting point in Arkansas. Act II: the wide-open fields and beat-up roadside stops of Oklahoma. Act III: the huge, impassive majesty of the Southwest desert and Grand Canyon.

Ridley decided to lean on the images he admired in the work of the midcentury realist painter John Register, a Californian who saturated his paintings of deserted coffee shops and bus stations with desolation. His work was often compared to Edward Hopper's, but the stark light and shadows of Register's weary interiors had a different feel, suffused by the blazing western sun outside the windows. It was bright but hardly cheerful. As Register himself has said: "I like the patina of things that have been battered by life."

Thelma & Louise's visual vocabulary would borrow that mysterious emptiness to foreshadow the ominous end for the heroines, as well as a sweeping, bright magnificence to celebrate the independence of their spirit. Ridley would start at the end and work back. It all depended on finding the right locations, beginning with the lip of that inimitable American landmark, the Grand Canyon.

WHEN THE LOCATION MANAGER, KEN HABER, arrived at that most crucial destination and plot point, he had been on the road for a month, driving from Little Rock to Arizona, taking photos to send back to Ridley—hundreds of shots of dated diners, sagebrush-lined highways and country-western bars. The woman in charge of public relations for the Grand Canyon, wearing a park ranger uniform complete with a Smokey Bear–style hat, led Haber into her office so he could lay out the case for shooting the climax of *Thelma & Louise* in the jewel of the National Park Service. For an hour and a half, she nodded absently while he explained that the crew was professional, that it would restore everything to its natural state, that the scene was absolutely essential to the film.

"What do you think?" he asked at length. "Can we do it?"

Not a muscle moved in her stony expression. "No."

Haber saw his job flash before his eyes. *This is the movie,* he thought. *If we don't have the Grand Canyon, we don't have the movie.* "Do you mind if I ask why?" he asked, his voice catching.

"I just don't like the story," she said. "I don't like that these girls go off a cliff and commit suicide."

Join the club, Haber thought. Gingerly, he pointed out that filmmakers enjoyed First Amendment rights, that legally they could say anything they wanted without a stamp of government approval.

She didn't budge. "This might get a lot of copycats," she said. "I just don't like it."

Haber broke the news to Ridley back in the production office on Melrose. They might try lobbying the Park Service or suing the government for permission, but they didn't have years to burn for that.

Ridley scanned the pictures Haber had taken of the canyon. "It's not going to work anyway," Ridley said. "The scale isn't right. See"—he pointed to the red rocks of the opposite canyon wall. "If the car goes off here, you'll lose it in the vastness of the space." In other words, the Grand Canyon was too big. Its source must start somewhere upstream, Ridley concluded. To find someplace smaller, Haber had to trace the canyon back to that source.

Meanwhile, when he had time, Ridley joined Haber and his production designer on the road to visit other sites Haber had selected. They covered some four thousand miles of southern heartland, listening to a cassette of songs that Callie had recommended to complement various scenes, including "Better Not Look Down" by B. B. King.

The scouting mission was an unlikely road trip—three mismatched outsiders in a car: Ridley, the Englishman of few words; Haber, a native of Brooklyn who'd never before been west; and Norris Spencer, the production designer of the film, well over six feet tall, who wore flowing scarves and smoked Marlboros with the filters cut off. Spencer, in particular, attracted curious stares wherever they went. Son of a Jamaican father and Chinese mother, he registered as a black Asian man with a thick British accent. "In Arkansas, that's not a good idea," Ridley says. "The racism was shocking." A menacing clerk in a village store looked them over and asked, "Where you boys from?" They beat it out of there pronto. Other encounters were more fruitful. They met a woman driving a cement truck with a pack of cigarettes rolled in her sleeve and a perfectly aged trucker hat, a black cap with a faded American flag on the front. Ridley bought it for Thelma to wear once her character had evolved and toughened up. For all the skill of the production crews, Ridley felt, there was no convincing way to properly age a hat.

While Ridley could be uncomfortable with actors, he relaxed with the crew, especially those, like Haber and Spencer, who helped him craft his proscenium, something he could understand and control. All three had been art students who started in commercials, and they had worked on *Black Rain* together. Yet hours in the car ground them down. "I wanted to show America the way I'd like to see it," Ridley says. "But Route 66 didn't exist anymore. It was gone. There were only ghost towns left running parallel to the freeway. The rest was now garages, hideous hotels and parking lots with big stores." *If the West looked the same everywhere,* he thought, *why drag a whole bloody circus of equipment across four states?* Grand Canyon aside, he could film everything within a couple hours of LA.

Armed with Haber's photos, other scouts sought out look-alike locations for Arkansas around Los Angeles and its suburbs. Ridley fixed on the agricultural San Joaquin Valley near Bakersfield to stand in for Oklahoma. "I love Bakersfield because of the vast, open landscapes of these huge farms where there are no walls, there are no fences," Ridley said. "It's almost like the Dust Bowl before it became the Dust Bowl... the middle of this great landmass you call the United States of America."

Laddie, a native Californian, was skeptical. No one admired Bakersfield for its scenery. But Ridley found beauty in what most Americans would consider mundane—fields of bobbing oil pumps, rows of spritzing irrigations pipes, pencil-straight highways lined with telephone poles. Cost was also a decisive factor. Ridley wanted to squeeze as much epic grandeur as he could out of an unimposing budget. Pathé had allocated just under $17 million for *Thelma & Louise* in an effort to hedge the risks for the female-led property. That was more generous than the allowance for the sort of independent film Callie originally had in mind, but significantly less than the $24 million average for a studio picture. It helped that Ridley had cast Susan and Geena. At $1 million apiece, their salaries were respectable for the time but less than the demands of top-tier stars. But Ridley calculated that with fifty-four locations needed to capture the women's journey, he'd have to make do with some cut-rate choices. He'd shoot most everything in southern and central California. Now all he had to do was track down a stand-in for the Grand Canyon.

ON A LITTLE PRIVATE PLANE over the desert near Las Vegas, Ridley turned to Haber and Spencer in the back and asked, "Have you ever seen Monument Valley?" He directed the pilot to take them down. They hired a Navajo guide to show them around, passing red sandstone buttes up to a thousand feet tall. The landscape offered depth and texture that were absent in a sprawling, flat desert. "It was so spectacular that I couldn't speak," Haber says. The men knew that John Ford had filmed legendary Westerns with John Wayne in the area, but not much in the way of filmmaking had happened there since. It could become the grand backdrop for Act III, the driving scenes near the end of the movie, but there was only one hotel in the vicinity—Ford had set up tent villages for his casts and crews. The logistics would be impossible. The three had to keep searching.

Then the Utah Film Commission suggested the area around Moab, Utah, a jumping-off point for Arches National Park. Haber found more red buttes and mesas and, better yet, a canyon in a neighboring state park called Dead Horse Point. The area practically vibrated with intense colors, orange-red monoliths against a sapphire sky. The canyon itself was small and broken up by formations that would provide layers of rock and contrast to highlight the car as it flew off the edge. A narrow strand of the Colorado River sliced through the bottom, well upstream from the Grand Canyon. A local guide led Haber to survey details like access roads and secondary locations, when suddenly, for no reason whatsoever, he broke down and cried on a stretch of highway, to the point where he had to pull the car over and stop.

"Don't be embarrassed," the guide assured him. "It happens all the time." Grown men often bawled like babies in the desert, she said. "Everyone here knows the strength of this place." Haber developed a theory that the fierce color contrasts in the brilliant light—he called it color vibration—stirred up uncontrolled emotions. Whatever the reason, he was the first of many working on *Thelma & Louise* who would weep when confronted with the intensity of the setting. He and Ridley had found the place that would hold its own with his epic vision.

CHAPTER 15

REAL CHARACTERS

James Caan toyed for a while with playing Hal Slocumb, the Arkansas cop who pursued Thelma and Louise despite an undertow of sympathy for their plight. The actor negotiated for script revisions that would add more detective work and other heft to the part.

Caan was a veteran of tough-guy movies whose battered face and vaguely sinister aura resonated from a history of seventies roles like Sonny Corleone in *The Godfather*. Caan as Hal Slocumb was the kind of unpredictable choice Ridley was looking for when he hired Lou DiGiaimo as casting director after admiring his work on *Tin Men*, another guys' movie populated with strong but unpretty faces.

Tall, with a scruffy beard and balding on top, Lou worked up a flight of rickety steps in a ramshackle old New York building on West Fifty-fourth Street, later home to *The Daily Show*. He hung out with ex-cops, not theater people. No one would think to hire Lou to cast *Amadeus* or *A Room with a View,* but he developed a niche. "His friends were a certain kind of guys' director—Barry Levinson, William Friedkin, Ridley—guys who smoked cigars and talked about girls and weren't going to musical theater," says his assistant Brett Goldstein. Lou favored New York–trained theater actors and even nonprofessionals, so long as they sported interesting mugs. "Realies," Lou called them.

Hiring Lou to cast a women's picture seemed like a head-scratching move, but aside from the two leads, the rest of the characters were almost all men. Ridley liked to think that, flawed as they were, each represented a different aspect of maleness. All of them could be rolled together to form a complete man, but the risk was that each one alone could skirt close to caricature. Lou's realies would keep them grounded.

Ridley also wanted to work with Lou because, coming from the instant-impression world of commercials, Ridley preferred actors who could quickly telegraph visually who they were, as Lou's picks usually did. And Ridley and Lou shared another point of view, says Goldstein: "They didn't give a crap about who was hot or famous."

But Ridley did choose actors with great care. "I am a very niggling caster," he says. "I believe if I do it right, half the work is done. In fact, more, because once the actors walk out on the floor, they've done all the work, you've discussed it and they are red-hot to do it. That leaves me room to do all my other things."

He met with James Caan, but by the end of their talk, Ridley backed away. Caan's demands would have turned the movie into *Thelma, Louise & Hal.*

In March 1990, Lou began to hunt in earnest for the roles beyond the leads. "Surprise me," Ridley said to Lou. "Bring me people I haven't seen before." It was possible that actors would hang back from signing on to an unfashionable, modestly budgeted chick flick when action-movie riches beckoned from every other production in town. Ron Howard, for example, was casting *Backdraft,* a firefighter action film studded with beefy male parts.

But it seemed that good actors were sick of running, jumping and grunting, and Callie's rogue's gallery of semi-dysfunctional males tantalized with the chance to explore something different. While not inciting quite the frenzy the search for the female headliners did, the male casting calls still attracted a who's who of performers who were up-and-coming, if not quite there.

As written, Detective Hal Slocumb served up a plum part, a good detective who performed his duty by tracking Thelma and Louise even as he became convinced that they were honorable women blown off course by circumstance. His growing protectiveness toward them made him the moral center of the movie. Lou and Ridley considered approaching the stalwart Sam Elliott for the role, and they made an offer to Scott Glenn, who took a part in *Backdraft* instead. But most of those Lou brought in to read were rugged-looking, lesser-known character actors with theater experience: Hector Elizondo, Robert Forster and Clarence Williams III, familiar as Linc on TV's *The Mod Squad*.

Ridley short-circuited the process when he got a call from the agent for Harvey Keitel. The intense New York method actor with a soulful, gnarled face specialized playing scary thugs in movies like *Mean Streets* and *Taxi Driver*. His most improbable role up until then had been in Ridley's first film, *The Duellists*, as a nineteenth-century French general, albeit a scary, thuggish one. It was regarded as nutty casting at the time, but it worked.

In the eighties Harvey had settled into supporting roles in lesser movies. He'd seen the script for *Thelma & Louise* when a friend up for one of the parts shared a copy, and its uniqueness spoke to him. "It was about women, in a real way," he says. "Their difficulties, our difficulties as men, what we have to confront with each other and within ourselves. There weren't a lot of movies about women, and there were a lot of problems that needed to be discussed. Callie was discussing it."

When his agent threw his name in the hopper, Ridley and Lou didn't focus on the obvious mismatch. Lou thought of everyone as a New Yorker, and Ridley didn't see the difference. Given Harvey's history of villainous roles, Ridley liked the idea of playing with that expectation. "The perception of Harvey was the antithesis of what I wanted him for," says Ridley, "which I thought was the right reason to go for him." Audiences wouldn't expect Harvey Keitel, of all people, to sympathize with the heroines. In real life, Ridley found Harvey touching. "He's a very sensitive man, even though he's nearly always playing against what he seems to be." They'd enjoyed a manly rapport when they worked together before, dining well on French food and sharing Cuban cigars at the end of the day.

"Why don't you ever cast me, you jerk?" Harvey began when they spoke about the part.

"You're going to have to play a good guy," Ridley warned. "It's a departure."

"That's cool," said Harvey. "But Goddamn, this guy is *really* sympathetic. Do you think it's a good idea?"

"Stop fucking about it," Ridley said. "Do it."

MEANWHILE, AN AWKWARD MIX OF knowns and unknowns avoided eye contact in the waiting room at the bare-bones Melrose Avenue production office where Lou, and often Ridley, too, heard readings for the other roles. Thelma's piggish husband, Darryl Dickinson, was one of the least evolved characters, a self-absorbed slob oblivious to his wife's happiness, so Ridley felt it was doubly important to find an actor with the comic versatility to make the character relatable. In an interview after the movie's release, Ridley admitted that Darryl was probably the character closest to himself, a guy too consumed with his own needs to listen to his wife. "We need to accept that these men are out there," he said after a nervous laugh. "On different levels, of course. These men are *us*."

Dan Aykroyd wouldn't be available until the fall, Lou found out, but

Bill Pullman, who'd made a strong impression in comedies like *Ruthless People* and *Spaceballs*, took a meeting. He was prominent enough not to have to read from the script, but others did: Paul Le Mat, Matt Frewer, John C. McGinley and Chris Cooper, still early in their careers. J. T. Walsh took an interest before he joined the *Backdraft* juggernaut, and Tim Robbins landed on the wish list until he refused to audition. Judge Reinhold didn't object. The fresh-faced comic actor, hot off parts in *Fast Times at Ridgemont High*, *Ruthless People* and *Beverly Hills Cop I* and *II*, showed up to read in a Darryl-appropriate polyester suit from Sears. "Do you know how hard it is to find a suit like this?" he said.

Geena had someone else in mind: an old boyfriend, she said, Chris McDonald, who had a theater background and top-shelf training—Stella Adler and the Royal Academy of Dramatic Art in London—and an acting toolbox stocked with hilarious comic shtick. It had yet to be fully tapped in roles like a guest shot on *Cheers* or a singing, dancing greaser with a pompadour and a flipped-up collar in *Grease 2*. "He is the funniest guy in the world," Geena promised Ridley. Her message got garbled, or else Lou was on a different track, because when Chris's agent called him, the invitation was to read for Harlan, the role of the rapist who attacked Geena and got himself shot.

Chris couldn't believe it. He thought, *I'd have to take whatever the money is and put it right into therapy.* Because while Geena had copped to a relationship with him in her conversation with Ridley, she hadn't hinted at its extent: the couple had bought a house together near Griffith Park and become engaged, with a ring on her finger and the dress already picked out, before she met Jeff Goldblum on location and broke Chris's heart. There was no way he was going to take on the thankless role of Geena Davis's rapist.

Heart sunk, he read the script anyway. He could see why his name might pop up. Chris could summon a manic intensity in his icy blue eyes and was tall enough to match up well with Geena, as he well knew. The dialogue grabbed him, and the people felt authentic, especially Thelma and Darryl. "I knew this woman was stuck in this relationship with maybe her high school sweetheart, who was a pretty big deal on campus and basically peaked there," Chris observes. "Now he's just trying to keep that going. He's a regional manager, a big deal! Just ask him, he'll tell you!" Chris agreed to the audition, but he showed up at the Melrose Avenue production office tricked out as Darryl and asked if he could please, please read for that part.

Ridley usually remained sphinxlike in auditions, saving a cryptic comment or two until the actor left the featureless conference room designated for casting sessions, but he couldn't hold in the laughter when Chris McDonald unleashed a wild mix-up of dimwitted deadpan and ridiculous comic tics. He appeared as the very vision of Callie's chauvinist carpet salesman in the requisite polyester leisure suit, absurdly sculpted bouffant hair and a gold necklace dangling a roman numeral number one that a friend had given him as a joke. Lou read the Thelma part in his gravelly *Goodfellas* voice for a scene where Darryl told her not to bother waiting for him for dinner. Then they read a scene where Darryl faked enthusiasm to hear from her on the phone with a patently insincere "Hello!" That's when Ridley lost it completely. He hadn't been sure, but there Darryl was. The character could be seen as creepy and vicious, yet Chris found the goofiness in him, maybe even a touch of desperate pathos, the preening of an empty-headed egotist.

CALLIE HAD SERVED UP ANOTHER IMPERFECT, multilayered character in Jimmy, Louise's musician boyfriend, who, as written, demonstrated a rather sweet devotion that finally, sadly, too late, overrode his chronic failure to commit. It was important to Callie that Jimmy come across as a vaguely inappropriate love interest for an uptight waitress like Louise. Her choice of a safe but unavailable man would reinforce the impression that the rape in Texas had hardened her to romance.

Ridley and Lou aimed to knock some of the sweetness off the Jimmy character by casting a rough-edged guy with enigmatic sex appeal. "I wanted somebody who on the surface appeared to be very much a man's man," Ridley said. "A bit of a shitkicker. Drinker, likes his cigarettes, has a band. But he's not high-end rock 'n' roll; he actually plays in lounges." *Loser* was too strong a word for what Ridley had in mind. Jimmy was more a man with a certain amount of talent who'd been disappointed with where it had taken him. "A lot of those frustrations probably come out and backfire in Louise's face," Ridley said.

Lou rounded up some actual musicians to read. The country singer Dwight Yoakam came in, and the rock 'n' roller Huey Lewis. Both were interested in pursuing acting, and later did, but this would have been a first credit for either one. Rubén Blades, the Latin music star who'd already won some movie parts, made the list, too. Lou also wrangled some rising, more typically handsome leading men from the era: John Shea, who'd made an impression in 1982's *Missing*, Michael Ontkean, who had secured a number of mostly romantic roles, and Jamey Sheridan, who was still working in smaller parts. One of the most out-of-left-field candidates was Joe Bob Briggs, a Texas writer-comedian who hosted a cable B movie show called *Joe Bob's Drive-in Theater*.

These actors mingled in the waiting room with the Darryl, Hal and other wannabes, including an array of sinister sorts up for the rapist role of Harlan. That crew was uniformly tall, with forbidding eyes. One of them, Michael Madsen, shambled into his meeting with an air of menace so masterful it would make Vito Corleone look like Mister Rogers.

Ridley saw right away that this actor had the tools, the résumé and the physical presence to both attract Geena's character and then try to rape her. In the last eight years, Michael had deployed hooded eyes, a looming physical presence and the raspy voice of someone who had spent too many nights in smoky bars to portray a series of dark characters in less than top-tier movies. He knew how the industry saw him: "Give Madsen a gun and a cigarette and roll the camera."

Michael slouched in a seat opposite Ridley and Lou, knowing what was expected of him at this audition, the psycho-killer persona that he'd raised to an art form, but he balked. "I don't want to play Harlan," he said, speaking softly as he fixed them with a sullen stare.

"Why not?" asked Ridley, taken aback, but intrigued.

"I know the routine, okay? We're going to square dance together, then I'm going to rape her in the parking lot and then Susan Sarandon is going to shoot me." He shrugged. "Where's that going to get me? I could do it," he stated with utter confidence. "And you'd *believe* it." The words hung in the charged and suddenly chilly air. "But I'm not going to do it."

"Well, who do you see yourself as?" Lou asked.

"Jimmy."

Ridley burst out laughing. He shook his head. He thought of the candidates they'd been seeing, with their dance cards full of amorous roles. "You really think you could do that?"

"Yeah," said Michael. He held the gaze of his interrogators without flinching. "Yeah, I do."

They asked him to step out of the room.

"There's a touch of Elvis Presley in there, isn't there?" Ridley noted. An Elvis, maybe, who never made it out of Tupelo. Sometimes, on instinct, Ridley liked to cast based on physicality in hopes that the person could pull off the acting. But here he also saw a natural, realistic talent and, behind the snarl, a vulnerability that hadn't found an outlet yet in pedestrian tough-guy roles. Maybe the ardent Jimmy would play better as a gruff, uninvolved guy with just enough softness to care about Louise.

They called Michael back in and posed a question: Would he mind taking Susan Sarandon to lunch? If the chemistry worked, they'd consider him for the part.

The odds seemed slim that Michael would strike a spark with the former Catholic school grad with a history of lofty moral stands. The actor's juvenile rap sheet—stealing cars, breaking and entering, gun possession—had put an end to his family's hopes that he'd become a cop in Chicago. He'd been working as an auto mechanic when he accompanied an actor friend to an audition there. The director Martin Brest spotted Michael, and he wound up with a brief part at the opening of *WarGames*—in a missile silo his character pulled a gun on another soldier who couldn't bring himself to turn a launch key. Utterly cold. The production got him a SAG card and put him up at the Sunset Marquis. He worked pumping gas and changing tires at a Union 76 station in Beverly Hills until other character parts came along, all the while running with notorious Hollywood wild men like Dennis Hopper and David Carradine.

Michael Madsen's biggest struggle was finding the humanity in the people he was asked to play. "If I had known how many times a gun was going to be put in my hand after that first movie, I don't know if I would've," he says. "I guess it's good to have something to fall back on, but that's why I wanted to do *Thelma & Louise* so bad, because I wouldn't have a gun." Jimmy was the closest to a romantic lead he'd ever had a shot at, an opportunity to break the typecasting. "You could sit there and focus on my being intimidating and dangerous," he says, "but you could also focus on the fact that I'm a sweet man, a good man, an honest man. I'm a father." He was a man who wrote poetry! The kind of person who was largely absent from the assembly line of crime movies that sought him out.

He picked up Susan from a house where she and Tim Robbins were staying in Santa Monica to take her to a nearby red-sauce pasta place, coincidentally called Louise's Trattoria. They talked about family, the world at large, not much about the movie. Michael admired that she was a woman with political opinions, but he tuned out the details. "A lot of what she went on about I wasn't keen on discussing," he says. "But I liked her very much, and we were fond of each other pretty quickly."

Susan agreed that he would make for good casting, as much for his singular code of masculinity as his presence. "He certainly was that character," Susan says. "He said he couldn't be with Louise if he knew she'd been raped."

His many contradictions made him right for the part, while also promising some interesting moments on the set, for while Michael liked and respected female coworkers, his approach to gender in the workplace wouldn't pass muster with the human resources department at the Acme Corporation. "Susan's the kind of girl you could give a swat on the butt and she'd probably laugh," he says. "In fact, I think I did that. To me, doing something like that to a woman in a situation where you're working is a sort of a test. It says a lot about a girl. I like women who are playful. I like women who are smart. If you put those two things together, that's Susan, for sure."

He got the word the next day. Michael Madsen won the part of Jimmy without even having to read.

CHAPTER 16

"THE *BLOND* ONE!"

Every twentysomething kid in Hollywood who fell somewhere on the spectrum from cute to handsome to downright pretty descended on the casting office in pursuit of the role of J.D., the sexy hitchhiker who gave Thelma the night of her life. The auditions churned up an abundance of Bon Jovi hair, shrink-wrapped T-shirts with rolled-up sleeves, dreamy eyes and plummy lips.

In a delicious twist, J.D. filled the customary girl part, the nubile sex object who beds the star and then disappears. Looks were just about everything here. But because J.D. ultimately stole the women's money, he needed a dark side, too. That was the casting predicament: this character had to radiate enough seductive heat to cajole a woman who had narrowly escaped a rape to hop into bed with a sketchy stranger. Yet he had to signal enough treachery to use her and turn on her once he'd turned her on. "Dangerously sexy" was the mission.

"It wasn't as easy as it sounds," says Ira Belgrade, an assistant casting director who screened the bad-boy candidates with Ridley and Lou. "There had to be a wild, interesting sexuality and charm for the part."

Throughout the month of March 1990, Lou set up a little camera on a table in the casting office to record the mixed results as actors delivered some mildly flirtatious dialogue from a scene in the car. Those who made the callback cut returned to deliver the seduction scene in the motel, where J.D. demonstrated how to perform armed robbery by slinging a hair dryer in place of a gun. This being a part with a racy lovemaking sequence in the offing, one would think the men would have been asked to take their shirts off, as actresses routinely did in auditions, but no one remembers any of that with the men.

Looking back, the applicants, most with few credits at the time, formed a who's who of future stars. Mark Ruffalo was only twenty-three, with just a single TV pilot under his belt. James Le Gros, thirty-two, had played supporting roles in a couple of cool indies, including *Drugstore Cowboy*. As if the procession of perfect cheekbones wasn't confusing enough, one day Dermot Mulroney read at three o'clock while Dylan McDermott took the three-thirty slot. At least McDermott managed to make an impression, if only for the wrong reason. "He made the biggest classic mistake an actor can do," says Ira Belgrade: he brought along his fiancée, a fairly obscure actress named Catherine Keener, to read the Thelma part, and she outshone him.

"Not him," Ridley said crisply as the actor left, "but what can we give her?" Keener wound up with the role of Sarah, the wife of Harvey Keitel's Hal, although ultimately her scene was cut during the edit.

The J.D. contenders mostly fell into two camps. Some adopted the spikey, tousled hair and winning charm of star of the moment Tom Cruise, while others went for the more retro effect of a shuffling, mumbling James Dean. Most fell short. The comments they left in their wakes ranged from "not bad-boyish enough" to "not good-looking enough." For while they represented the epitome of available hunks at the time, as Belgrade puts it, "There's gorgeous, and then there's Hollywood gorgeous." The role called for movie-star dazzle at a supporting-player salary.

A near beginner named Brad Pitt was twenty-six years old when Lou had seen him on the tube. The blue-eyed blond skewed toward the better-looking end of the scale, but he had managed only guest shots on shows like *Dallas* and *21 Jump Street*, not counting such movie gigs as "guy at beach with drink," "waiter" and "preppie guy at fight."

"I don't know who besides Lou would have thought of Brad Pitt," says Brett Goldstein, the other assistant casting director. "He was so good-looking that if he could act, we would have found out by then."

Pitt's reading veered into James Dean territory, with a nicely authentic accent and a certain slinky charm. But Ridley thought he seemed too young. They moved on.

One of the strangest tapes featured a twenty-eight-year-old with a résumé of supporting roles on TV shows like *Roseanne* and *The Facts of Life*. With his square face, heavy eyebrows, thick sideburns and dark, wavy hair that bulged out to the sides and hung down nearly to his shoulders, the overall effect was of a head that measured wider than it was tall. He hunched forward, fidgeted to the point of distraction and for some reason made the choice to chomp on a toothpick throughout the scene in the car, shifting the intrusive prop from side to side with his hand so it obscured his mouth as he spoke. It was impossible to watch the audition tape without wanting to say, "Dude! Sit still!" Or at least "What's with the toothpick?"

It was all too much, and certainly not dangerously sexy, although Lou found him faintly interesting. "You would never in a million years look at this guy and think that this was the next big movie star," says Ira. They thanked him and checked the name off the list: George Clooney.

Throughout this procession, all Ridley could talk about was William Baldwin. The twenty-seven-year-old's brother Alec had already played some major roles when Billy made the leap from modeling to playing the preppie murderer Robert Chambers in a television movie and went on to a smoky turn in *Internal Affairs*, a police thriller with Richard Gere. The rising star's acting range wasn't broad, but he was extraordinarily good-looking, with an air of mystery about him. When he nailed an audition at the end of March, Ridley called off the hunt. Billy Baldwin would play J.D.

MOMENTUM WAS RUNNING IN THE MOVIE'S favor toward a hard start date for shooting of June 11, 1990. Callie sometimes stopped by the production office, which hummed with the tasks of casting smaller parts and locking in locations. The choice of supporting actors pleased her. In fact, she had suggested Michael Madsen after he appeared in an indie movie produced by her boyfriend, David Warfield, with a typical Madsen title, *Kill Me Again*. "He could play the kind of guy who's too much of a kid," Callie says. "He doesn't even know that he's not coming through for Louise."

Callie felt the frustrating, disjointed moves of her life coalesce. Her agent fielded inquiries from studios curious about the new screenwriting name in town. She angled to school herself in directing by observing the filming of *Thelma & Louise*. And on June 2, 1990, at the age of thirty-two, the woman some would vilify a year later as the man-hating writer of a man-hating movie threw herself the southern wedding of her dreams, with the big white dress and all the trimmings.

She and David and 150 guests abandoned all pretense of Hollywood cool at the Belle Meade Plantation in Nashville, with a full southern spread of barbecue and ham biscuits. "It was hotter than the hinges of hell," Callie remembers. Amanda Temple flew in from London, and Pam Tillis served as maid of honor. By this time, the young musician who'd served as an inspiration for Thelma had recorded her first album and just signed with a new major label. Callie had helped write one of Pam's early singles about longing and loneliness, "Wish I Was in Love Tonight," but even the singer's breakup songs, like "Don't Tell Me What to Do," celebrated the hardy spirit the two friends had cultivated in many an all-night talk.

As they toasted Callie's wedding that weekend, the old running buddies were flying. They had finessed their way past the sentinels of the entertainment industry and stood poised to fulfill the promise they had seen in each other all along.

GEENA TOOK AN URGENT CALL. Would she consider pitching in on Saturday, two days before the start of production? It was a casting emergency: Billy Baldwin had dropped out. His first scenes were scheduled within days, and now there was no one to play J.D. It would help if Geena would read with four guys who'd failed to make the cut before, in hopes that one of them could muster some chemistry with the star.

Billy set this fiasco in motion when he was offered one of the much-coveted parts in Ron Howard's *Backdraft*, which, thanks to a final roster of names like Robert De Niro, Kurt Russell, Donald Sutherland and Scott Glenn, was still shaping up as the movie to beat. Pathé had failed to lock in Billy's contract, so he had left *Thelma & Louise* practically at the altar.

Ridley and Lou hadn't panicked at first. They turned to a solid backup: Grant Show, a twenty-eight-year-old who played a cop on a TV show called *True Blue*. But he was committed to twelve days on a Jackie Collins miniseries and couldn't get out of his contract. *Thelma & Louise* "was the best script I've ever read," said Show, "the cherriest role I've ever read. The worst actor in the world could have taken that role and walked away a movie star." Years later, long after a stint on *Melrose Place* and a dry spell of middling television roles, he couldn't help but second-guess how he'd honored the contract for the miniseries. "If there is one thing I wish

I could tell that young actor," he said, "it would be to walk off that set and say, 'Sue me.'"

The casting directors sent out a distress call to all the talent agencies and got an intriguing response. "Hey, Ira," Lou called out in the office one day, "CAA says Robert Downey Jr. will take it for whatever we have in the budget."

Downey was then twenty-five and already a certified star, but Ira had his doubts. "Isn't he too short? Next to Geena?"

Ridley scotched the idea over the phone. Now they had to scramble.

That Saturday they convened in a faceless office for a new movie Lou was working on because he was already supposed to have wrapped *Thelma & Louise*. Everyone felt the pressure. The actors had to drop straight into J.D.'s pivotal hair dryer scene, where sexual tension crackled under the surface. J.D. had to be cool—but hot. From the beginning, before a hundred male ingenues tried out, Lou had predicted, "Whoever nails the hair dryer scene gets the part."

Geena, always the sport, was happy to help out. She and three dark-haired guys proceeded through the reading without a hitch. Honestly, they blurred together for her. Abs. Hair. Slouchy delivery. "They were all handsome," Geena says. "They all did a great job."

When the fourth candidate sidled into the room, he came at the bad-boy thing a little sideways. Almost painfully polite, Brad Pitt presented himself as a perfect southern gentleman, with a few shy, sidelong looks toward the star. The deferential persona came to him naturally. Brad was the son of straitlaced Southern Baptists, born in Oklahoma and raised in Springfield, Missouri, so the accent was spot-on. Weeks before graduating from the University of Missouri, he'd left school when an itch to act propelled him to LA with nothing but gas money in his pocket and a mullet on his head. His approach to J.D. came from within, humble and attentive, a departure from the cocky style that might have been the more obvious choice.

Ridley noted his trim physique, that he was shorter than Geena—although not as short as Robert Downey Jr. To Ridley, the actor still came across as a kid. "I want to see a real sociopath," he insisted.

Brad dipped his head respectfully. *Sociopath?* "I was fresh out of Missouri," he later said. "I had to go home and look it up."

He had just lost out on one of the many roles in the ubiquitous *Backdraft,* another defeat in a long four-year slog. This *Thelma* script was so fine, the part so far out of his league, the presence of an Academy Award–winning actress and legendary director in that close office so pressing, his nerves could have gotten the best of him. He could have lost his cool. But then a strange thing happened. Geena lost hers instead.

Brad launched into the scene, which, naturally, he had memorized for an audition as crucial as this. *I'm just a guy. A guy whose parole officer is probably having a shit fit right about now.*

The room fell silent as Geena gawked at him. "Oh!" she exclaimed. She looked down at her pages, then looked back, simply staring at this knockout of a kid. She tried again, with an awkward stop-start shuffle that spelled disaster for Brad. *What!? Parole officer? You mean you're a criminal?* She sputtered, stalled and laughed.

"I'm so sorry, I'm screwing up your audition," she said. "There is no rhythm here."

"It's all good," he assured her. "Let's just try again."

They fumbled ahead, then broke off. "Don't worry about it," he said, and he meant it. He found her disarming and playful, which in turn helped him to feel loose. They relaxed into the scene as he wrapped it up.

I've always believed if done right, armed robbery doesn't have to be a totally unpleasant experience.

God. You're a real live outlaw! Geena's face lit up with giddy, ardent embarrassment.

Softly, Brad delivered the coup de grâce, looking straight into her eyes. *I may be the outlaw, but you're the one stealing my heart.*

"He had an incredibly calm and comfortable vibe," Geena recalls now that she's had a chance to collect herself, but still with visible enthusiasm. "He was so natural. There are people who can make it seem like they're making up the words as they go, and that was what he was like."

After the actor let himself out, Ridley and Lou debated over the various brunets they'd seen. Which one had the right look, which had a rougher quality? No one mentioned Brad Pitt, the one who still seemed young for the role.

Geena busied herself packing up her things, waiting to be asked to weigh in. *What*, she thought, *would Susan Sarandon have said in this situation?* She knew: *Why are you not asking me what* I *thought?*

Finally, she stopped waiting for an invitation. "Would you be interested in what my impression was?" she asked sweetly.

"Yes, yes, of course." The men recovered themselves.

"The *blond* one! *Hello?!*"

Later, Lou explained the thinking behind the call. "Here was this kid who set her sparks off." Or as Ridley says, "I saw her color up, and that was it." They wanted chemistry? They got the kind of chemistry you couldn't cook up in a jet-propulsion laboratory.

NEARLY TWENTY-FIVE YEARS LATER, Geena found herself seated next to George Clooney on a plane. They chatted as if they already knew each other, actors who enjoyed being members of their own exclusive club. At one point, he said, "That Brad Pitt, I'm never going to forgive him."

"I thought he was your big friend," Geena responded, genuinely surprised. "Why?"

"For getting the part instead of me," Clooney said. "You know, when I read with you."

He had been one of the nobody brunets. She's always wondered who the others were.

CHAPTER 17

THE GIRLS IN
THE THUNDERBIRD

The door to Thelma's garage flipped open first thing Monday morning, June 11, 1990, and the camera rolled as Geena Davis burst out, dragging enough luggage for a reenactment of the Lewis and Clark expedition rather than a weekend fishing trip with Louise.

The moment marked the official start of principal photography on a movie already freighted with more doubt than your typical multiplex fare. Yet *Thelma & Louise* had made it this far, and still none of the principals had given much thought to such weighty issues as whether this gender-bender road picture had something sweeping or controversial to say about women, men and the evolving deliberations over what constituted fairness or justice between them. Right now the set functioned pretty much like any workplace in America at the time—men and women bent to their tasks, collaborating, cooperating and bringing their various skills to bear.

This was a simple scene, but important: they had to get Thelma down the driveway to Louise's turquoise 1966 Thunderbird on a leafy suburban street in the Los Angeles suburb of Tarzana, ably standing in for Arkansas. It would mark the first time Thelma and Louise shared the screen in the course of the movie, setting the benchmark for their rich but complicated friendship.

After a 6:30 a.m. call for hair, makeup and costumes, Geena, Susan and Ridley met at 8:30 to roughly block out the action. Afterward, they'd let it fly. They shared the belief that rehearsal killed the adrenaline and the spontaneity they prized.

Geena, as usual, came prepared. She knew exactly how to play the moment: she would open the faucet on all her own bottled-up adrenaline, all the emotions on one of the most momentous days in her career, and let them flow into her character. She put to use her full awareness that she had spent nearly a year pursuing this rare and coveted female role, her first as a major lead, her first that wasn't a kooky girlfriend to a vampire or ghost or bug, a role that she'd spent hours prepping with an acting coach and with Callie, scribbling notes on every available margin of the script, spelling her lines out phonetically to nail the Arkansas accent. "I'll do whatever it takes," she said to herself, "not to mess up this brilliant part."

She believed that Thelma felt the same way she did. All the beleaguered housewife was doing in this scene was taking off for what most women would consider a commonplace jaunt, a weekend getaway with a friend. But for Thelma, Geena knew, the action carried uncommon significance. Although the scene was the first to be shot, in the film it would follow an earlier setup in which Thelma decided, for the first time in her life, to defy a domineering husband and skip out without his permission.

"It was a huge deal, a big, giant moment in my life that I was doing this," Geena says in a comment that applies equally to her character and herself. "It needed to be treated as such."

So while the props department had deposited a whole load of stuff by the door—suitcases, lantern, cooler, fishing pole, fishing net—and told her to choose what to bring, Geena opted for *everything*. She minced down the driveway, all elbows and knees and toothy grin, dragging the awkward jumble of paraphernalia toward the car, investing the character with her own over-the-top preparation, eagerness to please and fear of making a wrong step. She gave the simple scene a sense of momentousness.

We don't need the lantern, said Louise, jumping out of the car to help. *The place HAS electricity.*

Thelma took the lamp anyway, *just in case*. What if there was a psycho killer on the loose?

The final effect was perfectly comic. Done up with flouncing, curled hair, a ruffled white dress and a baby-blue jean jacket embellished with absurdly dangling strings of pearls, Geena looked like Big Bird dressed as Dolly Parton. But like any natural comedian, she didn't play it for laughs. "Thelma's not silly," she insists. "I'm serious about what needs to be done here. We need to be supplied, because who knows what we might do? It's new rules."

Susan's Louise met this spectacle with a fond, indulgent chuckle, but her getup indicated a very different character from her friend's. A scarf was wound tightly over her hair and tied snug at the neck. Sunglasses shielded her eyes, and a long-sleeved white blouse, buttoned to the top, masked the famous Susan Sarandon décolletage. Red lipstick turned her sensuous mouth into a strict line. As Geena heaped her bursting luggage into Louise's pristine trunk, Susan's brow creased with momentary worry. *Careful, careful*, she ad-libbed. In contrast to Geena's sweet, childlike Thelma, Louise already came across as bottled up and cautious.

Unlike Geena, Susan hadn't consulted Callie about her character's backstory. Much of the actress's preparation for the role had arisen from her own initial concern about steering clear of a Charles Bronson revenge fantasy. She thought Louise should be driven not by anger or vengeance, but by a will to understand what had happened to her in Texas, and an effort to regain control of her life, to get a grip. The actress had asked the set decorators to supply Louise's house with photo albums filled with images from the past, artifacts that Louise could study and decipher, even though the movie audience would likely never see them.

In keeping with that idea, Susan suggested that she and Geena take a picture together as their journey began, to document the moment. Before they hopped into the car, Louise whipped out a Polaroid camera, held it at arm's length, and the two flashed wide, winning smiles, heads together in casual intimacy. The shot came to be regarded by many as the first selfie. It certainly became one of the most famous. One scene in, and the movie was breaking ground.

Susan still intimidated Geena, a parent-child dynamic that Geena used in her performance. But Susan already felt during the coziness of taking that selfie that the two had the capacity to form a potent combo. "You know when somebody is going to be your equal, if not better," she says. "You don't have to take responsibility for them, because they're always going to be on time and prepared and have their own ideas, and they're strong and smart and sassy. It opens your heart. You're free to go full force."

RIDLEY COULD SEE THAT THE CASTING was working as he intended, which freed him to go full force on his end. "It was a good mix," he says. "Susan as the mother figure or older sister. And Geena as the child who makes all the mistakes." The contrast would be all the more striking when the roles reversed later in the film. He relaxed. With the actors taking care of their business, he could take care of his, finding the visual statement that would amplify the story.

He had twelve weeks to get everything in the can—a little over a month in Los Angeles to film the Arkansas scenes, a few weeks around Bakersfield for the road trip across the plains and a month in Utah for the stark endgame in the desert Southwest. To stick to the schedule, the cast and crew had to keep moving, keep it loose, catch each moment and move on. Not the ideal environment for a stickler like Ridley.

Nor was the everyday world of middle-of-the-road Middle America. Most of the settings for *Thelma & Louise* were planted squarely in the realm of the ordinary, and there could be nothing ordinary about a film by Ridley Scott. He and Norris Spencer had developed a shared mania for showy visual pyrotechnics on their other projects. "The fact that Ridley and Norris had television-commercial backgrounds gave them a visual style that was full of impact," says Michael Hirabayashi, the assistant art director on *Thelma & Louise,* who came from the same ad background as many on the crew. "They knew how to make an image punchy, make it pop."

Ridley invariably packed dimension and movement into every shot, filling the frame with layers of shiny objects, surfaces that reflected light and things that moved, like rows of ceiling fans. Even the very air took on texture in a typical Ridley Scott film, as he routinely puffed a cigar near the camera lens to saturate the shots with smoggy atmosphere. On *The Duellists,* says Harvey Keitel, he once had to say, "Get rid of the damn smoke!" He couldn't see Keith Carradine, who was trying to act with him on the other side of the room.

The director couldn't bear flat, frontal lighting, the TV-sitcom look that resulted from pounding light directly onto a set. Backlighting, which he preferred, lent more depth to an image, alternating darker and lighter areas within the frame and leaving more unsaid. The technique allowed him to create a rim effect, in which light from an obtuse angle outlines a body with a shimmery glow and separates it from the background. Ridley employed backlighting so often that Norris Spencer called him the Prince of Darkness.

That was all well and good in the murky atmospheres of *Blade Runner* and *Alien,* but how to achieve such effects in everyday settings, under relatively broad daylight, in *Thelma & Louise*? The budget wouldn't allow Ridley to wait for sunset every day in search of burnished light. And how to make a working-class home in Arkansas gleam? Or a flat road in Oklahoma?

The challenge was to raise ordinary settings and costumes to a more elevated plane while maintaining a grip on reality. "It's hard to find somebody who can dress ordinary," says Ridley, speaking of the art and costume designers who created the movie's look. "Grand is fairly easy. But to dress normal is the most difficult thing to do. What are ordinary people like?"

He and Norris plucked the relatively young Anne Ahrens for the key job of set decorator. At thirty-three, she thought Ridley might have chosen her for a film like *Thelma & Louise* because she was a rare woman in the field. Ridley demurs, saying he admired her for bringing flair to a conventional milieu in her previous work on *The Fabulous Baker Boys*.

Anne had entered USC film school, one of six women in a class of sixty, hoping to become a cinematographer, but her classmates wouldn't sit with her or invite her to join them on their projects, so she settled on more-solitary screenwriting instead. Even then she was criticized for material that was labeled as overly female. "We don't do anything about women and growth and that kind of stuff," she was told. After graduation, a friend got her a job set decorating for music videos, and from there, a stint on *Hardbodies,* a beach-bunnies exploitation picture. Working with director Wes Craven on *A Nightmare on Elm Street* boosted her into more-mainstream projects.

Still, her heart jumped when she took a call from Norris Spencer, on behalf of Ridley Scott. From Norris's voice, she pictured an older British gentleman with a top hat and cane, asking her if she wanted to set decorate a small film about two women on a journey. Ridley wanted a lot of layers, Norris explained, because the women had a lot of layers. "The denser the look of an image, the more interested we are in it," he said. She quit a TV job as soon as she hung up.

Set decoration is a crucial element in a film's overall design, both indoors and out. Anne prepared by assembling a truckful of fake tumbleweeds and road signs for locations on the road, and she wrote her own backstory for the characters so she could furnish their homes in character—Louise meticulous and even a little paranoid, Thelma disorganized and artless. Ahrens's screenwriting background drove her to invest the physical with the intent of the story. Her understanding of Ridley's aesthetic informed her shopping at swap meets and junk shops—she loaded up on lots of shiny things, the better to glisten in Ridley's backlight.

Her handiwork showed in the first shot outside Thelma's home, where lawn sprinklers twirled and spritzed, catching and refracting the sun. A jumble of odds and ends cluttered the driveway and yard—piles of wood and a cement mixer from a half-finished construction project, a garden hose, trash cans, lawn ornaments—making for a dense image. The disarray also illustrated the state of Thelma's marriage. "We wanted to show chaos in her life," said Ahrens. "She's trying to hold it together, but Darryl doesn't really care about the house. He doesn't provide for her." Thelma's car in the garage was a beat-up Honda, whereas an earlier sequence would show her husband leaving for work in a red Corvette.

The costumes hit the mark from the first scene, just as the decoration did. They were designed by Elizabeth McBride, a thirty-five-year-old who answered to the same heightened-ordinary imperative as Ahrens. Ridley had selected a woman for this job, too, but again based on past work rather than gender. He'd seen McBride master the art of dressing ordinary people, southern style, on *Tender Mercies* and *Driving Miss Daisy*. Like Callie, she was known for wearing cowboy boots and showing a bit of swagger. McBride's job would be to bring texture and interest to commonplace clothes, adding the pearls to Geena's jacket, for example, or later sewing rhinestones around the pockets of her jeans, and then evolving to a tougher style as the story progressed.

With those details in place, Ridley could turn his attention to the quality of the light. He had decided that each of the three acts in the film would have its own lighting signature. The Arkansas scenes would feature soft, gray tones, with a lot of rain and greenery, to distinguish them from the golden radiance of the plains and the blazing red sun of the desert. Ridley drew artistically accomplished storyboards for each shot, often on the fly on the set, to show the crew what he had in mind. The drawings captured the personalities of the actors and always indicated, through shading, the source of the light in any given shot. His director of photography, Adrian Biddle, a big, burly, amiable guy who had worked with Ridley before, knew how to create the lighting effects he wanted but also when to step aside, because Ridley preferred to operate the camera himself, starting on day one. "The magic goes through the viewfinder," Ridley liked to say. He needed to see for himself.

THELMA AND LOUISE PULLED AWAY from home as the last shots of the first day's filming wrapped up. Sun winked off the chrome of Louise's Thunderbird, gleaming like her pride and joy. Ridley thought of it as her dream vehicle. "She probably goes over it with a Kleenex and a toothpick after she's cleaned it," he explained.

Green trees waved overhead, reinforcing the verdant signature of the Arkansas scenes. More lawn sprinklers sprayed the street. A truck followed close behind, adding movement. Ridley squinted through the camera, riding on a platform mounted to the side of the car, capturing a close-up of Geena's face, the sunshine behind her creating a golden corona around her hair. Thelma explained that she hadn't told Darryl about the trip.

I left him a note. I left him stuff to microwave.

Susan let out a whoop of laughter and hit the accelerator. Ridley grinned on the other side of the lens. They were off.

CHAPTER 18

HOT AS A PISTOL

Day two was a whole other story. Two hundred fifty extras, a four-member rockabilly band, a fully festooned country-western bar with pools of shadow and colored lights and, not to be forgotten, Ridley's beloved smoke machines to thicken up the atmosphere. The heroines' fateful stopover at the joint where they met Thelma's rapist would amount to a full-out demonstration of Ridley's abilities to corral the elements of a big production—and a test of whether he could keep the focus on the characters at the heart of it.

At the beginning, before the story line turned dangerous and dark, the week of shooting at the Silver Bullet in Long Beach felt like a party. The location guys had managed to find an actual country-themed saloon and dance hall in the vicinity of LA. When they made a deal with the owner to use the bar's real name, it never crossed their minds that someday the Silver Bullet might raise the hackles of critics convinced they had sniffed out phallic symbolism.

The stars prepared by focusing on the finer points of drinking and cutting loose. Ridley gave them earphones that played loud music, freeing them up to shout the dialogue across a table even when the set was quiet. Geena adopted a tip from Susan—feign drunkenness by spinning until it made her dizzy. And the two of them conspired to steep their performances in tipsy realism by persuading the prop guy to sneak real tequila into their drinks. "Just so we'd get the taste and kick in some sense memory," Geena says. "So we were doing all these shots and takes, and we started to feel drunk, laughing that people didn't know we actually were. When it was done, we were just rip-roaring. We asked the prop guy, 'How much do you think we drank?" And he said, 'Probably like a third of a shot.'"

What Ridley saw through the viewfinder looked pretty freewheeling. *I've had it up to my ass with sedate!* Thelma exclaimed over the supposed noise and the band, her eyes shining like headlights. *You said you and me was gonna get outta town and, for once, just really let our hair down. Well, darlin', look out, 'cause my hair is comin' down!*

No one was more dazzled by the extravaganza than Callie. She blended into the crowd as unobtrusively as possible—no one was eager to engage with the writer in the midst of this crush, she knew—but stopped short when she saw Susan and Geena together at the table.

There they are, Callie thought.

The feeling was exhilarating, thrilling. "It was also so weird, because something lives in your head, and then suddenly it's outside of your head and all around you," Callie says. But she also felt a profound intimation of no longer being especially necessary. "The train was leaving the station, fast and furious."

NORRIS, ANNE AND THE WHOLE art department crew had knocked themselves out to heighten the reality of the dance hall, which looked like a large, empty, beer-stained box before they got to work. They'd turned it into a Ridley Scott playground: crate loads full of clear glassware, neon beer signs on the walls, pool tables with blue billiard lamps suspended overhead and a dance floor beckoning under red and blue lights that spun from the ceiling. Dancers and drinkers animated the foreground, middle ground and background with constant motion. "We had a lot of opportunities to backlight them," says Michael Hirabayashi. "It allowed us to make more silhouettes to give depth to the image."

Over the bar in the center of the room, the decorators had dangled rows of glasses under red, white and blue neon, to give off an effect like an American flag. "We were going for super Americana," Ahrens said, "but not in a cutesy way. Just a real bar, gritty and dirty, like it had been there for forty years." The beer stains stayed. The scene would come across as authentic, right down to the waitress, Lena, played by Lucinda Jenney, a thirty-six-year-old who had won a number of supporting roles in movies like *Rain Man* and *Born on the Fourth of July*. She weaved expertly among the tables, picking up the light in a blouse embellished with a Native American design of fringe and polished paillettes.

Because this was a waitress in a screenplay written by a former waitress, Jenney wasn't expected to play some movie bimbo in a tight uniform. The part was small but had personality, including some of Callie's own qualities. She'd written Lena as a bit jaded, and smart about sizing people up. *It's a good thing they're not all as friendly as you,* she said to Harlan, signaling to the audience that the charm of the man who was hitting on Thelma had its limits.

Ridley recognized these straight-shooter qualities in Jenney at her audition and hired her without looking much further. She knew others had declined to read because the role occupied too few pages, but when Lou sent her the script, it was the best one she'd read in ten years, with a part, finally, that wasn't just "the girl." An accomplished theater actress in New York, Jenney had run up against a whole different environment when she moved to Hollywood. "The opportunities were entirely based on my looks; it's that simple," she says. "I just stuffed my bra and prayed to God my ass didn't look too big."

Jenney projected a fresh, pretty, girl-next-door quality, but agents peppered her with suggestions, few of them about acting. "They told me to dress a little hotter and make my boobs look bigger," she says. "Understood: get a boob job. I never did." But she appreciated the reasoning. Once, when she played a "very booby" character in a tight costume, she was amazed at the attention she received on the set. "It's a visual art, so to cry boohoo is foolish," she says. "I like to look at lovely people, too. I just wish there were more stories that had parts for women, any parts for women, whatever they looked like."

While *Thelma & Louise* became known as a quintessential women's film, Lucinda Jenney's Lena was the only other female character in the cast, besides the leads, after Catherine Keener got cut during the edit. Jenney appreciated that Susan, a female role model in the flesh, hung out with her between takes, an unaccustomed opportunity for an actress on a movie set. And Geena lived up to the name Thelma, Jenney felt. "It's a tough name to pull off. She's childlike yet bright. That's a lucky thing for an actress."

Looking back later, she says, she viewed *Thelma & Louise* as a little spaceship that made it through a wormhole. "At the time, I didn't have enough perspective to realize: this is a magic carpet ride."

THE ACTOR WHO FINALLY WON the steeplechase for the thankless job of Harlan the rapist was Timothy Carhart. The long list of potential heavies had included Viggo Mortensen and various action-movie veterans. Carhart specialized in making a vivid impression in small parts, like a paranoid corporate executive in *Working Girl*. Tall, thin, handsome, with cold blue eyes, he was "a Janus-faced guy," says the casting assistant Brett

Goldstein. "He looked likable, but then he could also look psychotic and evil, like one of those holographic pictures where you turn it and go, 'Whoa—what is that!' Like you see the skull under the skin."

"I'm not sure you're threatening enough," Ridley had told Carhart during the audition. The actor figured he'd lost out. *I can't turn into Snidely Whiplash*, he thought. But the director decided Carhart did possess an unexpected elegance that would appeal to Thelma at first.

He could appear pleasant or predatory at will, but in real life Carhart was a tender-hearted guy. Playing this role would exact a price. Nevertheless, he didn't hesitate to accept the offer. "It's a Ridley Scott movie," he says. "I said I'd do anything."

He kept himself apart from the others during breaks at the Silver Bullet and tried to play his first encounter with the two women as if convinced his winning ways would bowl them over. When Susan, recognizing the creep beneath, blew smoke in his face, unrehearsed, he was genuinely surprised.

Music and dancing dominated the scenes, which Ridley pulled together like clockwork. Patsy Swayze, a dance teacher and choreographer, the mother of Patrick Swayze, corralled the extras on the floor while Charlie Sexton, a rising young guitar player, performed with a popular local bar band called the Broken Homes. As they bashed away during a break, the extras, many of them regulars at the club, taught Geena and Susan how to perform a line dance called the tush push. Ridley had them repeat it, unrehearsed, so it would look ragged, while he sent handheld cameras up and down the rows.

Through the four days of interiors at the Silver Bullet, the mood for cast and crew was rollicking. The visuals popped, but the center of the story held. Ridley had learned that lesson on previous films. "It's very easy to drop the ball or just get lazy or get swamped on the process of how that film looks," he said. As the revelers stomped and twirled, Louise edged toward chucking some inhibitions, dancing with a stiff, fuzzy-haired stranger Ridley had plucked from the band. Thelma relished her momentary freedom, oblivious to Harlan's controlling grasp. They finished the week on budget and on point.

THE FOLLOWING MONDAY and Tuesday nights marked one of the most precipitous curves in movies, the attempted rape in the parking lot. As darkness fell on the exterior of the Silver Bullet, the first order of business was to shoot an earlier scene that depicted Thelma and Louise pulling in from the road out front. The crew added extraordinary interest to such a seemingly basic shot, wetting down the street for shine and lining up tractor trailers with their lights on, illuminating airborne pockets of exhaust. In the lot itself, where the attempted rape would go down, Norris ordered stacks of fifty-five green oil drums to block an ugly fence, then switched them out for black ones. Right before the cameras rolled, he changed his mind again and asked for black plastic sheeting to cover the whole pile, just enough to kick off reflective glints. Ridley approved tungsten movie lamps mounted on stands in the background. Even though they'd be visible on-screen, they would emit a stronger glow than streetlights to backlight the parked pickups and cars. Ridley cared more for the effect than for realism. He thought if anyone noticed the mechanics, the scene wasn't doing its job.

It wasn't until almost four in the morning on the second night that setups were complete and the rape scene itself was called. "We need to go quite a way down the road to make it understood what's going on," Ridley cautioned Geena and Carhart before they began. "We can't just cut away."

They blocked out the action and got down to it. Thelma, spinning from drink, Harlan groping her, Thelma pushing him away, Harlan smacking her sharp across the face and throwing her down against the trunk of a car. At first, Carhart felt invigorated to be playing a scene with an Oscar-winning actress. "Geena has the most insane talent in the sense of her belief that what is happening is actually happening," he says. "As an actor, it becomes real for you because it's so real for her. Which is why you want to do things with Academy Award–quality people. It was wonderful— maybe the first couple of times."

Then the ugliness began to sink in. It got physical. It got rough. "Grueling, just grueling," he says. When they finished, Carhart went straight home with a massive headache.

Geena tried to keep it professional, although the assault left her with bruises and cuts on her knees that were visible throughout the rest of the film. "Doing it was upsetting," she says. "But I'm not one of those people who takes stuff home, or has big hangovers from things. It's whatever it is at that moment. I'm always able to let it go." Until the next time. Toward the end of the entire production Ridley would decide the scene needed a greater boost of violence to justify the rest of the women's actions. They would have to go at it again, in a fashion that would be even more harrowing.

Before closing out the Silver Bullet shoot that night, the unit still had to tackle the scenario that most disturbed Susan—Louise's shooting of Harlan, clearly unjustified because she had already stopped the rape by holding a pistol to his head. In rehearsals two weeks before, she had repeated her objections to performing a revenge killing. "What bothers me is, it's not a necessary death," Susan had insisted. "We don't want this to be a genre where taking a life is superficial and flip." She wanted the moral price to be evident, for Louise to recognize that she would have to pay.

Susan and Ridley negotiated how Louise would fire the gun, as if she weren't fully aware of what she was doing. "She points her finger, but the finger has a gun in it," Ridley explained. "It goes off—*bang*—which is why she startles and then realizes what she's done."

Moments later, Louise spits out at Harlan's inanimate body: *You watch your mouth, buddy.*

Susan approved the approach, especially that line. "She's just trying to shut him up, and because she speaks to him afterward it shows she almost doesn't understand what's happened," Susan says. The way she played it, it was all on her face, the trauma that drove her to shoot, the shock that she had really done it, the horror at the realization that she'd made an irrevocable mistake.

The night ended with Thelma and Louise tearing out of the parking lot, Geena at the wheel, hysterical, her clothes torn, fake blood pouring out of her nose. "I have to run to the car, squeal back to pick her up, peel out, then slam on the brakes and hit the mark exactly next to the camera," Geena said. "I have no recollection of how I was acting. I was just driving—it was all I could think about."

CHAPTER 19

BAD BOYS

Chris McDonald strutted out the front door to the smokin' red Corvette emblematic of his character, Darryl Dickinson, buffoonish husband of Thelma, regional manager of Carpeteria and all around Big Swinging Dick. The actor was white-hot to make an impression in the first take of his first scene, and all signs pointed to the positive. He looked snappy in a peacock-blue polyester jacket and slick new shoes from the costume department, and he congratulated himself that Ridley had adapted "The 1" idea from Chris's audition necklace and embossed it on the license plate of the car.

Next thing he knew, those new shoes slipped on some lumber from the household's lackadaisical home-improvement project. Chris fell smack on his ass, his head ringing like a gong on a metal tank amid the mess on the driveway.

Ridley saw that the actor was hurting but didn't yell cut. Chris rallied, threw his briefcase into the car and ad-libbed a tirade at the construction workers. *I want you out of here by five!* he hollered. *No, three, get outta here by three today!*

He winced and shot a chagrined look at the director. Ridley was laughing his head off, along with most of the crew. "That's the funniest thing I've ever seen," Ridley said. "We could do it again, but *that's* in the movie."

After the ordeal of the rape scene, the mishap was a gift. The production badly needed some comic relief as it backtracked to pick up the earlier threads of the story. For the next couple weeks, *Thelma & Louise* settled back in the comedy groove.

Some early scenes set before Thelma and Louise took off on their odyssey served up a showcase for the art department to define the characters through decor. A brisk montage of Louise packing for the weekend, sealing everything in Ziploc bags, highlighted her spotless apartment. There was a photo of Jimmy in a silver frame, and one of Louise as a child, twirling a baton, an actual picture of a young Susan Sarandon. In the immaculate kitchen, she rubbed a drinking glass dry and set it upside down on a neatly folded dishtowel, because leaving a wet glass in a dish drainer just wouldn't do. Ridley's camera lingered for a moment as sunlight filtered through the blue glass.

The designers went to town on Thelma's place. Thanks to her taste for frilly, ill-considered kitsch, the home exploded with texture and color, mostly pastels. Clear plastic sheeting had emerged as Norris Spencer's favorite design trick, so he draped it over the Dickinsons' perpetual construction work to pick up shine. Anne Ahrens packed the set with recipes taped on the stove, a TV game show playing in the corner and motley flea market finds. "Thelma's life was out of her control," Ahrens says. "She was trying to control the chaos with ruffles."

The set decorator shopped in the mind-set of the Thelma character to pick out one-of-a-kind pieces, but once, at a store that specialized in zany Lucite furniture, Ahrens spied the one thing, a lamp, that she thought

Darryl might have chosen. Under the shade was a clear base filled with water, where pretty live fish swam around and around. "That's how I saw Thelma," Anne says. "She was trapped in there."

The scenes before Darryl departed for work dispelled any concern that the formerly engaged Geena and Chris could work together. They conveyed good-natured respect for each other's skills as they invented comic business that supplemented the script. Geena snatched a candy bar out of the freezer, took a guilty bite, returned it, then repeated while she talked on the phone. And Chris, preening in front of a mirror, perfectly executed the script's instructions for fussing with his hair.

On camera, they played off each other with finesse, as when Geena, all innocence, commented on Darryl's suspect plan to stay out late:

Funny how so many people wanna buy carpet on a Friday night. You'd almost think they'd want to forget about it for the weekend.

Chris blinked hard before delivering a reprimand: *Well, then, it's a good thing you're not regional manager*—he twirled a jumbo set of keys like a cowboy with a six-shooter—*and I am.*

Geena, done up in one of those floral print bathrobes that seem to be sewn together out of terry cloth towels, managed to make Thelma not only amusing but also poignant as Darryl found exasperating her every effort to please. And Chris located the core of his self-absorbed jerk right in the text. He saw Darryl as a man who had let himself forget that he loved his wife as he took her sweet nature for granted. From there, Chris had fleshed out details with research, flying on his own dime to Arkansas, where he hid behind sunglasses to observe a guy at an airport, the very model of Darryl. "He was on the make with some woman, and he had a big key chain with him," Chris says. "He's saying, 'this one is for the Porsche'—it's obviously a GM key—'and this one's for the beach house, and this is for a couple apartments I own.'"

A truly important man, Chris decided, must flaunt it with a bloated batch of keys. Tacky jewelry added to the effect, he says, "because that makes a lion like me even more spectacular." He capped the Darryl look by growing a mustache and asking the stylists in the hair trailer to duplicate the airport guy's do, a big blowout, combed over and sculpted into a helmet. Darryl, Chris knew, was very proud of his hairline, and somehow he managed to anticipate the self-regarding aesthetic of Donald Trump. Ridley was delighted when he checked in on Chris in the makeup trailer. To encounter him off camera in his full Darryl regalia was to laugh.

CHRIS MCDONALD KEPT THE DIRECTOR, cast and crew entertained through the rest of the Los Angeles shoot, which skipped ahead in the plot to the police investigation while Thelma and Louise were on the run. That meant that for two weeks, the story line of *Thelma & Louise* veered into the exclusive territory of men, and the production switched to a typical movie shoot, a bunch of guys horsing around and yukking it up. Ridley brought in rain machines so the audience would understand it was back in Arkansas when he cut away from Geena and Susan. "The girls," as everyone referred to them, had some time off.

Harvey Keitel cracked up so often while playing scenes with Chris McDonald that Ridley gave up and used the takes, deciding Detective Slocumb might as well react naturally to such a dunderhead. Darryl in a fuzzy blue bathrobe, Darryl swatting at an invisible fly, Darryl taking a beat to flash a look of vacant incomprehension before delivering every line, Darryl playing the dick, switching the channel while the cops watched a soapy late-night movie at his house. When Darryl carried on a conversation with his feet planted in stale pizza that littered the floor, Harvey, Ridley and everyone else bit their lips to keep from cracking up completely.

"I kept falling off the dolly at the end of every take, laughing," said the director, "and not a lot makes me laugh." Ridley hadn't anticipated just how funny Chris McDonald would turn out to be but happily let him run with the ball. The director stuck to his principle that if he cast well, he should let the actors do their thing.

Chris, for his part, worried about going too far over the top. "Ridley was the best audience an actor could dream for," says Chris. "He'd say, 'I love what you're doing,' but otherwise he left me alone." The actor had to trust that Ridley, who wasn't known for his comedy expertise, would pull Chris back if he skirted too close to making a fool of himself. The script provided his only other assurance. For all the added funny business, Chris kept to the dialogue in that script. "So often you have to work overtime to bring a script to life," he says. "It wasn't work with this one."

In some respects, Ridley granted even more license to Harvey Keitel. Insisting he drive himself, Harvey called the production office most mornings when he got scrambled on the way to the location. He kept his own dialogue coach at hand, and he ate up time parsing the motivations of his character with Ridley, who preferred his actors to hit their marks and make their own choices. Harvey took seriously his responsibility to represent the more caring end of the male spectrum. He stopped Lucinda Jenney during rehearsal for a scene when he questioned her character after the shooting to suggest that she act friendlier to Hal, the better to establish his bona fides as a good guy. Ridley let Harvey diverge from the script to ad-lib lines like *Excuse me, you're standing in your pizza* or an incongruous *Happy birthday, lady* when he spotted a photo of Louise in her apartment.

WITH CHRIS AND HARVEY CUTTING UP all over the place, the character actor Stephen Tobolowsky resolved that his role as the FBI agent Max was to keep the investigation, and the story, on track. "Chris's performance did a lot; it set a parameter," Stephen says. "It set a fence the other actors could work within. If you didn't have Chris out there, you might have thought Brad was too big, Michael Madsen was too big. But now those performances were right down the middle, because you had Chris out there holding down the edge." Stephen chose to calibrate his performance by playing the kind of law enforcement official who showed no emotional response to events, a guy just doing his job. His deadpan delivery would create tension by virtue of juxtaposition.

A tall, bald, pop-eyed actor with a nudgy demeanor, Stephen, thirty-nine years old, played such a recognizable type that he worked constantly, everything from Caveman Carl in the TV show *Alice* to a Klan leader in *Mississippi Burning*. In 1991 alone, he appeared in twelve projects—playing, for example, a cop, a lawyer, a baker, a warden and the alternative healer Tor on *Seinfeld*. Lucinda Jenney, in contrast, had worked twice. Stephen understood that gender played in his favor. "It is a business that is unkind to women," he says. "It chews up and spits out the young. They don't have as many good roles."

No one could accuse him of sucking up to get the part of Max. Stephen may have been the sole auditioner, aside from Susan Sarandon, who openly criticized the script.

"I don't think it's bad," Stephen had said to Ridley, "but I find it odd." He thought it was brave to make a movie so out of the Hollywood mainstream, and the writing was out of the box, but the idea that it was a traditional buddy movie with women in the leads? "I just thought that was horseshit," he says. He saw the screenplay as a Greek tragedy in which, instead of following a typical three-act structure, events were set in motion so that little changed through the course of the film. Once Louise shoots the rapist, he said, "the women are cooked."

Ridley smiled and asked, "So how do you see yourself in it?"

"I see myself as the undertaker," Stephen replied. "I am strictly professional. You send the corpse to the undertaker and he dresses it up, because that's what he does. I am not a character so much as a force that moves from state to state and fulfills the job of catching the women, regardless what anyone thinks."

He didn't admit as much to Ridley, but Stephen objected to the tone and morality of the script as well. He was sympathetic to the quandary the women found themselves in—up to a point. "The underlying violence between men and women was something that I experienced a lot growing up in Texas," he says. "You see it in the country-western mentality of women being honky-tonk angels and getting knocked around, and guys getting too much to drink and being violent, and a woman's place is in the home and keep your biscuits in the oven and your buns in bed."

But when Thelma and Louise locked a state trooper in his trunk, he says, "It shocked me; it beyond shocked me. It horrified me. I'm thinking, *These women are monsters.*" The same with killing the rapist in the parking lot, bedding a hitchhiker and blowing up a truck. The underlying rage of the main characters disturbed Stephen. He didn't get the point.

All of this fed his portrayal of the relentless Max and his annoyance with Harvey's Detective Slocumb. "He didn't seem to be doing his job protecting the public," Stephen says with visible irritation. "He wanted to protect the women at the expense of his job. I felt he was like so many of the men in the script—not true. They're all cheaters and liars. Thelma and Louise are desperately looking for something that is pure."

His first day on location he could appreciate the art direction that Ridley brought to the story. Stephen walked onto the set and thought, *This is an ugly kitchen. It is not a female kitchen. There is no place for a woman in this house.* The temperature soared over a hundred degrees that week, and Elizabeth McBride, the costume designer, had fully embraced his undertaker take on the part by encasing him in an anonymous dark blue wool suit. He would wear that same suit with the same striped tie every day in every scene, another nod to his view that he was playing a force rather than a character.

His objections to Harvey's Detective Slocumb spilled over into the work. At that point in his career, Stephen wasn't comfortable with improvisation, and he didn't find Harvey as approachable as the other actors or as generous during close-ups. A couple of times Ridley told Stephen that Harvey wanted to improvise, and then with the camera running Harvey took some of Max's lines. "I tried to use my frustration over the fact that we didn't have the easiest relationship with thinking that this was perfect for the part," Stephen says. "He was trying so hard to be sympathetic, I thought it tilted the film in an odd way. As Max, I didn't trust him. I felt like he was a loose cannon. As my character, I went, *This is a guy I have to watch.*"

Every morning Ridley assembled the guys like a general coordinating troops for an assault on a beach. "What are you going to do?" he asked everyone in turn. When the cops hunkered down in Darryl's house, hoping to intercept a call from Thelma, Ridley turned to Stephen, "What are you going to do?" he asked. "I want you to come in and take over the room."

"Absolutely," Stephen said, racking his brain for some standard-issue *Law & Order* dialogue. In rehearsal, Ridley looked vaguely displeased when the actor barked out some fake cop talk along the lines of "Okay, you get on channel two; you stay on channel seven." But waiting outside the door for the camera to roll, he thought, *FBI guys would already know how to do their jobs, but they wouldn't know where their next meal was coming from.* So he burst in and started taking deli orders—*Okay, who wants turkey? Who wants corned beef?* From then on, Ridley instructed Max to eat while the action swirled around him in almost every scene. The self-interest played into Max's heartlessness. So did the line he delivered when the cops advised Darryl to sound affectionate toward his wife if she phoned, the better to buy time to trace the call: *Women love that shit.*

"You read a line in a script like that," Stephen says, "and you know if you just say that line it will be funny." He gave it Max's standard deadpan delivery. "You don't have to do anything more than that."

Ridley approved of Stephen's take. "Steve talks in the film as if he knows about women," Ridley says. "Clearly, he was a virgin."

The spirit was festive on the set during the guy scenes at Thelma's house. A shift to the Water and Power Building in Burbank, selected as the location for Hal's police department, would bring a new, completely unseasoned performer into the mix. Some kid playing a hitchhiker, a third-string player after the first two choices fell through. The men on the varsity team had never heard of him. They wondered if he had what it took to play in their league.

CHAPTER 20

THE KID ENTERS THE PICTURE

When Lucinda Jenney stopped by the production office for a cos-tume fitting the week of June 18, a male figure had just slipped out, dissolving like a ghost as he turned a corner at the far end of the hall. Elizabeth McBride and four or five of her female costume assistants poked their heads outside the office, tittering as they watched him go. "If you run after him, you can *see* him," one of the dressers urged Jenney.

Jenney felt deflated. *How typical,* she thought. *Cute guy in Holly-wood, and all the girls are behaving like ninnies.*

They chattered and teased each other about him throughout her fit-ting, exalting a Polaroid they had taken that was pinned to a board. Jen-ney dutifully took a look. He wasn't even famous.

"Okay," she admitted, "he's good-looking, but can we get off it now? I mean, he's blond and sort of Midwestern, but he's not even very *original* good-looking."

"There's something about him," the others insisted.

"I certainly experienced what a movie star's effect is on people," Jenney says later. "I saw the electricity that followed behind him. I saw the damage he did."

Callie happened to visit the set during the actor's first day on the picture. Somebody said, "The guy who's playing J.D. is here." She knocked at the tiny honey wagon where he'd been assigned to dress. In full wardrobe—skintight jeans and a flannel shirt open over a fitted T-shirt—Brad Pitt answered the door.

That's good, Callie thought. She took a step back and let out a long, slow breath. She reconsidered and spoke aloud: "Perfect!"

THE GUYS WEREN'T SO SURE about Brad Pitt. "Nobody knew him from the bellman," says Michael Madsen. "He was just this guy walking around." They often got stoned together waiting for the van to take them to the set. "I just thought he was a good-looking kid. I don't see what the big deal was about. I still don't get it."

This scruffy kid, this Pitt, showed nothing but deference to his elders, calling them sir, offering to serve them, cowboy hat in hand. "Would you like to sit in my chair, Mr. Tobolowsky? It's very comfortable." (*Really!*) Or "Would you like me to get you some tea from craft services?"

"I never felt so old and ugly in my life as when I was sitting next to Brad Pitt," Stephen Tobolowsky recalls. "But I didn't know if he was an actor or if he wanted to wash my car for extra money."

In his first scene, shot out of sequence on July 5, J.D. got hauled into the police department for questioning after he'd split from Thelma and Louise. Shy and understandably nervous, Brad said, "I dealt with staying focused, knowing I was in a new league." A league with Harvey Keitel, no less, the master improviser, determined to cut loose. Harvey wanted to demonstrate his growing protectiveness toward Thelma and Louise, "not necessarily a show of extreme violence," he said in some notes, "but a demonstration that Hal does not intend to be 'fucked with' by this kid."

The tension mounted when Brad met the grilling with brazen insolence, and Harvey did his thing. "By the end of the day, Harvey was beating me over the head with my own hat—unscripted," Brad said, "and I was having as much fun as I've had on a set since." By now he had figured out the nature of a sociopath. His eyes drifted off, disconnected, even as he turned all fake polite and started to cooperate.

The next day the crew moved to a hallway for a setup that called for an accidental encounter between J.D. and Thelma's outraged husband. Everyone expected some more ripe histrionics from Chris McDonald, but the guy playing the petty thief almost managed to steal the scene.

I like your wife. J.D. smirked as he passed by Darryl next to a stairwell. Brad's sly tone left little doubt that he'd cuckolded the dumbstruck Carpeteria manager.

Come back here, you little shit! Darryl bawled.

Chris was supposed to lunge toward J.D., with Harvey Keitel and an extra playing another cop holding him back. But Chris knew that for Darryl, the cock of the walk, someone touching his wife—touching his property, the woman he really did love (after his own self-involved fashion)—would be the ultimate provocation. Chris's history with Geena, the broken engagement, fresh again after they'd just worked together, flooded his brain. His face flushed purple. Steam blasted out of his ears. He dove for Brad headlong down the stairs, heedless of injuring himself or anyone else who got in his way.

"I was vicious, like a rabid dog," Chris says. "I would have ripped his clothes. At that moment, I really wanted to freaking kill him."

Harvey was truly alarmed. "He was too strong," he says. "He rolled over me like a car."

Ridley swapped Harvey out for two beefier galoots, and they went at it again. After four more takes, Chris was sore and gasping for air.

Then Brad capped the scene with an improvised coup de grâce, a sneaky taunt. He jumped down the stairs, just out of Chris's reach, and rocked his hips in a lascivious humping motion, a blissed-out look on his face. The kid had more than held his own.

The guys had to admit they were impressed, even if they still didn't grasp the sex-appeal thing. Ridley thought Brad's intuition was the key. "He's got great taste, he's very smart," Ridley said, "but again, it's intuition. I think with actors, intuition is probably everything."

INTUITION. RIDLEY CERTAINLY LET the actors run with it. The scenes between the men turned more and more into displays of dominance that weren't necessarily spelled out in the script. Sometimes they went overboard, as when Michael Madsen's Jimmy turned up at the precinct for some unscripted questioning from Harvey. "What are you going to do?" Ridley asked them.

"We were like, 'Let's just fuck around,'" Madsen says. They tried a number of variations—Harvey flashing some mug shots, improvising questions about the missing "girls" and missing money, asking if Jimmy loved Louise. Michael refused to turn on her, as befit his character. Bit by bit, both men upped the attitude, and the tone turned increasingly hostile. Then Michael lit a cigarette and started flicking ashes around.

"You're not going to smoke in here," Harvey ad-libbed.

"Why the fuck not?" Michael leaned back toward a window. "Is that better?"

Harvey flipped out and leaped on top of his desk, prepared to launch himself at the sulky antagonist.

"Okay, guys, that's enough," Ridley broke in. "What are you going to do, get in a physical fight?" The scenes had allowed the actors some showy fronting, but they were starting to divert from the central story, where the Jimmy character needed to occupy the more sensitive portion of the male continuum. When it came time for the final edit of the film, none of those interrogation scenes made the cut.

On the set at least, Harvey got the last word. He spun toward Michael with a good-natured growl. "You know, if this was a real situation in a police station, you'd be eating that cigarette butt by now."

ONE MONTH INTO THE SHOOT Ridley felt relaxed. Gone was the screamer from *Blade Runner* and other high-pressure productions. He felt looser, even playful, on this smaller, simpler lark. "Ridley was generous with people, and people were generous with Ridley," says Stephen. Sometimes it seemed the director wanted to perform every job on the set himself—moving the props, setting up craft services. He chatted with the guys, talking to Chris McDonald about how well he thought Geena was doing so far, telling Michael Madsen how the studio felt about the ending: nervous. Ridley puffed on his Macanudos and Partagás and handed them out to the actors to smoke offscreen. (For Ridley, a cigar was never just a cigar—the excess smoke veiled the shots in his favorite blue haze.) The actors bonded. Michael later appointed Harvey godfather to one of his sons and signed on to *Reservoir Dogs*, where the actors could put their sinister rapport to good use, so they could work together again.

The guys loved Ridley, and so did the crew. "Ridley's a really masculine guy," Madsen later told a magazine. "I thought, *Wow, somebody like him—I need to be with him*. We guys were: 'We're here to do this chick flick, but don't forget when the testosterone comes into play.'"

For a couple of weeks, they had been taking the script and making it theirs. On July 9, "the girls" would return, and the estrogen would come to the fore. Then everyone would find out how comfortably Ridley Scott could pivot back to the women's point of view, or if Geena Davis and Susan Sarandon were forceful enough to wrest it back.

CHAPTER 21

WHAT THE FUSS IS ABOUT

Geena Davis peered out the window of her trailer at a lineup of Playboy Playmates outside Ridley's adjacent door. He was screening for someone to serve as a body double in Thelma's sex scene at a no-star motel.

Inside, the women stripped down one by one and spun in a circle. One of the hopefuls, Julie Strain, knew the director wouldn't object if she kept her underwear on. "But it's just easier to show the whole thing," she said, "because if they're going to shoot a love scene, they need to see there are no scars or marks."

"Very nice," Ridley said to each in turn. "Thank you very much." He settled on Strain, a Penthouse Pet who billed herself as "Six Feet Tall and Worth the Climb."

Geena had never appeared nude on-screen, but something about this procession of voluptuous beauties galled her competitive nature. After a couple hours of this, she marched over to Ridley saying, "Goddammit, nobody's going to double my body. I'll do it." Once she committed, the bashful newcomer playing J.D. could hardly demur.

Discomfort with sexy scenes was one of the reasons Ridley himself had nearly demurred from directing *Thelma & Louise* in the first place. Now there was no getting around it, and he had to hope that the sizzling chemistry between those two at the casting session would carry the day.

To add to the challenge, the encounter would be filmed out of sequence, before any other scenes where the actors might have a chance to meet and kindle a little rapport. The three days scheduled at the motel would be their very first together, starting on what was only Brad Pitt's third day on the entire shoot. Oh, and the action had to be mind-blowingly, convention-shattering hot, beyond anything Thelma had experienced before, just in case the stakes weren't forbidding enough.

"Oh my God, this is going to be weird," both players agreed when they sat down with Ridley. The action wasn't really spelled out in the script, Geena said. "Ridley just blocked out two days and said, 'we'll make stuff up, we'll make stuff up.'"

Anne Ahrens had recommended the location, the Vagabond Motel near USC, for its down-market retro vibe. Palm trees and skyscrapers showed in a couple of quick shots of the exterior, but such was the price of keeping the budget in check. For other shots, Adrian Biddle masked the urban view with a large overhead mirror that reflected the sky.

Ridley chose to make it rain while the characters holed up inside. Perhaps due to his Northern England upbringing, he saw wet weather as comforting, adding to the coziness indoors and a sense of a temporary respite from the wider world. Ahrens dressed the room in womblike, fleshy colors and gold-flecked wallpaper, so far out of style that she snapped it up on sale. Mismatched furniture filled out the glowing co-

coon along with a weird assortment of junk-shop lamps that were never in style, in particular a timelessly horrible one with a base like a stone fireplace and a fake flame flickering inside. Ahrens figured it would comment on the hot situation. Ridley opted to let it share the screen with Brad during the much-anticipated hair dryer scene.

The actors emerged from their trailers on the morning of July 12 knowing they had to heat up fast. They had put in a couple of days filming preliminary dialogue in the scene, but this entire day would cover just about an eighth of a page in the script. (Direction: "J.D. turns out the light.") That's when the music would crank up and all but the essential crew got lost. Susan sent her ward off with best wishes. "You go ahead, honey, you have the sex scene," she told Geena. "I've had plenty."

"Lovemaking scenes are always a little tricky," says Steve Danton, the assistant director who was charged with making everyone comfortable. He assured Geena and Brad that the atmosphere would be professional, that only half a dozen people could access the closed set, that robes would be at hand to whisk on between takes. Ridley would operate the camera. He lit the room based on where the actors would start and where they would end, leaving it up to them to figure out the rest.

For the early buildup, Geena wore panties and a T-shirt, and Brad went shirtless in his jeans, but eventually they both got down to full-body makeup and little else. "It's a long day when you're running around with a patch on your personals," Brad told a British publication afterward.

Such forced intimacy was pretty much standard procedure for a movie love scene, but just about everything else in this one cracked the mold. Jaded crew members had seen all the typical elements before: slam-bam, foreplay-free sex; a younger, less experienced female actress paired with a veteran man; plenty of close-ups of the woman's body while he took cover under the sheets.

But in this scene, Callie's dialogue stoked a seduction where the characters actually talked to each other, with humor, affection and interest.

Geena and Brad, for their part, devised foreplay that was literally play. A hand-slapping game gave Brad an opportunity to slip off Thelma's wedding ring, and a take when he jumped on the bed as if it were a trampoline flaunted his tantalizing physique.

Even more unusual, the ingenue here was the *guy* for a change. On-camera lovemaking represented a career first for Brad, and he seemed so shy that Geena felt protective toward him. "I'm sweating, *oh I'm sweating*, and she's actually sitting in my lap," he said. "We're basically naked, which is a really odd experience with everybody standing around doing their job like it's another Monday. I just remember her talking to one of the guys about the shot and where they needed her to be. And all of sudden she just looks at me and goes—" He demonstrated a smile and a shake of the head. "She was just really cool about it."

After a buildup, the players tried out different scenarios on the bed, the floor, the top of a dresser. Chairs, lamps and props went flying. Brad had more than the mechanics of the action on his mind. "One of the dilemmas an actor faces in those scenes is what happens if the 'soldier' starts to salute," he said, admitting, "I ran into that predicament as well." At times, his nerves took a toll. He knew the hair dryer scene was the showpiece for J.D., "but I flatlined that day and failed the scene by a few degrees," he said. "It was Geena's performance that made mine. Her ability to be carefree and comfortable in each take led the way for me."

Ridley gave Brad the full ingenue treatment, lighting him to perfection and personally spritzing Evian on his abs, the better to make them glisten as the camera panned up his torso. "Muss his hair up a bit," Ridley said. "Wet it down. Twist to the left a bit, *yeah, yeah*, just to catch the light." One of Ridley's talents was making beautiful people look even more beautiful than they did in real life. His painterly eye turned Brad Pitt into a celluloid Caravaggio.

Ridley, hello! Geena wanted to say. *I thought I was the girl in this scene!*

Callie Khouri brought her southern style to Hollywood.

Her friend Pam Tillis, model for Thelma.

Khouri (center) with would-be producer Amanda Temple and her daughter, Juno.

Players who sealed the deal included the D-girl turned studio executive Rebecca Pollack

. . . Pathé Entertainment studio boss Alan Ladd Jr.

. . . and ICM agent Diane Cairns.

Sigourney Weaver shook the status quo in Ridley Scott's *Alien*.

Jack Nicholson in *The Witches of Eastwick* with top contenders Cher, Susan Sarandon and Michelle Pfeiffer.

Geena Davis and Alec Baldwin in the outré *Beetlejuice*.

Louise, Thelma and the original selfie.

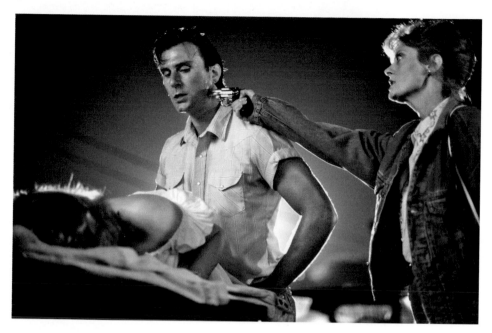

Harlan (Timothy Carhart) and Louise in the movie's second most controversial scene.

Darryl (Christopher McDonald) and Thelma in their kitschy kitchen.

Stephen Tobolowsky's stone-faced FBI agent.

Detective Slocumb (Harvey Keitel) tried to rein in Darryl.

Louise and Jimmy (Michael Madsen) broke up in backlight.

J.D. in the sack with Thelma.

A Polaroid of newcomer Brad Pitt delighted the costume department.

The star-making hair dryer scene.

The director preferred to operate the camera himself.

Ridley Scott sought to convey the open spaces of America

. . . and the patina of the Old West.

One of five vintage Thunderbirds tricked out for filming.

Blocking out the action with the state trooper (Jason Beghe).

Preparing to blow up a truck, the marketing department's favorite scene.

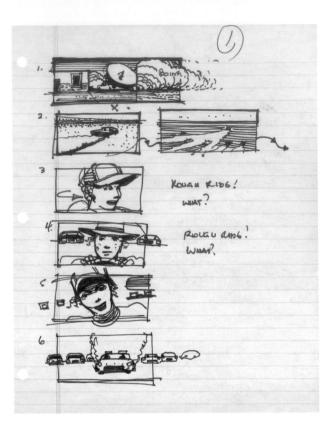

Ridley Scott's hand-drawn storyboard for the car chase

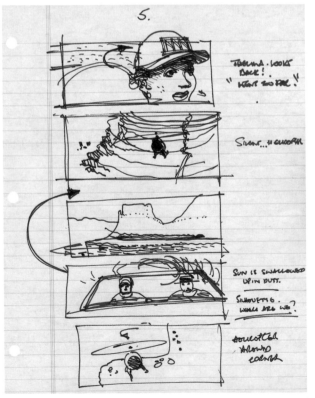

. . . and a final drive, sketched on the fly.

Set decorator Anne Ahrens and production designer Norris Spencer
dressed the cliff for its close-up.

Last day, last scene.

Producer Mimi Polk (center) toasted the stars on the final day.

Polk, Davis and Scott lit up the Cannes Film Festival.

Callie Khouri
scored the Oscar.

Thelma & Louise lives on.

Ridley doesn't remember paying less mind to the female star. "No, she looked pretty damn good," he says, replaying the scene in his head. "Maybe she was watching him and not me. All I had to do with Brad was, well, he put on his hat, and of course he had that six-pack. You can't miss his six-pack. The rest was all on her."

That may be so, but the most heralded aspect of that scene was that it marked the blazing dawn of Brad Pitt, Movie Star, and launched him into the firmament of leading roles. Ridley's camera work had a lot to do with it. But lost in some of the sensation Brad set off with that scene was the importance of Geena's reaction to him. She ogled his body with such libidinous, googly-eyed wonder that her gaze of clear delight made him a sex symbol as much as those Evian abs and easy charm. The audience saw him through her eyes. Together, Geena, Brad, Ridley and Callie had invented a new language: they had created a movie sex scene from the woman's point of view.

THE LUNCH BREAK DRAGGED ON. Susan Sarandon cooled her heels waiting for word about whether she was needed in the afternoon. "What's going on?" she asked a crew member.

"They're still watching the footage of that scene." It was perhaps the only time the crew ran over schedule from watching dailies. Word was they were so racy, the movie's rating would have shot past R if Ridley had left the sequence uncut. Hans Zimmer, who saw a full fifteen-minute version during editing, said, "It was truly the most incredible love scene since *Don't Look Now*," a 1973 film so notorious for its graphic outtakes that they once won an award at an underground porn festival.

MEANWHILE, IN ANOTHER ROOM at the motel, Susan Sarandon and Michael Madsen grappled with how to approach their own encounter, the one that had bothered Susan from the first. Meant to be intercut with Thelma and J.D.'s erotic romp, the original romantic scene in the script had once featured Jimmy proposing to Louise and references to their making love. It had been through a couple drafts since then. Jimmy still presented Louise with an engagement ring, but the final version had cut such touches as Jimmy's setting the mood with a dozen roses and champagne and the two of them singing a lovey-dovey song before acting out some half-serious impromptu "I do's."

Callie had defended her original draft following earlier read-throughs. She wanted a nice moment for Louise, she said, after the years she'd spent waiting for her lover to commit. "They kind of agree to be together for the rest of their lives or until it gets light, whichever comes first," Callie explained. But in Susan, Ridley and Michael Madsen, the script had run up against collaborators who were incapable of sentimentality. This would be the only sequence in the film to be reworked almost entirely on the set.

Even with changes in the final draft, Susan still believed that the proposal scene would relax the tension of the story so much that it couldn't recover. "It's too much of a leap out of the pressure that is needed to make driving off a cliff feasible," Susan said when she and Michael met in the motel room to plan the scene with Ridley. The room, just down the row from Geena and Brad's, had the same dated wallpaper but harsher light and less comfortable furniture for a less comfortable situation. "I don't know if I could get back into that state of mind after this scene." More than ever, she was convinced that her character's guilt over killing Harlan and the anxiety of life on the lam would overpower any inclination toward romance. And however intriguing, the orgasm-breakdown scene she had once suggested would have been too much.

Susan found she had an ally in Michael Madsen. The laconic, sleepy-eyed actor had objections of his own. "It's not real," he said gruffly. "It's just stupid. Nobody would do this."

"Why not?" Ridley asked. He didn't mind eliminating the Jimmy-

Louise love scene, but as a practical matter, something had to be intercut with Thelma and J.D.'s tryst.

"Because I'm a heterosexual male, and I know a little bit about women," Michael responded. "I don't think that Louise would have anything to do with anybody who wasn't a little volatile, or didn't have a little bit of balls. I can't play Jimmy as a dummy or a pushover, like Chris McDonald's part." The prospect of making an ardent proposal to a reluctant Louise struck him as emasculating.

Michael believed that among the roles he'd played in his career, the Jimmy character was the one closest to himself. He couldn't see Jimmy doing anything Michael Madsen wouldn't do, especially anything that made him appear vulnerable or weak.

"I understand masculinity," he says. "There's a physicality to it, there's a body language, there's a tone of voice. You either have it or you don't. I also understand tenderness; I understand love; I understand forgiveness. I have a duality in my own personality that comes out in spades in Jimmy." He understood Jimmy's conflict—he probably did love her, Michael thought, but was disinclined to be tied down. "You feel her slipping away, and you're just trying to take a shot at holding on to her," Michael says. "Maybe the reason she loved you in the first place was because you were a little hard to get, so you want to maintain that attitude."

The clock was ticking as the three of them thumbed through the script.

"Look, I think I would get kind of mad at the whole situation," Michael finally said.

"Yeah, I guess you would," Ridley agreed. At the time, he thought Michael's instinct might be to slap her. "She's afraid of him at that point, I think," he explains later, "because he may be a bit of a beater." But to Michael, he argued against striking Louise. "No, you're losing something of great value to you. Your life will change once you've lost her." He left the two of them together in the room to make something up.

When he returned, they acted it out for him once, then put it on film.

Michael found an outlet for his urge toward violence by flipping over a table with abrupt force. "If you're having trouble with dialogue," he explains, "it's always interesting to take it out on an inanimate object. In the environment I grew up in, furniture is fair game in a situation like that."

Susan darted toward the door, but Michael, realizing the mistake, stopped her with a conciliatory gesture. The moment had arrived for him to propose, but he had his own ideas about that, too. He wouldn't pose a question as he held out the box with the engagement ring inside, not even the half-hearted one in the script: *Will you wear this?* Instead he shoved it in front of her without looking her in the eye. The script didn't call for him to fall to one knee, but still, the custom was on his mind. "I never understood that whole thing," Michael says. "What a dumb way to start a relationship. I wasn't going to be that guy."

Ridley liked this lukewarm approach to courtship—"It's classically difficult for a man to say he loves a woman," Ridley says. The little bit of gallantry Callie had tried to insert into the story bit the dust.

Susan continued along the same lines. Instead of acting flabbergasted, as the script suggested, and telling Michael the ring was beautiful, Susan substituted a jaded *Why? Why now?*

Michael did keep the next line Callie had put in the script: *You didn't see that one comin', did ya?*

The scene evolved into an all-night back-and-forth between a couple combing through the shards of a broken relationship with resigned affection. By this time, Ridley saw Susan's point about the characters not making love. He thought Louise was a fair-minded woman who wouldn't give Jimmy false hope. Michael wasn't so sure. "In true life, I probably would have fucked her, to be blunt," he says. "If only for old times, or one for the road." But he saw the logic in not having every character in the hotel going at it at once. "I suppose Jimmy could have forced the issue," he says. "But at least we kissed, and that was nice. Susan's a good kisser, for sure."

The actors were pleased with the way the scene worked out, impressed with each other's ability to improvise. Susan told Michael there were only two men in her life she would allow to call her a broad, and he was one of them. "I took that as a compliment," he says.

But it didn't sit well with Callie that they had gutted the scene and turned one of her more sympathetic if flawed male characters into the kind of bruiser who busts up furniture. "I thought it was a mistake," she says. "Louise would have been out of there in a second. She would not have been with a guy who was acting like that."

The end result was freighted with competing perspectives and a jagged sense of cross-purposes. Each collaborator had contributed a different note: Callie's desire for romantic wish fulfillment, Susan's concern for the consistency of her character, Michael's defense of the male ego, Ridley's natural embrace of pessimism. There was certainly a male-female split on the import of violence between men and women, not to mention what constituted a proper proposal of marriage. The scene ended on a minor chord of disillusioned attachment, especially in Susan's final close-up and her tender delivery of the line *Chalk it up to bad timing*.

THE SCENE WHERE SUSAN AND MICHAEL parted in the motel coffee shop the next morning proved to be one of Ridley's favorites in the entire movie. Susan's kindness as Michael slid the ring back across the table to her was heartbreaking, and Ridley loved a good heartbreak. It was clear she knew the lovers wouldn't see each other again, that she was destined for a desolate fate. Ridley lit her face around the rim to highlight a few fine lines, and her complexion and large oval eyes beamed radiance. "She was particularly brilliant in that," Ridley says. Michael's tough-tender duality came through again. Susan thinks it was "a nice little scene-scene, with people talking to each other. Ridley was probably happy we weren't in the car for once." He also loved the gleaming surfaces of the diner as the sun washed in, and he moved Michael to one side of the screen to pick up rays on the tufted leatherette banquette beside him.

Geena as a walking sight gag signaled a quick change of mood once he left. The hairdressers had created a tangled masterpiece of morning-after hair for her arrival at breakfast with one of the widest, goofiest grins in all of movies to tell Louise about her first-ever world-shaking sex. Michael thought she looked like a cross between Daffy Duck and Grace Kelly.

I finally understand what all the fuss is about, Geena said.

Susan delivered the next line like a proud mama: *You finally got laid properly.*

THE MOTEL LOCATION HAD BEEN challenging for all the actors, but there was one more morning-after setup to go before the whole production left Los Angeles. It was a scene that would test the actresses' mettle and establish their characters for the rest of the film. When they realized J.D. had made off with all their money, Louise had to break down in the love-nest motel room, and the flighty Thelma, for the first time, would step up and take control. She would order Louise to get herself together, to gather her stuff, to *Move!* Ridley saw it as the most crucial turning point in the story, when Thelma ceased to behave like the child or little sister and the two became true friends.

The sequence would be challenging for Geena, whose character had never witnessed her rock-steady friend fall apart before, but even more so for Susan, who would have to sob for hours. They were scheduled to film in the afternoon, when her acting juices were flowing, but the light was wrong, and Ridley asked if she could pull it off at eight o'clock in the morning. He stepped between the two of them, his arms around their shoulders. "If you can't get to that, we'll try to do it again later," he said.

Susan got there, and Geena fed off it, summoning convincing power as the roles reversed. Ridley grinned with satisfaction. The transition worked just as he'd intended when he cast them in the film.

The men may have exerted some muscle in molding their parts, but it was clear the women weren't taking a backseat in this picture. "A lot of people were saying very chauvinistically, 'What is this chick flick, who are these girls? They're not going to blow up a truck, are they?'" Michael Madsen says, looking back at the production. "There was a general feeling that this was like an episode of *Scooby-Doo*. But the movie set the bar for women. It said, 'Hey, man, these gals are pretty cool.'"

CHAPTER 22

OWNING THE ROAD

The T-bird barreled down a highway with tractor trailers screaming along on either side, horns blasting, chrome gleaming, headlights piercing the darkness. Susan Sarandon at the wheel and Geena Davis in the passenger seat shouted their lines over the noise. Scene completed, skidding to a stop, they turned to each other and shrieked, "We're in a Ridley Scott movie!"

On Friday, July 20, their simple road picture hit the road. The move to central California hurled the production into the core of the story, where the relationship between the characters deepened and transformed. Louise would push forward in the face of guilt and fear, her big saucer-shaped eyes looking into an abyss. Thelma would morph from homebody ditz to Amazon road warrior. The friendship of the characters would reach a level of feeling rarely achieved between two women on-screen. This was the moment when the creative tension that started to simmer when Callie entrusted her baby to a grandiose action director could reach a rolling boil. Would *Thelma & Louise* emerge as a thoughtful character study or a flashy action film?

For the most part, mutual respect prevailed. Ridley stuck to the script as he lavished attention on the visuals. Geena and Susan worked to stay true to their parts. But they all had to broker underlying tensions as Susan, in particular, fought to defend the values of her character and the conscience that would give meaning to all the dazzle.

An activist actress, a guy's-guy director—it was a classic yin-yang matchup. "The experience was an interesting collaboration, because you had me at one end of the spectrum and Ridley at the other end of the spectrum," Susan says. "The atmosphere was very male. The guys on the crew were all shirtless with their T-shirts around their heads, like a band of cigar-smoking marauders. They adored Ridley and would follow him off a cliff." Together they chased sunrises and sunsets, making spectacular shots of the two women in the car. "The joke was the whole movie would be voice-over," Susan says. "Because he was getting such fabulous footage, why do scenes?"

Nothing in the script indicated that the intimate story needed such an opulent stage. "He brought that to it," Susan says. "We filled in the emotions and the people." Once she saw the finished film, she understood: "Because Ridley put us in this heroic setting, the film had the impact it did," but that wasn't so apparent at the time.

The actresses would plan subtle emotional adjustments for a scene, only to arrive on set and discover that there would be a train passing through the shot. "Or now there's a *cattle drive* all around us while we're having an intimate talk about sex," Geena said in a newspaper interview when the film came out. "We just did it. We just said, 'Well, okay, I guess we're shouting this scene.'"

"We were shouting all the time," Susan agreed. "Every time Geena and I got on the set, we were shocked by what was going on around us."

Their concerns for their characters distracted Ridley, prompting him to grumble in the same interview: "Every scene was a bloody debate."

THAT DIDN'T STOP HIM from sticking to his storyboards and packing every shot with trademark visual density, a particular challenge in the San Fernando Valley, which had to fill in for the Oklahoma flatlands for seven shooting days. The wide, flat agricultural fields and long, straight highways wouldn't crack any guidebook lists of scenic drives. Their visual interest would probably strike some directors as nil. But Ridley Scott was fascinated with settings that most Americans would consider plug-ugly— "All those watering machines and those railway lines, where any Englishman goes nuts because he doesn't see that in the UK."

He dug into his bag of favorite tricks. Instead of smoke, now he had... *dust*! Instead of ghastly furniture and kooky lamps, he sought out backgrounds with irrigation sprinklers, telephone poles and oil pumps that bobbed like feeding birds. A sorry motel off a highway in Gorman hit all the right notes as a one-night shelter for the fugitives. The ground rumbled from trucks on the too-close freeway as Thelma, wearing an absurd ruffled bikini and still trying to salvage a sort of vacation, tried to sun herself beside a pool surrounded with cracked concrete, a John Register painting come to life.

Norris and Anne added layers of artifice to enhance even the most barren settings. They didn't go anywhere without their supply of fake boulders, tumbleweeds and strips of reflectors to line the highways and make them shine. They brought along weather-beaten billboards and a stash of satellite dishes to project the feeling that no matter how remote the territory, the outside world was encroaching, even watching, as the heroines tried to disappear. Ahrens dressed up a gas station with shiny pinwheels that spun in the wind. She etched graffiti into the glass of the phone booth where Thelma called her husband and said, *Darryl. Go fuck yourself.* And to break the monotony of the open space, the prop people designed little structures, like a concrete sinklike form for Brad Pitt to sit on when the women encountered him on the road.

It wasn't only the backgrounds that were loaded with interest. There was constant motion to keep the scenes spinning. When the crew saw a crop duster working at a nearby field, the pilot accepted two hundred bucks to fly by the car as the women waved. He let a camera ride along for free to film from above as the plane swooped away.

Most of all, the boy in Ridley delighted in trucks, American eighteen-wheelers that were bigger, shinier and louder than their counterparts in Europe. "These gigantic trucks covered in lights—he thought they were better than sliced bread," says Ahrens. But ordinary trucks weren't enough for him. Crew members souped them up with extra chrome and borders of red lights that outlined their curves.

Whenever possible, Ridley garnished his already lively tableaus with human props—colorful extras like a cowboy on a rearing horse, an oiled-up bodybuilder lifting weights or guys with potbellies and shaggy hair gunning their Harleys. "That's all just part of America," Ridley says. "I tried to show America the way I like to see it."

He pushed for more, then more again. "When the script said we pull into a gas station," says Susan, "it didn't say we floor it backward with a guy pumping iron and smoke everywhere and he's half naked. That's what Ridley brought to it."

GEENA AND SUSAN PROVED formidable enough to claim their share of the screen, however many moving parts Ridley crammed into it. For the Central Valley locations, the women would mostly carry the story on their own, save for some traveling scenes with Brad Pitt. Ridley also brought

Chris McDonald and Harvey Keitel to the set a couple times so they could deliver lines from a few feet away in scenes when the leads phoned them from the road. The plan lent immediacy to the conversations.

It took greater focus to bring intimacy to dialogue when the car zipped along the highway, top down, wind roaring, but Ridley did his best to help there, too. The production spent $115,000 to buy five vintage Thunderbirds and trick them out to various degrees. Some looked pristine riding on their own. Others were set up so a rig could pull them from the front, or cameras could be mounted on platforms on any side.

Ridley operated the camera from a side mount for one of the first speeding-car scenes, when Thelma and Louise discussed whether they should hightail it to Mexico rather than turn themselves in. *Goddammit, Thelma,* Louise said, *every time we get in trouble, you go blank or plead insanity.* Their hair tossed around their faces and other cars kept pace with them, yet they managed sensitive, even tentative line readings. Ridley smiled encouragement from behind the lens.

"It was the only experience I've had, and I loved it, where the director was the camera operator," Geena says. "He loved our characters. He was smiling the whole time. He was on the periphery, and we had to tune him out, but to see him smiling was so comforting and warm, and very intimate. He just made it very comfortable." He often set up scenes so two cameras filmed at once, the better to let the actresses work off each other's performances. It took greater skill to light such scenes, but it also saved money and time.

It was even harder for the actresses to concentrate in the seemingly delicate scene when Thelma questioned why Louise wouldn't travel through Texas, with the intimation that she had been raped there. *If you blow a guy's head off with his pants down,* Louise said in the script, *believe me, Texas is the last place you wanna get caught.* They were flummoxed when Ridley had the car pull to a stop in front of a railroad crossing, and the women delivered the lines as a train roared by, because ... well, Ridley wanted a train to roar by. The actresses soldiered through.

But they balked at a request that Geena herself embody a visual diversion in a forthcoming scene. Thelma and Louise, having resolved to make a run for Mexico, would feel a liberating sense of release as the car sped along next to farmland while they bopped along to the Temptations' song "The Way You Do the Things You Do."

When the crew broke for lunch beforehand, Ridley pulled Geena aside. "This afternoon," he said, "you two are driving along and listening to music and you are feeling just great. This is the time when it all feels right. So what would you think if your character just sat up on the back of the seat, and you took your top off? You're exhilarated and you're throwing your shirt around or something."

"You know what?" Geena fumbled. "I think they need me at lunch. Ah... I think I better go." She cleared her throat. "I think they want me to eat. Yes! They want me to eat." She kicked herself that she'd bungled the moment, that she couldn't come up with a better excuse to avoid the question, let alone answer it.

Geena found Susan at a picnic table. "Susan!" she said in an exaggerated whisper. "Ridley says for this scene he wants me to take my *top* off."

Susan stopped midbite. "Oh, for heaven's sake," she said. "Can you think of any reason why you should?"

"No." Geena gulped.

"Then that's exploitation," Susan said. She marched over to Ridley and said flatly, "Ridley, Geena is not taking her top off." That was that.

Susan walked straight back, and Geena thanked her. But she kicked herself again for not finding a way to stand up for herself. "As it turned out, he was not bothered by the answer," she says. "It was just so built in for me to be worried about offending anybody, or somebody not liking me because I said no."

Susan shared no such scruples. But they all remember Ridley's reaction a bit differently. He says he simply answered, "Yeah, fine." But in Susan's memory, he came up to her later and said sarcastically, "Thanks a lot."

AFTER EIGHT YEARS IN THE BUSINESS, this was the first time Geena had found herself every day on a movie set with another woman, an equal, someone to emulate. "I wanted people to like me, above everything," Geena says. "I always had to make sure to dance around to get what I want. Ever since Susan, I've always tried to be like her."

Susan reveled in the companionship, too. It fed the real affection and comfort of the performances. "I hadn't really done a part before where it was two women and it was about their friendship so much. We really did hit it off and get along terrifically, in our real lives as well. It was very impactful and important for me."

With so many remote locations, there was no retreating to a trailer between takes. The two of them often hung out in the back of the car, gnawing on beef jerky sticks that were always on hand as props, a patio umbrella overhead to ward off the heat and sun. They planned their upcoming scenes, strategized or just talked. Sometimes they killed time by asking the makeup artists for tweezers and then plucking hairs from their legs.

They entertained the crew by making kitty noises, a nutty contest of meows and purrs, even as they upended the clichés about catty female stars undercutting each other to compete for glory.

"Isn't it fun with girls?" Susan said several times, apropos of nothing.

"Oh God, yes," Geena replied.

Once, they pranked Ridley when he was shooting one of his sundown beauty shots. He panned from the vista to the two leads, only to find an empty seat as they ducked onto the floor.

In their personal lives, the two stars found themselves in different places. Susan was fully occupied when she wasn't on the set. She had brought her kids along, and her brother and manager, Phil Tomalin. Tim Robbins sometimes visited on weekends. Geena got the crew whispering by spending some downtime with Brad Pitt during the few days he was on location. The whispers got louder the more time they spent together. Geena was in the final stages of her three-year marriage to Jeff Goldblum and was already separated. She filed for divorce at the end of the shoot, insisting that the split had nothing to do with a Thelma-like rebellion.

To the crew, Geena was the funny one, Susan the troublemaker. "Look, she's more diplomatic," Susan said of her costar when the film came out. "But she's a strong gal. She was in the midst of a relationship change, and that figured in there." As they filmed more scenes in the car, some members of the crew thought Ridley focused on his art-direction thing while Susan pretty much directed the performance, but Susan insists it was an equal collaboration all around. "Ridley pretty much listened," she says. "He trusted us to take care of the stuff that was in our jurisdiction, and he took care of the stuff that was more than we could have imagined."

THE PRODUCTION OF *THELMA & LOUISE* had wound up in the hands of a male director, but there was no question that women's voices were being heard. Back then, women usually made up only about 20 percent of movie crews, a statistic that has remained about the same ever since. The *Thelma & Louise* workers, outside of the cast, were 22 percent female, not much of a variation from the norm. Many of them filled slots typically occupied by women—costume design, script supervision, makeup, office work. But a number of others wielded untraditional authority.

Mimi Polk, as a first-time producer, continued to toggle logistics throughout, bouncing between the home office in LA and the set. Some found her warm and enthusiastic, a strong advocate for the film. Others regarded her as cool or scary depending on which face she chose to show to get what she needed done. Lisa Dean, the art director, worked closely with the production designer, Norris Spencer, and supervised a crew that constructed sets. Kathy Nelson, the music supervisor, chose the widely admired "needle drops," popular songs that set the mood of the story along the way. And Anne Ahrens ran the team of half a dozen guys who arranged the sets.

While the number of women wasn't great, it felt to members of the crew as if there were more around than usual, perhaps because they had greater say than usual, led by the two female stars. They also weren't exposed to the kind of denigrating treatment that held them back on other movie sets. "*Thelma & Louise* had a different feeling," says Ahrens. "Because it was such a women's story, women were respected on and off the set."

One member of her crew, Ken Turek, performed a function called lead man, responsible for supervising the placement of Anne's set decorations. He had worked on a dozen movies before, but never one written by a woman. The female-centered story struck him as refreshing, he says, in part because his girlfriend, who worked in the same field, turned down a project at the same time called *Boxing Helena,* about a woman imprisoned with her limbs cut off. "*Thelma & Louise* was the opposite of that," he says.

Turek had worked with a few female set decorators before and witnessed their struggles to be taken seriously. Sometimes, he says, a set decorator gave instructions, then left to scavenge for props, only to find when she returned that the men had taken off right after she did, without accomplishing a thing. "They were almost insulted by having to work for a woman," says Turek. "They didn't know how to react to a female telling them what to do. It was like their wife telling them to do something."

The eighties corresponded to the influx of crew members who had studied film in college rather than worked their way through the trade, and that made it harder for them to win respect from seasoned blue-collar hands. Traditionally, Turek says, there had been many gay male set decorators, but the crews were accustomed to them and less likely to give them a hard time. But a woman? "She must be on the rag," guys said when she gave an order. Or "She's crabby. Her husband must be out of town." Turek had seen and heard it all.

"The female set decorators had to be tough," he says. "They tended to be more on the ball. They made better lists—like things were actually legible—and they were better educated. But they had to prove themselves every day."

Crew members in various departments recalled other shoots where they witnessed or heard about disrespect and harassment. Stories circulated about people like the female assistant director Candace Allen, one of the first African American women to hold the job, who once was ordered to stand in the rain until her T-shirt was soaked and to jump up and down so the director could watch her breasts bounce. She tried lowering her voice at work to come across as less feminine, and she always addressed her colleagues as "Gentlemen," hoping they would take the hint. Kathy Nelson resolved to underreact to affronts. A music executive once chased her around her office and forcibly kissed her before she broke free. The next day she tried to pass the incident off as some kind of accident so they could keep working together.

On some of her other films, Anne Ahrens says, she encountered "guy banter and gags, boys-will-be-boys stuff, which I didn't get on *Thelma & Louise*. On this movie, it was like we were all on a journey together and everybody was just as important." While some directors' methods could be more rough-and-tumble, Ridley held meetings where softer-spoken workers could have their say. "Everybody's voice was heard, which I don't think happens much on other films," she says.

If Ridley set such a tone from the top, it wasn't a conscious effort to promote a gender-free utopia so much as a reflection of his personality and mostly gender-blind management style. Some practices on the set were stuck in the typical Hollywood groove. Memos all referred to Geena and Susan as girls, and in one of Ridley's hand-drawn storyboards of a car chase later in the movie, he depicted Geena without a top on. Like many men in many a workplace, he was more comfortable talking with guys. But his all-business approach to directing meant that everyone's contribution got the same degree of respect, and it was based on performance. "I don't think the guys on the movie looked at it as a women's picture," says Steve Danton, the first assistant director. "They just looked at it as good filmmaking."

The crew agreed that Ridley Scott set an example for a smoothly functioning shoot. Utterly confident, decisive and experienced, he didn't act out of insecurity or play favorites. "I don't think he was buddies with anybody, except maybe the camera crew," says Tracy DeFreitas, who helped manage the office on location. "He had to be focused, and he had to stay on a really tight budget." He also worked harder than anybody else, but then he let it go at the end of the day to enjoy a good dinner before he watched the dailies.

"He was mischievous and, I would suspect, a kind of gentleman hedonist," says Jason Beghe, who played the state trooper who stopped Thelma and Louise for speeding. Beghe was one of the few members of the cast or crew who had personal conversations with Ridley. "Ridley enjoyed life. He was a discreet guy, but wine, women and song were things he embraced, I don't think to an unhealthy degree. He was not overly serious, but he was professional as hell and knew where his talent lay. If you think about that, it's a healthy and intelligent recipe for any artist."

The production process had turned into one long, rolling negotiation among director, actors and crew as they strove to settle on the right details and, more important, given the loaded subject matter, the right tone. Susan Sarandon even raised the possibility that the picture benefited from the leadership of someone who didn't necessarily share her point of view. "Ridley is pretty interesting," Susan said in a newspaper interview a year later. "I don't trust him as far as I can throw him, but I love him, and I would work for him again in a flash. Our agendas were not always the same, our priorities were not always the same, but it was not a question of what's right and what's wrong. If anything, this movie shows that you can have people coming from completely different perspectives creating a third thing. If this had been directed by a really serious feminist trying to make some kind of statement, it may not have had the air that it needed."

The usually dour director told people he had enjoyed himself more than on any other film. "Part of what made it so good," says his friend Hans Zimmer, "is that it was almost like a hobby for Ridley to direct it. There was an ease about it, a complete lack of cynicism."

On time and on budget, it was all going so well that Ridley had to wonder, as the production sprinted toward its denouement in the canyonlands of Utah: *Was this all too good to be true?* When he got to the editing room, *would there be a movie there?*

CHAPTER 23

SOMETHING'S CROSSED OVER

When the cast and crew rolled into Moab, Utah, on August 1, they knew they were in the presence of some powerful juju. Merciless heat and sun pounded the parched desert landscape. The hallucinogenic color contrast—burnt orange mesas and lapis lazuli sky—that had thrown the location scout's mind into disorder soon worked a spell on others, too. Anne Ahrens, for no other reason, broke down sobbing while driving to the set and had to pull off the road more than once. Norris Spencer and art director Lisa Dean crashed into a ditch, so distracted were they by the monumental rock garden jutting skyward on every side. With no time for repairs, coated with powder from the exploded airbags, the two stuffed them back into the car and sealed them in with duct tape.

A memo to the crew had already broken the bad news about Moab itself, once a uranium-mining town, now a sluggish center for tourists: no liquor was served in restaurants, the few bars sold only beer and "dining is poor to fair." It was a lights-out-by-eight kind of place, which was just as well given the fifteen-hour days on the schedule. Aside from Ridley, who stayed in a resortlike ranch outside of town, and Geena and Susan, who rated rented homes, the rest sacked out at a mixed bag of cut-rate motels and even some camping trailers. Actors who played minor characters killed time at the production office, an old oil-company building furnished with folding tables and chairs. Hollywood tinsel was in short supply.

But Ridley felt certain this remote, almost forgotten pocket of the American West offered him the epic proscenium that could transfigure the final scenes of the film, turning them into the stuff of myth. For four weeks, a place where John Ford filmed some classic Westerns would frame controversial set pieces destined to blow the usual ladylike movie mandate to smithereens. Ridley's antiheroines would lock a state trooper in the trunk of his cruiser, blow up the rig of a sleazy truck driver, lead the cops on a car chase and skyrocket off a cliff, if the studio would still let them. Ridley's plan was set, the storyboards drawn, but Geena Davis, Susan Sarandon, Callie Khouri and Alan Ladd Jr. had opinions of their own.

GEENA AND SUSAN STRODE ONTO THE locations looking wild, tanned, windblown and looser without traditional makeup. In fact, it took the makeup artists longer than ever to prepare the stars each day, layering sunscreen, followed by bronzy fake tans, followed by smudges of dirt and even tiny individual painted freckles. Every night, the costume crew dutifully washed their clothes, now swapped out and ripped apart. Every morning, Susan and Geena rolled around on the parking lot to dirty them up again—jeans and a jean shirt with the sleeves ripped off for Geena, jeans and a white tank top for Susan, with strips torn from Geena's sleeves to knot around her neck. Ridley loved how they looked—more truly themselves, as Callie had envisioned. His camera seemed to worship them in close-ups that outshone the scenery.

Members of the crew appeared more than ever like a band of land-locked buccaneers, bare chests brown from a daily blast of vitamin D, wet rags tied around their necks to deflect the 100-plus-degree heat, an eccentric collection of hats to shield their heads. Ridley seemed impervious. In long sleeves and a cap with flaps, the freckled redhead said he'd never felt so fit in his life in the dry, magnificent air. Geena and Susan won respect by toughing it out. They often had to forgo head coverings or sunglasses so the camera could see their expressions, and every night they had to rinse the grit out of their eyes to stave off infections from desert fungus that festered in the ever-present dust.

This was the most action-oriented portion of the screenplay, but Callie had provided grace notes along the way. Thoughtful moments appeared amid the mayhem so the characters could reflect on what they had done and become. One such moment that was scripted near the end had already been filmed in LA. During the women's final scramble to escape as the police zeroed in, Callie wrote a short, wordless scene for Darryl, staring dully into space back home. Chris McDonald welcomed the opportunity to show that Thelma's husband realized the enormity of what had happened. "This gave him some humanity," says Chris. He let a stream of thoughts flow through his mind as he played the scene next to the horrible lamp with the goldfish trapped inside. "How he'd lost this thing he'd taken for granted, his girl, who he really did love and also saw as his property. How he was going to be alone now. How this was all so far outside his parameters. It was a beautiful thing that Ridley left it in."

Other moments allowed Geena and Susan to show their own nuanced emotions, an anomaly for most action films. Elation at escaping their pasts ran parallel with premonitions of the end.

I don't remember ever feelin' this awake, Geena said in a conversation in the car. *You know what I mean? Everything looks new. Do you feel like that? Like you've got something to look forward to?*

We'll be drinking margaritas by the sea, Mamacita, Susan replied with false enthusiasm. Their expressions conveyed simultaneous layers of optimism and hopelessness.

The script gave Susan another actorly opportunity when she waited in the car outside while Thelma held up a convenience store. Susan began to apply lipstick, but thought better of it. Ridley added a touch: two weary-looking older women who looked like subjects in a Dorothea Lange photo watching Susan through a window. It seemed to spook Louise. *Is this what life holds in store for me?* she seemed to wonder before she tossed the makeup away.

Later, in an effort to take her character beyond time, Susan suggested that she trade away her jewelry and watch for a hat. "I knew I was not going back," she says. "I was cutting off my links with everything." Ridley had spotted just the person to play her trading partner, an elderly man pushing one hundred. He was a prospector who lived with a pet chicken— an attack chicken, the crew called it—in a ghost town an hour out of Moab. "You gotta get me that guy," Ridley said to Ken Haber, the location manager. "I want him in the movie." The man refused, embarrassed that he was missing teeth, but he relented after Geena and Susan made a fuss over him and invited him to join them for lunch. He didn't have to act in the scene. He merely looked at Susan, and the rest—the isolation and melancholy—was all in his expression.

Susan craved one more moment of stillness for Louise that wasn't present in the script. "We've been in the car forever," Susan said to Ridley. "Can't she just get out and experience a little note of quiet, where you don't know what she's thinking, she's just looking out?" She was surprised when Ridley agreed and set up the shot at night in Arches National Park. It meant bringing in a Musco light, a huge multidirectional fixture on a flatbed truck, usually used to light up football stadiums, to penetrate the darkness and illuminate the mountains and monuments. The effect was unreal, like silvery sideways moonlight, reminiscent of the time Callie drove through Monument Valley at night and rethought her own life. Susan appreciated the effort. "Actors offer suggestions all the time, but lighting something in the desert that takes seven hours was a huge thing," she says. "Ridley could be a great collaborator."

Meanwhile, Thelma, the formerly insecure flake, now owned the road. She held herself with new authority, vaulting into the car over the side, too cool to open the door. When Louise seemed to waver while talking to Harvey Keitel on a pay phone, Thelma hovered silently in the background, summoning all her stature to boost her friend's resolve. Yet Geena still conjured up a soft, melting delivery to imbue one of Thelma's signature lines with heartbreak: *Something's crossed over in me and I can't go back,* she said, her eyes searching toward the sky. *I mean... I just couldn't live.*

Ridley framed her face with dreamy late-day light, and her tangled hair formed a shimmery crown around her head. A second camera captured Susan's reaction in real time.

I know, she said gently. *I know what you mean.*

Years later, Thom Noble, who edited the film, still chokes up when he remembers seeing that footage. "I actually cried when I cut that," he says. "Tears streaming down. It cuts to your heart."

THE PERFORMANCES OF THE TWO STARS gave the story weight, but Ridley never forgot that this was to be popular entertainment, so he lavished attention on the action sequences, always with an eye for sparks of comedy. He was stoked when the cast and crew met on the side of a road two miles outside Moab for the scene when a New Mexico state trooper stopped Thelma and Louise for speeding, and Thelma's transformation to badass would be complete. She would pull a gun on the cop to stop him from calling them in, order Louise to shoot out his radio and lock him in his trunk, taking his gun to shoot airholes in the lid. The light was harsh and flat that day, but Ridley looked forward to the scene regardless. He liked that Thelma would become the authoritative Louise, and Louise would become the hapless Thelma, shooting out the wrong radio. *The police radio, Louise!* Thelma would admonish her. He liked the idea that the audience would feel torn and anxious, unsure whether Thelma would really shoot the cop. And Ridley had been talking up an actor he loved for the one-day trooper role.

Jason Beghe wasn't a typical bit player. A native New Yorker who'd grown up as a private-school buddy of John F. Kennedy Jr.'s, he'd taken a serendipitous approach to his career, becoming a model almost by chance when he posed for the photographer Bruce Weber. That took him to Europe, where he spent a couple years as the Armani man, his dark looks and square jaw turning heads. When he decided to act, his second audition landed him the role of a boy toy in *Compromising Positions.*

A standout audition sealed his casting as the trooper. Ridley thought the actor had the perfect look for the part—fit, fascistic in demeanor, threatening without being too threatening. Ridley arranged chairs like the seats of the car in the audition room and asked Beghe to act out the scene. "I have a different take on this, do you mind?" the actor offered. Ridley nodded assent, and when the gun got turned on him, Beghe burst into tears. "Underneath, he's just a little kitten," he reasons. "It's endearing, but it's also funny." Ridley couldn't stop giggling. He didn't look further.

Beghe turned up on the roadside looking even better than Ridley had hoped, a bit like Batman, in a tight black uniform, his hat pulled low over his mirrored sunglasses. Ridley had asked the actor to shave again and again and put oil on his skin, so he'd look smooth and shiny. "I looked rigid and vain," Beghe says. "The more you set that up, the better the fall will be."

The scene clicked. Geena stepped up, Susan fumbled comically and Beghe delivered an arc from intimidating to cowering. *Ma'am, please,* he begged. *I've got kids... a wife.*

You do? Well. You're lucky, Geena said. *You be sweet to 'em. Especially your wife. My husband wasn't sweet to me, and look how I turned out.*

The women tore away on a high note. *I know it's crazy, Louise,* Thelma said, *but I just feel like I've got a knack for this shit.*

Ridley had one more comic flourish in mind: on the way to one of the locations during scouting, he'd spotted a Rastafarian on a bike. A mile later, Ridley had his driver turn the car around so they could photograph the guy. Callie had written that an older Mexican man in a pickup truck would stop to free the cop from his trunk, but Ridley told her when she visited the set that he wanted to substitute a Rastafarian mountain biker in Day-Glo gear. She argued against the change, found it distracting and irrelevant, but Ridley went ahead, and the encounter capped the trooper sequence with added absurdity. Beghe poked his finger through the air-hole in the trunk, trying to point out where the women had thrown his keys. The biker took a long pull of ganja and blew the smoke through the hole.

Beghe cut his finger on the metal, but he didn't mention it. "I suppose today we'd have a stunt finger," he says. And he couldn't reach the level of all-out bawling he'd managed in the audition, but he didn't ask for another take. He figured he was there to do his job without making a fuss. "Ridley is a consummate gentleman, but I think that stuff is irritating to him," Beghe says. "He wants you to shut up, plant your feet and talk." After working together that one day, Ridley told him he'd hire him again. He did, six years later, to play Demi Moore's boyfriend in *G.I. Jane.*

RIDLEY WAS HAVING A BLAST, but he still didn't like friction that slowed him down. Once the production left LA, he granted Callie just one opportunity to visit the set. The limitation galled her, but her presence, when she showed up, galled him. He figured their prep work together more than sufficed to school him on her point of view, and now he needed the freedom to add improvisation as he saw fit and to get the film in the can. He didn't want to hear more of her strong opinions or resistance to anything that messed with the text, like her objection to the Rastafarian character. Ridley shot down a suggestion from the studio that she give press interviews during the shooting, citing concern that there might be changes that displeased her.

"Once I've chosen a script, I always spend quite a lot of time with the writer," Ridley says. "I spent a lot of time with Callie initially, because I read it, I liked it and there was nothing to be done except talk to her about women generally. Once I've got that, I go out and make it."

Writers at that time were rarely welcome on movie sets, but Callie didn't see why that should be. Directors valued the expertise of costume designers and hairdressers on location, she reasoned. If there were changes to be made in the dialogue, why shouldn't the writer be consulted? "There were a lot of people who wanted to be the final authority on this movie, and I make that really difficult for people," Callie says. "I don't think you can look at Ridley and say this is definitely his movie if I'm in the picture. Or Susan, or anybody else. It's so much mine."

She did make a few minor alterations in the script—when asked. "I think she proved a certain mettle that she could write on the fly," says her agent, Diane Cairns. "But it wasn't a lovefest."

BACK IN THE OFFICES OF PATHÉ, the staff could hear Laddie laughing his head off when he screened the dailies every day after lunch. Given his largely nonspeaking role around the studio, this was the best available measure that he liked what he was seeing. The beauty of it, the humor—it was a relief to find it there in the rushes, especially given that there wasn't money in the budget for reshoots. He and Becky could see that Ridley's vision was clear, and he was sticking to it. When Becky visited the set, she mostly held her tongue and let Ridley stay in the groove. But there were jitters, mostly emanating from the studio marketing department, about how it was supposed to sell this thing. Was it an action picture or a women's relationship picture? There was no category out there for a hybrid of women and action, comedy and drama.

And that ending. Laddie never told Ridley to change it, but the two of them held conversations about whether to shoot an alternative that they could test with audiences. "I think it's the perfect ending," Ridley said, despite his own concerns.

"Yeah, but they'll hate it," Laddie said, thinking of the paying customers.

They circled the options for the characters—ten to fifteen years in jail? The chair? An implausible escape? They all seemed even more depressing. But that wouldn't stop the director and the studio head from hashing out the same dilemma every time they spoke, right up until the last day of shooting, when the last scene had to wrap.

Thelma & Louise dominated most of the discussion among everyone else at the studio, too. One of the atmospheric charms at Pathé was that a private chef prepared Italian family-style lunches in the conference room, where the executives engaged in family-style debates. "We spent a couple hours, all of us, talking about movies and sports and arts and culture and laughing and fighting, all around that table," says Greg Foster, the young vice president who handled market research. "We must have had fifteen movies that year. Half the time we talked about the other fourteen, and half the time we talked about *Thelma & Louise.*"

Foster and the higher-level marketing managers fretted constantly about how they were going to entice what they called mainstream commercial guys to see this movie. "Your traditional young male moviegoer was not going to watch a couple of women in their mid- to late thirties kick ass and shake it up," Foster says. "And a huge amount of the movie takes place in a car with two ladies talking. I remember a fairly intense argument about how this was really designed more as a play than a movie, and how it was up to the director to give it scope." The marketers were disappointed that there wasn't more traditional action so far, and no sexy scene for Susan Sarandon in the dailies mix. Ridley, they thought, had to deliver enough kinetic action sequences to flesh out the movie trailers and ads. They wanted the illusion of a huge buildup of cops chasing the heroines, Foster says, "because that's what guys are attracted to when they go to the movies—they want to see activity." Not to mention explosions—big, loud, fiery explosions. More than anything, the marketing department pinned its hopes on Ridley bringing his A game to blowing up that truck.

Ridley was on the same page. He decided to make the truck driver as broadly funny as possible and to make the explosion of his truck as big and loud and fiery as possible. Overblown humor and overblown action. The studio would love that. Callie and Susan would not.

CHAPTER 24

READY, STEADY, BLOW

The only dailies that didn't please Ridley were of the attempted rape, the film's most grueling scene. On the night of August 11, he reshot five takes, all close-ups. The production cut off access for all but essential crew to the parking lot of the production office in Moab and dressed it up like the exterior of the Silver Bullet. The setting wouldn't match up perfectly, but once again Ridley figured no one in the audience would notice the details.

Neither Geena Davis as Thelma nor Timothy Carhart as Harlan looked forward to revisiting the painful encounter, especially because it was likely to be nastier this time. Most everyone was told that the reason for the retakes was trouble with the focus on Harlan in the original footage. But Ridley felt that it hadn't been violent enough to justify the rest of Thelma's and Louise's actions through the rest of the movie. Carhart steeled himself to tap deeper into the character's darkest impulses for the five takes:

Harlan's hands hike up dress, he slams her on trunk, pulling panties down.

Tight shot of same.

Thelma slammed on trunk.

Medium close-up and close-up of Harlan, just face.

Carhart had to wait it out for a week in his Moab motel room, sometimes venturing into the parkland on a rented mountain bike during the day, until a night opened up for the reshoot. It was another bleary four a.m. kind of affair. "They didn't tell me to be rougher in so many words," Carhart says. "Ridley gave me a certain allowance to go for it. He did it with a wink and a nod. It went beyond the action to a realm that was a really ugly part of humanity." He saw how it affected Geena. "Geena is really brilliant at the kinesthetic part of acting. She's really emotionally vulnerable to suggestion. I guess it was pretty rough for her."

So much so that she walked off the set, clearly upset, a stunning departure for the usually accommodating actress. All these years later, she is still reluctant to discuss it, beyond saying that she felt genuinely terrified, and Carhart still expresses regret that she was placed in such a hostile scenario. They parted without speaking after the scene. He called her later to apologize.

"I WON'T GET A DATE FOR A YEAR," the actor Marco St. John bemoaned to Ridley before they shot his scenes as the truck driver.

Ridley looked at the actor with pity. "Try five," Ridley said.

If Harlan the rapist was the movie's most thankless role, the trucker wasn't far behind. When Ridley first met with Callie, he hadn't believed there were guys out there who made such lewd, crude, rude remarks and gestures to female motorists. But after Callie assured him this was an everyday occurrence on American roads and Mimi Polk weighed in with her own examples, Ridley was now fully on board, doubly sold because there was an explosion involved. The truck driver, and that photogenic fireburst of his gasoline tanker truck, would provide welcome relief to the grim endgame with the police in the final section of the movie. The script called for several encounters with him along the road before the women flirtatiously suggested he pull off to the side. They would spar with him before shooting out his tires, then shoot the tanker to make it explode in a ball of flame. "I think Ridley did the movie to blow up that truck," Susan Sarandon says. "He loved that scene."

Ridley told Marco St. John to let it rip, the lewder, cruder and ruder the better. This was hardly the sort of direction St. John was accustomed to receiving. "I was mortified that I was such a dork," he says. He had been a New York theater actor, Shakespearean, no less, until a horrific tragedy derailed his career in 1971. Playing Alcibiades in a production of *Timon of Athens* at Shakespeare in the Park, he was summoned offstage midperformance to the news that his wife had been brutally assaulted and shot in their Greenwich Village apartment. The crime was never solved, but St. John believed she died fighting to save herself and their seven-year-old son, calling out to him to stay outside while she struggled to fend off the attacker. Afterward, St. John left New York and its acting opportunities to take their son to live with family in Mississippi. His career never regained its former trajectory.

Lou DiGiaimo called St. John in for the part of the FBI agent, but Ridley liked the actor's comic delivery and suggested he read with all the leathery-looking guys up for the trucker. He was pleased to be offered a role, even this one, in a film that broke the mold for women. "My wife was very courageous," St. John says. "She fought to the death for her son. She fought for her life. So I have great respect for women. Susan and Geena were the real deal, and the way Callie dealt with men, nobody had done that before."

St. John followed instructions and kept it broad—too broad, according to many critics when the film came out. He waggled his tongue at the women as they passed him on the road. Like some cretinous good ole boy in a *Smokey and the Bandit* movie, he delivered lines that were slipped into the script on the spot, like *Hey baby, I'm your Captain Muff Diver!* and *You ready for a big dick?* Geena and Susan amused themselves by suggesting raunchier ad-libs that didn't make the film, like "How would you like a come shampoo?" The art department gave the trucker the shiniest possible chariot, a chrome gasoline tanker with silhouettes of naked women on the mud flaps and an interior perked up by just enough gold spray paint to give off little kicks of sparkle. Gold mirrored sunglasses completed his look.

"I thought he pulled it off brilliantly and outrageously," Ridley said in defense of the performance. And St. John says, "I know guys who make that look like I was underplaying."

Brett Goldstein, the assistant casting director who suggested St. John for the part, offers a more nuanced justification for the trucker. "Yes, there is something clownish about it," he says. "I think men *are* broad when it comes to the prospect of easy sex. This is not a subtle country. Men can be big, dumb, loud idiots in a lot of ways. And it's like the gravediggers in *Hamlet* or the porter in *Macbeth*. People need a little escape, to lose some steam before you go back into the drama. Ridley instinctively got that in terms of film structure. It was justified." Goldstein gives it a beat. "And people love explosions."

But Callie was still visiting the set during the scenes, and she couldn't stomach the cartoonish version of the statement she wanted to make. Her demeanor on location struck others as withdrawn, "like there was a glass case around her," St. John says, but everyone understood that she had wanted to direct the movie, and they knew she would have ditched the Rastafarian and toned down the truck driver if she could. Callie didn't mind the Rastafarian so much after she saw the finished film, but she could never reconcile with the troglodyte trucker. "He was a caricature," Callie says. "Any woman on the set could have told them that a guy like that is a real guy, but the way it was played wasn't real. It was disappointing because it engendered criticism of the movie that it was making fun of male characters in a way I didn't intend." She ends on a wistful note. "I still wish there was a way to fix all that stuff."

Callie had no power on the set, but Susan Sarandon did, and she objected to the trucker scenes for reasons of her own. The sequence fed her ongoing concern about the film skewing toward a revenge fantasy. She opposed a script direction calling for Thelma and Louise to "howl at the top of their lungs" after the explosion—too celebratory. "I wanted to be somber in the moment," Susan says, which wouldn't have been music to the marketing guys' ears. And she wanted the dialogue with the trucker to be more thoughtful, more an attempt to understand than to lecture. "She's trying to figure out," Susan says, "why men think that sticking out their tongues or talking about your body parts would in any way be a positive experience for a woman."

The script already hit some of those notes.

We think you have really bad manners, Thelma said when they confronted the driver.

We were just wonderin' where you think you get off behavin' like that to women you don't even know, Louise added.

But Susan insisted on a line she devised: *How would you feel if someone did that to your mother or your sister or your wife?*

Ridley suggested St. John respond as if he didn't understand what she meant. *Huh? What are you talking about?* When he refused to apologize, they let the bullets fly.

Ridley appreciated the businesslike quality of the two actresses in the scene. "It's not threatening," he said. "It's authority. It's equality."

Even with flashy pyrotechnics in the offing, the designers still dressed the set. Geena and Susan would stand in the T-bird to shoot, but to keep the background interesting, Ridley asked the art department to build an awning of some sort behind them. The crew slapped together an odd metal structure, then attached scraggly pieces of gauze, aged with paint, to flap in the wind, and some splinters of Norris Spencer's signature plastic sheeting for the requisite shine.

On August 20 a couple hundred crew members and locals gathered to watch the big conflagration, positioned well back because of the real danger. With only one $79,000 tanker to blow up, Ridley stationed half a dozen cameras behind safety barriers to catch every angle. St. John took his position closest to the blast, about fifty yards away. "You don't have to do this," Bobby Bass, the stunt coordinator, told him. "We could use a stuntman."

St. John replied, "Hey, today is as good a day as any."

Geena and Susan were the next closest, about a hundred yards back. "Um, you've cleared everybody away for miles," Susan said to Ridley. "Why are *we* so close if it's dangerous, and the camera's behind us so you can't see us anyway?"

"It's not safe for the camera here," Ridley answered.

"Well, get stunt people or figure out how to make it safe," Susan said, drawing on her best no-nonsense voice. "This is the only time we'll see this, and if you put a camera in front you can get our real reactions."

Ridley spent another hour with the safety coordinator, setting up a view of the actresses' faces and telling them what to do if debris flew their way. Then the director crawled under the car to get near the action himself. He told St. John he'd call, "Ready, steady, go," but the blast was rigged to detonate at "steady." "It had to go before he knew it would happen so it would scare the shit out of him," Ridley says.

The truck blew on cue, flames licking well over a hundred feet in the air. St. John rocked on his heels, mouth gaping, and felt the heat smack his back. Later he realized he'd lost some of his hearing. Geena and Susan were so stunned that they looked completely blank.

"What the hell was that?" Ridley asked after he saw them on the monitor. "You didn't do anything!"

"It was just too amazing to react to," Geena responded. "I think we forgot."

The crew had to set up some fans and flashing orange lights, and the actresses went wide-eyed for close-ups, Susan keeping it on the solemn side, as she had planned. But first they filmed her whipping the car in circles around St. John before the women peeled out under the smoke, Geena delivering the final insult by swiping his hat. It was the beat-up cap that Ridley had bought off the woman trucker on the scouting trip to Arkansas, and Thelma would wear it in the penultimate scenes.

Back at Pathé in Los Angeles, Laddie invited the nervous marketing guys to the dailies. They couldn't contain their joy. "It was a giant explosion like you'd have in *Beverly Hills Cop*," Greg Foster says. The sharp script, the humor and now this. "At that point, it was like having your cake and eating it, too."

Meanwhile, Marco St. John flew out to his next gig at an arts festival in Pittsburgh. He played the title role in that most poetic of Shakespeare's love tragedies, *Antony and Cleopatra*.

IT WAS A TOUGH SHOOT, everyone agrees, what with the six-day weeks, the heat, the scour-proof dirt and the long drives to remote locations. While the cast and crew baked between takes, a second unit tooled around the area for added beauty shots with a matched set of Thelma and Louise doubles in another car. After long days of shooting, Geena Davis and Susan Sarandon had to sit still at night as a makeup artist made plaster casts of their heads, models for the dummies that would be sent over the cliff in the final scene. Tony Scott, on location to shoot a Marlboro commercial, joined his brother for a few days. Otherwise, Ridley, recently divorced, mostly kept to himself when he wasn't on the set, watching dailies over takeout food and keeping his focus. Occasionally he went horseback riding on a day off.

The rough conditions nurtured a general camaraderie. "It was like an extended camping trip," says Mimi Polk. Geena and Susan hosted a party at the local bowling alley, where Ridley obsessively perfected his initially pathetic game. He threw gutter balls until an assistant director approached with questions about the next day's shoot. As soon as Ridley's mind clicked back into his usual world, he started throwing strikes. On the set, laughter and practical jokes prevailed, with water balloon fights and competition to find phallic references in the rock formations.

Susan enjoyed her kids visiting Moab, at times with Tim Robbins, and she was always laughing and happy in the makeup trailer. "It was something I hadn't done before," she says, "and I felt very open and expansive and energized and had a lot of fun." But members of the crew detected spiraling tension between her and Ridley as the shoot progressed toward its controversial conclusion. Some say the two barely spoke from the trucker scenes through the end of production.

The differences seemed inevitable given their polar-opposite sensibilities. One of Ridley's favorite lines was to tell an actor after a shot, "Oh, you're one of those one-take Johnnies." It was intended to make the player feel confident while letting Ridley move on. "I'll interact to a point," Ridley says. "I'm like Clint Eastwood in that way." He'd heard that when an actor asked Eastwood for another take, the director liked to say, "Yeah, if you want to continue wasting everybody's time." Ridley favored actors like Matt Damon, who worked with him years later on *The Martian*. When Ridley told Damon, "I tend to do two takes. Is that okay?" the actor answered, "Whatever."

With Susan, the issue wasn't that she wanted endless takes but that she tossed out so many opinions before the cameras rolled, and so definitively. Geena stayed true to the text and had already planned her scenes when she arrived each day, but Susan was a dynamo about asking for changes and making sure her point of view came through. There were members of the crew who thought her shadow direction kept the performances just where they needed to be. "Because this was a women's film, and Ridley is about as far from a feminist as you could get," says one, "Susan was leading the way."

None of this struck her as unusual. "I'm always like that," she says. "I don't feel like that's being a director necessarily. The director has so many other things to do." She likens a movie shoot to a car trip, with the director driving and the actors in the backseat saying, "Let's take this road. Or how about that one." The actors aren't responsible for getting the movie where it has to go, she says, "but we throw out suggestions. Sometimes they work. Sometimes they don't. Sometimes they lead to a third thing." Given how much else Ridley had to worry about, she said at the time, he didn't have the luxury to think about whether a line was too sentimental or it was appropriate for her to have a sex scene. "Sometimes I would have to be the one who said, 'No, I absolutely won't.'"

It wasn't that the two of them weren't speaking by the end, she says. "I don't remember it that way at all. There was so much technical stuff, and because there was a time factor and it was the end of the movie, there was not a lot of conversation." She suggested lifting some dialogue about friendship from the final scene and putting it during an earlier driving scene, and Ridley agreed. "So we ended up fine. We would kid him and he would kid us. It wasn't like he was finishing my sentences, and there was definitely a divide between the men and the women—the guys were hanging out together. But Ridley listened, and we contributed when we could."

Most of her coworkers admired her forthright style. Some of them, accustomed to working with actresses who were insecure about their looks or their lack of authority on the set, got a kick out of Susan's crystal confidence. "Susan Sarandon is like *the* tough woman actress," says Ken Turek. "There is no stepping on her. Both on camera and off, she could go head-to-head with any of the guys. She was not going to be some female who would sit in the car and look pretty." She was never apologetic about expressing herself, but she also never raised her voice, and she often took the edge off with well-timed humor. No one remembers the actress and director having words on location.

"I didn't notice her bossing anyone around," says Michael Madsen.

Ridley Scott's feelings about her seem to vary depending on when he's asked. "With two very collaborative actresses," he told a reporter who visited the set, "I keep everything open. They chuck in their ideas, and it all goes into a melting pot. I'm having more open and, I think, better discussions with these two than I've probably ever had." But years later, during a moment of reflection, he says, "I listened, yeah, yeah, yeah, but I knew exactly what I'm going to do." He added, "She just knows more about anything than anybody." He agrees that they never had words at the time.

His views may be colored by interviews Susan gave when the film was released, including an article that quoted her as saying, "The only way to find out what was going on was to batter him, just completely abuse him. And that's what Geena and I did." According to Ridley's account, he called her up and gave her an earful after one such feature appeared.

Susan's opinions about the script and interviews about her role in making changes led to some frosty moments with Callie, too. "Susan saved the picture," Callie says in a moment of sarcasm. "We've marveled for years at what kind of a ham-fisted mockery we would have made of it if it had not been for Susan."

As Ridley Scott movies went, though, the tension wasn't all that notable. And it was understandable that emotions would crest as the final days of August loomed and the crew rigged the precipice of Dead Horse Point for the much-debated end of Thelma and Louise.

CHAPTER 25

OFF THE CLIFF

The last week of August. Time to settle the argument that had bedeviled everyone who came into contact with *Thelma & Louise* since Callie brought the screenplay into the world. By now one or both of her leading ladies had shot a rapist, robbed a store, blown up a truck, had sex with a stranger and drunk Wild Turkey while driving a car at a ridiculous speed, but would they be allowed to gun that car off a seven-hundred-foot cliff? If so, they would play out Callie's vision of liberation, sacrificing themselves as an ultimate act of resistance to the place they'd been dealt in society. Staged grandly enough, they'd fulfill Ridley Scott's concept of a passage into legend. But there was no getting around it—they would also be killing themselves. The scene would test all known limitations on what was acceptable for women on-screen.

Laddie spoke with Ridley again two days before. Had anyone come up with another ending, if only to give them options in the editing room? The answer was no. The two men agreed: they would let the movie be what it was supposed to be. If preview audiences rebelled, that might be another story.

On Monday, August 27, the production descended on Dead Horse Point, thirty-five miles outside Moab over rocky, barely graded roads, following an exhausting three-day shoot of a car chase. It had taken more than sixty complex setups to film some dozen police cars, a cavalry in hot pursuit of the Thunderbird, barreling through an old ghost town, home of the old prospector and his attack chicken. A stunt driver handled some of Susan's chores, although she sometimes had to steer for close-ups. Geena often hung on for dear life as the passenger.

Time was running alarmingly short. When tire tracks from rehearsal marred a field where a wedge of police cruisers would pursue the T-bird, the frantic crew ran out with brooms. "Stop," Ridley ordered. He directed a helicopter to make low passes over the ground. The downdraft from the rotors smoothed out the dust to render it tidy enough, if the audience didn't look too closely.

The chase reached a smashing conclusion thanks to a police pileup at a railroad crossing. Then the car broke free for a momentary respite as it headed toward the lip of the canyon. The scene offered the last chance for the heroines to get away, Ridley thought, but if so, the legend would die instead of them. This had to be the final leg of the journey.

Thelma and Louise pushed forward on that bit of road, grim, determined, with bursts of near-hysterical laughter, the car skirting the edge of the cliff. In ravishing close-ups, their movie-star faces looked burnished against the red-rock landscape, their eyes shaded by their battered hats. Geena's strong jaw jutted out in profile under the bill of her trucker cap. They shared a cigarette.

I guess I went a little crazy, huh? Geena said.

You've always been a little crazy. This is just the first chance you've had to express yourself.

Watching on video, Ridley thought them handsome, for want of a better word, handsome and strong. To him they seemed sexy, businesslike, heroic. *Women would like to be like this, secretly,* he thought. It killed him that time pressures didn't allow him to film that scene in the car, that he had to watch it later, once removed: "I wanted to be there with them."

CAST, CREW, STUNT DRIVERS, HELICOPTERS and multiple versions of the Thunderbird converged at the final location with only four days and a daunting thirty quick scenes to go. "It was sick how much we still had to shoot," says Steve Danton, the first assistant director. That included shots of swarming police, a confrontation over tactics between the law enforcement adversaries Harvey Keitel and Stephen Tobolowsky, the last words of Thelma and Louise and, of course, the plummeting car. No one could be sure whether it would fly into the canyon as the production hoped, or tumble ignominiously to finish the epic with a dud. Only three vehicles were available to launch, one for a test run and two for usable takes. This *had* to work, and fast—everyone was booked to fly out to other commitments by the end of the week. Ridley had already scheduled prep work for his next project. If filming on *Thelma & Louise* ran over through the weekend, it would carry the production more than $600,000 beyond the budget.

Dead Horse Point, with its glorious vistas of mountains, canyon walls and the Colorado River two thousand feet below, had once been used as a natural corral for wild mustangs, with a narrow neck of land serving as the only route in or out. The name stemmed from a legend about a herd that died there once, unable to find its way to food and water. The film unit set up on a plateau called Fossil Point, midway between Dead Horse and the river. It took five months for the production to secure all the permissions and permits to film on the parkland, including promises to roll camera only when rafting trips were halted on the river and to clean up the remains of the totaled cars. The crew arranged hundreds of bushy weeds to lend texture to the sandstone promontory.

Plans for shooting had to be airtight. The temperature topped a hundred all week, which meant that the helicopters that appeared in some shots and carried cameras for others couldn't take off without reducing their weight, carrying only enough fuel for ten-minute sorties. Everyone swallowed the red dust that gusted through the air. "It was physically taxing," says Stephen Tobolowsky, who stood out amid the tumult in his standard-issue wool suit. "It takes a really experienced general to command this sort of thing. I remember thinking, *Who better than Ridley to be at the helm? This is what he does.* Geena and Susan were focused and professional, too. Given the brutal conditions, Tobolowsky says, "Thank God the people in the lead on this movie weren't assholes." He allowed himself to break his affectless character just once. Concerned that he would have to reloop his dialogue later because of helicopter noise, and frustrated at Harvey for stepping on his lines again, Tobolowsky yanked Harvey up by the lapels to shout at him.

Ridley's greatest concern was how to marshal all the moving parts to lift the final scene into a realm of nobility. Since his talks with Meryl Streep, he'd considered saving Thelma at the last, letting her emerge from a cloud of dust after Louise went over the edge. But he decided they'd earned the right to die together, and the stars heartily agreed. Now they would have to deliver on a tall order, investing their final scene with enough heart to grant the characters their immortality. Ridley was also determined that the car should defy the laws of physics and take off on an upward trajectory, which would look more positive than a dead drop or a stomach-churning somersault. The crew had to manage it all without the benefit of special effects, which the production could not afford. That car had to fly for real.

The crew stripped everything of any weight, including the engine, out of the three Thunderbirds and built a ramp at the brink of the cliff to slingshot them off at an angle. The plan was to yank each one forward with a heavy cable. After looping through a pulley at the ramp, the cable would continue at a right angle to be hauled by a speeding sixteen-cylinder Jeep. If all went as planned, at the last moment the cable would release and the T-bird would soar.

The first afternoon at the point, the production prepped for two hours, then cranked up the mechanism and let it fly. The car barely cleared the cliff top, wobbled at a weird angle and tumbled like a rock. There was a thud a long moment later, then a soft collective groan.

Nothing for it but to try again the next day. "I didn't believe we were going to pull it off," Ridley says. At four o'clock, in perfect light, cameras in place, Thelma and Louise dummies in the front seat, the crew cranked up the whole Rube Goldberg contraption again. This time the car sailed away in a perfect state of uplift. One hubcap detached and trailed off behind. The crew never launched the third car.

THE LAST DAY OF PRODUCTION looked impossible, one of those "bloody huge quandaries" Ridley claimed to love. "We were going to have the plug pulled, and that was it," Ridley says. "I think we had forty setups, which was insane." First thing in the morning, he tried something he'd never done before. The son of the brigadier general gathered the entire unit, a sunbaked, disheveled gang, hardened by three months of down-and-dirty roadwork, in a circle around the car and insisted, "We are *going* to make this [deadline]. The light is going to go away, and we've got to be out of here by five—or else."

Among the shots to capture before the final scene of dialogue was one of the women grasping hands as the car careered toward the edge. Susan stepped aside for a stunt driver, but Ridley wanted Geena on board. "I'll operate, so if there's an accident, I'll die, too," he promised.

It's almost unheard-of for the stars' last scene in a movie to be the last one filmed, but Ridley wanted them at the height of their golden-hour beauty. He played chicken with the sun by scheduling their final moments, when they would make the decision to die, as the last of the light threatened to disappear. With only forty-five minutes left and a few rays scarcely peeking over the hills, they had time for only two takes. "This was it," Geena says. "There was no getting it another day."

It's hard to imagine a moment when the emotions of a story and the people tasked with telling it would so mirror and magnify each other. Geena and Susan were saying good-bye to their characters, to each other and to the experience of making this extraordinary movie. So was the entire crew. Even after many years, Ridley couldn't watch the footage without feeling a stab. "Everyone had become so close on this fabulous project, and now we would go our own ways," says Anne Ahrens. "Thelma and Louise had become real people to us. It was devastating that they would be gone."

The hair-and-makeup team fluttered over them nervously and then cleared out. Two cameras operated simultaneously, framing heroic close-ups that nearly burst the boundaries of the screen. With an army of police behind them and the canyon in front, the stars turned to each other, awash in russet light.

Let's keep goin', Geena said, hope, fear and epiphany written on her wide-open, childlike face.

What do you mean?

Geena cocked her chin toward the cliff. *Go.*

You sure? Susan dropped her shield and looked incandescent, as happy as she had ever been through the story. She reached across and kissed her friend on the mouth.

Yeah, said Geena. *Hit it.*

"We did two takes," Geena says. "And then the sun went *bip!*" It was over. Just like in the movies.

CHAPTER 26

KEEP ON FLYING

Ridley placed the raw footage in the hands of the British editor Thom Noble, an Academy Award winner for *Witness* who was known for his strength with character and dialogue, for placing the beats between the lines just so. Like Ridley, Noble was a foreigner who had fallen in love with the script of this extravagantly American and profoundly female story and was determined to keep it true.

He knew right away that what he'd been given was gold. "A perfect picture is rare," says Noble. "The two perfect pictures I've done are *Witness* and *Thelma & Louise*, because the material was fantastically good." All that wonderful dust, the unforeseen beauty of Bakersfield, the performances—"the performances were rock solid," Noble says. They fit together like a charm in the assembly, a first stab at putting all the scenes in order. Noble focused on hewing to the essential core of the story, which meant the first thing to go was much of the ad-libbing by the men. "Harvey was the most difficult to cut," says Noble. "He loves to improvise, and the improvisations were just crap. I had to keep cutting it back and back until Harvey became this wonderfully sympathetic guy. If I'd let him run, he would just be irritating."

In September 1990, Ridley picked up and moved to London with Noble and the composer Hans Zimmer to fine-tune the director's cut. Scenes of glorious desert sunshine tormented the director, editor and composer while they huddled in the perennially cold, damp Pinewood Studios. Ridley's mind wasn't on the picture much anymore. His head was into prepping his next epic, the story of Christopher Columbus— deciding whether to cast Michael Douglas or Gérard Depardieu in the lead—and filming a Perrier commercial on the side. "People make fun of me for making commercials," Ridley said to Noble, "but then I show them the Bentley." Noble laughed.

Ease, confidence and a sense of humor had been hallmarks of Thom Noble's career from the beginning. A native of London, the lanky editor broke into the movie business there by blithely asserting fluency in Swahili when it was required for a film-library job. No one would ever learn differently, he figured, and no one else would apply. He used similar guile when he made the leap from assistant editor to a prestigious editing job with the French director François Truffaut on *Farenheit 451*. Its producer had asked Noble to help find a woman editor (Truffaut preferred working with a woman) who spoke French. Noble sat on his hands but kept offering that he spoke French, which was true this time, until he got the assignment.

He established a reputation for a relaxed approach to finding the heart in the footage. Noble was also a charming raconteur, so people enjoyed his company, which was no small thing in the tight quarters of a cutting room. "It's a personality issue," he says. "You are going to be with these people day in and day out, so directors want to know, do you have a sense of humor, are we interested in the same things? Then it all flows."

Because Ridley had used two simultaneous cameras so often on the shoot, Noble could match up the performances with ease, free to use the best take and still stay in sync. Then it was a matter of picking up the pace by removing redundancies. He cut a couple of conversations between Geena and Susan, including one about a TV movie that starred Linda Blair in a women's prison. Callie had included it to show why the women wouldn't want to go to jail, but Noble felt the point was already apparent. Otherwise, most everything he removed had derived from improvisation rather than the original script. His objective wasn't to adhere to the screenplay per se, but when he selected the strongest, most entertaining material, that's how the edit progressed, a testament to the quality of the writing. A few off-the-cuff lines made the grade, including Brad Pitt's hitchhiker drawling, *I'm kinda stuck here like stink on stink.* But most of the acting flourishes that Noble kept were humorous physical bits that didn't stray far from the text: Geena sneaking bits of the candy bar, Brad Pitt taunting her husband with a little bump and grind, and just about everything Chris McDonald ventured as Darryl. "That guy was perfect," Noble says.

Decisions got tougher with the sex scene between Geena and Brad. "When we first assembled it, you think, *Okay, yes!*" Noble says. "It was an extraordinary moment for Geena. It took her out of her body almost." Noble, Ridley and Zimmer agreed it was a sex scene for the ages— incendiary, gritty, graphic yet grounded, with many appreciative views of Brad's well-toned behind. But it did run on. "There was more about this than any other part of the picture," Noble points out, and Zimmer agrees. "If we had left that scene the way it was, it would not have stayed on the story," Zimmer says. "It would have become *too* big a moment."

With a scene that showy, that certain to galvanize an audience, it took discipline to back away, but Ridley and Noble decided to trim the encounter to its essence and move along.

As for the problematic ending, Mimi Polk believed the final shot should be a freeze-frame of the still-buoyant T-bird after it took off from the cliff. Noble found the idea too similar to the end of *Butch Cassidy and the Sundance Kid*, when the heroes froze just before a hail of bullets struck. He fell in love with another scenario he pieced together. After the Thunderbird took the plunge and went completely vertical, he cut in footage of Harvey running to the edge, where he picked up the Polaroid the women had taken at the start of the journey, now blown from the car. As he studied it, the camera moved in, and the image faded and faded until it reverted to the blank exposure before a photo begins to appear. Thelma and Louise were... gone. "It was absolutely beautiful," Noble says, and the magical alteration of the image seemed appropriate for a passage of the characters into myth. But Mimi remained convinced that the additional shot detracted from the women's final, shining farewell. After Noble left the picture, she swapped out the actively falling car for the freeze-frame. Its finality left no place to splice in the Polaroid shot. She substituted some happy flashbacks from the past instead.

Noble, Ridley and Zimmer often repaired to the composer's London studio that fall to listen to music and consider its placement in the film. Long before he began to shoot, Ridley had sat down with Kathy Nelson, the MCA Records executive in charge of putting together movie soundtracks, to ask her to choose songs that would help tell the story. Kathy adopted some suggestions Callie had made, including "Drawn to the Fire" by her friend Pam Tillis, and Ridley had listened to the picks to establish the mood during location scouting and throughout the summer of filming. The eighteen tracks they ultimately selected would support and reinforce most of the action in the final cut, because, while Hans Zimmer would compose an original score, the main theme wouldn't be heard until the fourth reel of the movie.

Nelson, the niece of Ozzie Nelson and cousin of teen heartthrob Ricky, had worked her way up from a receptionist job thanks to a good ear and a knack for letting the excesses of the music business roll off her back. Petite, with short, spikey red hair, she had kept her cool working with some of the eighties' most flamboyant movie personalities, including Don Simpson, Jerry Bruckheimer and Ridley's brother Tony. Regarding all the offscreen shenanigans she witnessed, Nelson says, "I knew everything, and I didn't say a word. I'm not a crybaby." Although sometimes she did allow herself a good ladies' room cry, she played the voice of reason among her colleagues. "We're not curing cancer, guys," she often reminded them. "It's entertainment."

She found Ridley considerably politer than her usual collaborators, his vocabulary less prone to obscenity, but he presented a particular challenge with this film—finding music with punch on a bantamweight budget. Nelson rooted out artists obscure enough for the production to afford while seeking a country-rock or R & B sound that wasn't sentimental or corny. If songs showcased a woman singer, so much the better. When Nelson had plopped down on the floor of Ridley's LA office and hit the button of her cassette player to play him her first selection, it fit the bill perfectly: "House of Hope," featuring the flinty, barking voice of Toni Childs over a driving roots-funk background. The song was little known, raucous with a rough edge. Later in London, Ridley placed it over the early scene when Thelma and Louise drove away from home. The uncompromising, almost dark lyrics—"Is there a house of hope for me and you?"—signaled that this would be no saccharine girlfriend getaway.

The only original song, Glenn Frey's "Part of Me, Part of You," was a fairly ordinary ballad that would play over the closing credits, but that was standard for soundtracks. Others were more distinctive. Ridley chose the thoughtful, melancholy "The Ballad of Lucy Jordan" by Marianne Faithfull for the scene of the women driving through Monument Valley at night. After fiddling with other options, Nelson was relieved to snare an obscure track that perked up the montage of the women packing before their journey began. It was "Wild Night" by Van Morrison, about dressing up for a night out, in a full-throated, barrelhouse version by Martha Reeves of Martha and the Vandellas. "I Can See Clearly Now" by Johnny Nash underscored the humor of the Rastafarian biker delivering a blast of marijuana smoke to the state trooper.

Most of the music functioned just as planned, but Noble, Ridley and Zimmer hit a wall with what to play over the final leap into the canyon. In the script, Callie had specified B. B. King's "Better Not Look Down." Its lyrics reinforced the attitude she had in mind, urging listeners to "put the hammer down" and "keep on flying." The infectious arrangement—a blend of R & B and boogie, with B. B. King's signature chicken-scratch riffs underpinning the rhythm section—further fed the sense of optimism. The filmmakers assumed the song would work until they cut it into the film. Then the lyrics sounded too literal, the tone too jaunty in the face of the somber grace of the images. "The movie dictates," Zimmer says. "It's like a living organism, and it will reject things. It rejected that song." They switched it to one of the driving scenes instead.

Nothing else played any better over the perpetually troublesome ending. That left only one option. Hans Zimmer had to stop procrastinating and come up with a score that would carry the film, suit the final scene and balance the many conflicting imperatives of mood, expectation and commercial viability to send the audience out on a calibrated, rueful high.

ZIMMER RELISHED THE OPPORTUNITY to bring an outsider's perspective to the Americana he saw in the images. Born in Germany, he'd moved as a teenager to London, where he played synthesizer and keyboards in a number of rock bands, most notably with the Buggles, whose one-hit wonder, "Video Killed the Radio Star," launched the first MTV broadcast. By 1990, Zimmer had attracted notice as a film composer who mixed electronic sounds with traditional instruments. Ridley had worked with

Zimmer on *Black Rain* and knew that his skill with a synthesizer would do wonders for the flimsy budget—no need to hire a soundstage and orchestra. They aspired to a score that expressed a touch of sadness, a romantic yearning that nevertheless steered clear of Women's Picture clichés.

"I knew Ridley wasn't going to make a movie about 'the weaker sex,'" says the voluble Zimmer, who liked to share memories with Ridley of their formidable mums. "We respected women. We saw them the way Callie saw them. I didn't want to do girly music. Get rid of the strings, the feminine chords, get rid of the patronizing quality of all that stuff. Nothing could be cute."

What he did want to emulate was what he considered the great music of the United States—the blues. Ever since his youth, Zimmer had appreciated how English rockers like the Rolling Stones and Eric Clapton absorbed the lessons of Muddy Waters and Lightnin' Hopkins and delivered them back to America. "There's a rawness of emotion in that music, and it doesn't just belong to males," Zimmer says. "Think of Etta James and Big Mama Thornton, people like that. It belongs to America. The blues are real. It is the opposite of Las Vegas or Disneyland. America has this really honest music and doesn't quite know what to do with it." Zimmer knew the blues offered the perfect accompaniment to Ridley Scott's unpretty but beautiful images, a wailing expression of the characters' working-class disappointments.

But after letting those images wash over him, Zimmer couldn't rise to the task. When Ridley stopped by on a Saturday, Zimmer played him a theme he knew was weak. "I'll be back on Monday" was all Ridley had to say.

Zimmer pulled out some recordings from a favorite group of his teenage years, the British hybrid blues-rock Climax Blues Band, with the nimble-fingered slide guitarist Pete Haycock. The composer used to slow the records down to learn the soulful solos. He offered Haycock a train ticket from Birmingham to London to play a new theme that soared. "He gave wings to the music," Zimmer says. They performed the new score for Ridley late into the night, marveling "at a bunch of foreigners coming across a script written by an American girl, and going, 'We completely get your story.'"

Looking back, Zimmer thinks it was a bit much that he mixed in the voices of a chorus at the very ending, as the car went over the edge. "I was a lot younger then, so a lot less thoughtful," he says. But otherwise the theme hit the right note of longing, and it had a sense of open spaces about it. Ridley decided at the last minute to feature a fleeting riff of Haycock's guitar over a single additional shot at the beginning of the film, a black-and-white image of a road running toward a distant mountain, foreshadowing an end.

CHAPTER 27

MASSACRE AT THE MULTIPLEX

The custom at Pathé was for everybody to celebrate over dinner after a test screening. Following a nail-biting trial run to see whether ordinary Americans took to a film at a typical suburban multiplex in Illinois, the director, editor and all the key studio executives repaired to a favorite restaurant, Gene & Georgetti, a clubby, old-school steakhouse in downtown Chicago. There they feasted on rib eye, sautéed spinach and the restaurant's famous garbage salad, served family style with lots of red wine. No amount of alcohol could numb the pain at the first reaction to *Thelma & Louise*.

Creative people tend to disparage the test-screening process, tend to claim it dumbs down the daring aspects of their work, but it's still a punch in the gut if the audience doesn't approve. When only 20 percent of the crowd rated *Thelma & Louise* a must-see on the night of October 29, 1990, the dinner plunged into gloom. What had gone wrong? How could it be fixed? And how was the studio supposed to market this potential turkey in the face of an audience accustomed to something else entirely?

At a loss at how to pitch this movie all along, the guys in the Pathé marketing department had looked to a string of test screenings for answers. Everyone at the studio loved the finished film, but a female-buddy dramedy? It fell outside all the usual marketing templates. In the female realm, Pathé had found success with some Goldie Hawn movies, says Greg Foster, who set up test screenings for the studio, and had learned that those movies "worked, sort of, but we had to pretend they were bimbo-ish." There was no use pretending *Thelma & Louise* checked that box. The marketing department knew how to address the kind of crowd that enjoyed action set pieces like car chases and truck explosions, but no one could predict how it would react to the more subversive elements.

"Most movies were made for somebody like Geena Davis's husband, Darryl," says Foster. "That was our audience. So if that kind of guy didn't like the movie, whatever it was, we were screwed." With an offering that made fun of core moviegoers, the studio had to hope there was some other audience out there, too, one the marketers didn't fully understand or know how to reach.

Fingers had been tightly crossed that one would show up at the Cineplex Odeon Cinema in Arlington Heights, Illinois, one of Laddie's favorite locales for gauging the mood of Middle America. Ridley Scott, Thom Noble, Laddie, Becky Pollack and a slew of Pathé executives scanned the mostly white crowd of 330 that trooped in on that Monday night. Fewer than expected had accepted the offer of free tickets to a movie mystifyingly billed as a cross between *Bonnie and Clyde* and *Beverly Hills Cop,* but starring women. Younger men were conspicuously underrepresented.

To say that the filmmakers were anxious was an understatement. They understood the danger they were courting with a film that had scared off everyone who bought into business as usual in Hollywood. Even Sam Cohn, Susan Sarandon's agent, had flown in from New York to see how his client fared in this singular turn. Becky Pollack paced in the lobby, as nervous as anyone had ever seen her. She'd believed in the power of the movie when she saw it complete in London, but she couldn't be sure how it would play. "The trick was not to undermine what worked, but also be able to listen to the audience if that's what we needed to do," she says. "The danger was, if you had a bad audience, how lethal would that be?"

The crowd responded politely from the start, displaying enthusiasm for the humorous scenes. There was an audible gasp when Susan shot the rapist in the parking lot. Greg Foster, from his perch in a back row of the theater, thought people weren't opposed to what she'd done, but they weren't quite sure what they were in for yet. Clearly, the movie was something they hadn't seen before. Soon women, especially, were laughing again. *Okay, they're with the movie,* Foster thought. *It's new, it's different, they haven't been conditioned for this, but everything is good.* They applauded like crazy when the truck blew up. He relaxed. *We're gonna make it,* he thought. *They're with the characters.* Then the police cornered those characters, Susan hit the gas and Thelma and Louise flew into the Grand Canyon. "And you could hear it—'Oh my God,' intermingled with clapping and gasping and . . . and . . . it was just *emotion*," says Foster. "The audience was invested in those characters. It had been provoked. It was responding to this movie. I'm sure some responded incredibly well, and some responded not so well, but the movie was the impetus to release strong feelings, whatever those feelings were."

The car drifted downward in slow motion, Harvey ran to the lip of the cliff and then a shot appeared that Ridley had added for the test screening, a brief shot, a few seconds at most, of the two women still driving the car, a metaphorical survival, or so he intended.

Cries of "No!" and "Awe, *man!*" broke out. Laddie, the ever-silent Laddie, jumped out of his seat on the aisle near the back. "What the fuck is that?" he thundered. There was a smattering of tepid applause, and the crowd filed out, along with all the air in the room.

"It changed," says Foster. "Whatever was there, in an instant, not for everyone but for a lot of people, it was gone."

Foster couldn't read the comment cards on the way to the dinner for fear of getting carsick. When he arrived, the wine was already flowing, but the mood was funereal. Everyone was tearing the movie apart even before he could flip through the data and frame his dismal report. The overall "excellent" score of 11 percent was well below the usual average at screenings of 25 percent. Even the most enthusiastic group, older females, trailed the norm at 17 percent. While a few, mostly women, wrote in the comments section that they found the movie an original spin on a "tired" genre, someone else wrote in the comments section: "What kind of movie *is* this?"

Foster whispered to Laddie, then addressed the rest of the group with the grisly results—very high poor-to-fair ratings, so-so positive numbers and virtually nothing in the middle. "It was polarizing," he told the group. "They either hated it or loved it." Mostly hated it.

Sam Cohn, known for an eccentric habit of chewing on paper napkins under stress, went through a stack of them as everyone started suggesting scenes to cut, with the truck driver as the first sacrifice. Suddenly it seemed to Ridley as if the character had driven in from another movie. "It was a disaster, just terrible," says Laddie. "We said, 'Let's cut this, let's cut that.' We had the picture down to about twenty minutes." Ridley, fast losing faith in his creation, was one of the leaders in suggesting a massacre. "He was crestfallen," Laddie says.

Becky Pollack tried to keep everyone calm. "The preview process is a critical stage when you can become afraid and try to hedge your bets," she says later. "You wind up destroying what you originally envisioned the movie would be." She told the group, "We have to be careful to hang on to why we made this movie in the first place." With so many people insisting on alterations, she was afraid the film would wind up like a sweater with six-foot arms and no torso.

Foster, who had conducted focus groups with some viewers who remained behind, was convinced that the ending was the problem, and it had affected their opinion of the entire film. What the cards couldn't answer was *what* the audience hated about the end—the women going off the cliff, as everyone had feared all along, or the little snippet that followed of the women still alive. Foster sensed during the screening that there was support for the original downer, but he thought the crowd didn't get the metaphorical intention of that additional shot, that it thought the women had somehow landed safely and driven on. Some of the comments slammed the ending for its "Hollywood spin."

Everyone dreaded a second preview scheduled for the very next night in San Francisco. It was too late to cancel, and too late for a wholesale redo of the film. Laddie, who'd objected to the added shot the moment he saw it, suggested a simple experiment—cutting off those frames and leaving everything else unchanged. Sam Cohn seconded the plan, which was enough to sway the others. It was with heavy doubts and even heavier hangovers that the group flew out from Chicago the next morning, not before Laddie made note of the theater they'd used the night before, to make sure he never tested a picture there again.

THOM NOBLE ARRIVED A COUPLE HOURS early at the projection room of the Syufy Century Plaza in South San Francisco, where he snipped off the offending final moments with the care of a mohel at a circumcision. Then the whole group hunkered down again in the back, walleyed with apprehension, noting that the crowd that night seemed a bit more blue-collar, maybe more open-minded and liberal.

Once the movie started, something different was in the wind. "When people in the audience realized where the movie was going, they cheered, they laughed, they were incredibly vocal," Becky recalls. "They became *unglued* with the trucker. You could feel the movement in the audience. People absolutely over-the-top loved it."

Everybody from Ridley to Laddie to the projectionist was elated. "People applauded, they cheered, they were invested," says Foster. "The movie played through the roof." The excellent rating hit 30 percent, the overall positive rating 82 percent, a whopping 27 points over the norm. The must-see rating more than doubled to 49 percent. Nearly three-quarters of the viewers scored Geena's and Susan's performances as excellent.

Asked about their favorite scenes, the viewers singled out mostly humorous ones: the truck explosion; Thelma robbing the convenience store; the women locking the trooper in his truck; the Rastafarian rescuing him; J.D. telling Darryl, "I like your wife"; Darryl stepping on his pizza. On the other hand, Louise shooting Harlan also made the list.

As for the off-the-cliff ending, Greg Foster's report noted that the responses were outstanding, with comments calling the finish "uncompromising," "un-Hollywood" and "appropriate." Although a few found it too sad, others wrote in, "They did the right thing!"

"From that moment on, we knew we had something," Foster says. "It was everything we hoped it would be. The relief was unbelievable."

The movie rolled through the rest of the test screenings with the same kind of charged reaction. Perhaps the Illinois audience had been a bit conservative, Foster says, but the only other explanation for such a dramatic change in the outcome was the little snip that Thom Noble made in San Francisco. "Everything about that movie had been authentic," Foster says, "except for that little glimpse at the end."

Apparently, the audience would be satisfied only with what Callie had envisaged all along, with what had deterred every studio but Pathé all along. The movie itself seemed to demand the dark fate she had chosen for her heroines, to reject any attempts to jolly it up, just as it rejected the cheery B. B. King song during the edit. Standing fast in the face of that first preview had saved the film. "The center of it held true to what it was always intended to be," says Becky. "This was a special movie because it stayed where it started. It was never compromised."

FOR ALL THE BENEFIT OF aligning with a studio that stood by the filmmakers' intentions, they soon felt the drag of its debt-hobbled status. Giancarlo Parretti, the Italian tycoon who controlled the company, turned off the spigot of money at the most crucial moment for the picture. For a while the processing lab held the negative hostage when Pathé couldn't pay the bill, and no one knew whether funds would be forthcoming for advertising. Laddie was personally embarrassed when he had to postpone the release date, which had been set for March of 1991, a nice little spring-break niche for a smaller film that needed time to build an audience. The soundtrack album was doomed—shipped to stores and returned unsold before anyone could see the movie. "It was a nightmare," Laddie says. "The check is in the mail, that kind of thing. If I was Ridley, I would have sued somebody, if I could ever find Parretti to sue him." Laddie wrote some personal checks to try to keep the operation afloat.

Thelma & Louise was by far the best movie in the Pathé pipeline, the best shot at saving the company, so the executives moved forward with planning, unsure how long the film might linger on the shelf. The previews had not only raised the possibility that Ridley and Pathé might have a hit on their hands, but the testing also helped settle the long-running argument over how to market the film. Pathé would go all in on the female-buddy dramedy angle, whatever that was, with posters prominently featuring the two women. Comment cards from the screenings demonstrated enthusiasm for this previously nonexistent genre and for the sight of women in nontraditional roles. Fewer men had turned up to see the film, but those who did, especially the younger ones, liked it nearly as much as the women did. "This was a word-of-mouth movie," says Foster. "The only way that people were ever going to understand it was to see it." More sneak previews were scheduled to get people talking, and they did. "What a great, radical movie," said one viewer's comment in Houston. "It was like the sixties and nineties combined." Someone in Atlanta declared, "I wish Davis had shot her husband instead."

Ridley made a few more nips and tucks to the film in response to pacing concerns from the screenings. He pared back Susan Sarandon and Michael Madsen's improvised encounter in the motel, along with some of the line dancing at the Silver Bullet bar and the sex scene between Geena Davis and Brad Pitt, which, even trimmed from its previous spectacle, some still found too graphic, gratuitous or even offensive. With Pathé unable to pay Thom Noble, the editor was off the picture, so Mimi Polk oversaw the final cut of the ending. That's when she substituted the freeze-frame of the car in the air, followed by the montage of happier times.

The one audience member whose reaction seemed to intimidate Ridley most was Callie Khouri. She wasn't invited to screenings—filmmakers weren't required to invite writers back in the day—but Diane escorted Callie to one in New Jersey, sharing a New York hotel room to save money. Diane and Sam Cohn claimed seats on either side of the outspoken writer to provide a buffer from Ridley in case she didn't like what she saw.

Seeing Susan and Geena inhabit the roles, hearing the audience laugh, feeling the surge of emotion in the theater, Diane whispered to Callie, "Ridley really *did* get this movie." When Susan played the shooting scene perfectly and the audience clapped and even cheered, the agent and client exchanged a bug-eyed look. "They *cheered*," Diane remembers. "That never happens, never!" She stifled a laugh at the Rastafarian scene, knowing that it still annoyed Callie. Afterward, Diane leaned toward her client and said, "It doesn't matter what anyone thinks now. This movie *plays*."

For Callie, the experience was overwhelming. Tears streaked her face.

She had been afraid of feeling embarrassed at how much the movie re-vealed about her, or upset at how much Ridley had altered her vision, but she knew that as a *movie* it worked, with or without the Rastafarian and the vulgar trucker. This being a Ridley Scott version of her work, the ma-jestic imagery and sheer commotion of it astonished her as much as ev-eryone else. The director, she thought, had made the most commercial possible version of the script, and for that she was glad. "It wouldn't have been the movie that I would have made," she says, "just because I never would have had those resources—a helicopter and all those stunts." More than that the writer couldn't put into words.

She felt shell-shocked at the screening, she told her friend Amanda Temple later. "It was so much more heightened than we'd ever pictured it, it took some adjusting," Amanda says. "After a while it was possible to chill and go, okay, the movie is still there, the heart is still there."

Diane planned to scoot with Callie out of the theater to avoid any dicey back-and-forth with Ridley, but they did speak for a moment before she left, and he saw the tears. "I've been waiting a long time to see this movie," Callie said to him, which was just enigmatic enough to leave him wondering.

For more than two decades afterward, Ridley remained unsure of her real feelings. "When she saw the cut, she was very emotional," he says when he recalls that night in New Jersey. "I could never work out whether she was disappointed or whether she loved it." ICM offered to pay Callie's way to the Cannes Film Festival, where *Thelma & Louise* would cap the closing night on May 20, 1991, but it was up to Ridley and Mimi to decide whether to include the writer. Mimi reported back to Diane that Callie wasn't invited.

THE STUDIO HAD BIGGER WORRIES. After the joint entity of MGM and Pathé flirted with bankruptcy in April, the chief creditor, Crédit Lyonnais Bank Nederland, put Laddie in charge instead of Parretti and started to parcel out just enough cash to keep things afloat. The release of *Thelma & Louise* was back on, even though there wasn't even enough money at one point to pay for the poster. Ultimately, the company was able to spring for some all-important television ads, but the publicity budget was still 60 percent less than it should have been.

More critical was the release date, which had now been pushed to Memorial Day weekend, the kickoff to the 1991 summer season. Over the next few weeks, Callie Khouri's everyday women would face a murderer's row of fully loaded action and comedy summer blockbusters, including *Terminator 2* with Arnold Schwarzenegger, *Robin Hood: Prince of Thieves* with Kevin Costner and *City Slickers* with Billy Crystal. On opening day alone, Pathé's little genre buster would run smack into its longtime nemesis, the $75 million *Backdraft*, not to mention *Hudson Hawk*, a $70 million Bruce Willis spectacular. *Thelma & Louise* was showing up in the middle of a circular firing squad armed with nothing but a slingshot budget, a couple of midlevel female stars and one exploding truck.

CHAPTER 28

THE SNOWBALL EFFECT

Thelma & Louise landed in theaters like a depth charge on May 24, 1991. The shock waves rippled out for weeks, months, even years. Watching the movie proved a profoundly riveting and personal experience for the American audience. It entertained, but also electrified.

And divided. The film touched off a catharsis for viewers who identified with the heroines, and a roil of controversy for everyone else. It was possible to encounter couples who actually split up after arguing over whether Louise should have fired that pistol. Feminists debated into the wee hours whether driving off a cliff was a defiant statement of self-determination or a capitulation to the view that the only way for women to win was to lose.

Critics showered the picture with raves, at long last proving that somebody out there would celebrate the idea of women carrying a film that delivered some shocking twists. *Variety* led off with praise for the movie's "reckless exhilaration," saying, "Even those who don't rally to [the] pic's fed-up feminist outcry will take to its comedy, momentum and dazzling visuals." Janet Maslin of the *New York Times* wrote, "It reimagines the buddy film with such freshness and vigor that the genre seems positively new." She heaped accolades onto every element—Callie's "sparkling screenplay," Ridley's "previously untapped talent" for "exuberant comedy" and the performances of the stars, "whose flawless teamwork makes the story gripping and believable from start to finish." *Newsweek* labeled the film "a genuine pop myth" that "goes way beyond the Butch [and] Sundance syndrome in warmth and complexity."

In *New York* magazine, David Denby got the movie's intentions completely. "I don't know why it took so long, but this is the first feminist buddy-buddy movie, or at least the first one that matters," he declared. "The relationship between the two women is the central thing, volatile and always funny, and a triumph for both actresses. The movie itself, coming at a time when Hollywood has just about abandoned such essentials as experience and character, is like a gasp of pure oxygen in a vacuum-pumped room."

In the *Washington Post*, Rita Kempley delivered a backhanded slap to other women's pictures, insisting that "this is one chick movie that isn't about to whine, bitch or backseat drive."

Even the critics who demurred found much to praise. Roger Ebert of the *Chicago Sun-Times* withheld half a star only because he thought the cheery flashbacks followed the final freeze-frame with unseemly haste, as if the filmmakers were afraid of their true intentions.

Standing apart from the general love bomb, a minority of reviews found some measured fault with the feminist implications. Terrence Rafferty of the *New Yorker* praised Geena's and Susan's performances to the sky, along with Ridley's masterly vision. "The movie has the look of a mirage, a jeweled shimmer that keeps us half hypnotized," Rafferty wrote. But he also called it "a crazily overstuffed Hollywood entertainment" that used "dopey ideas" to drive an implausible plot. "The feminist justification that the script provides for the heroines' behavior doesn't make their actions any less preposterous," he said.

AND THEN CAME THE BACKLASH. After critics had their say, cultural commentators went to town, scandalized and outraged by visions of man-bashing killer women on the loose. On opening day, the *Los Angeles Times* critic Kenneth Turan had praised the movie for being "provocative, poignant and heartbreakingly funny," and managing "to seamlessly blend political concerns with mainstream entertainment." But a week later, the paper ran lacerating side-by-side he-said, she-said critiques, both of them negative. Such a film was inevitable, allowed the writer Peter Rainer, because it plugged into the anger and frustration of women working in Hollywood and beyond. But he called it a "sisterhood bash-a-thon," "as vague and negligent as any macho shoot 'em up." Next to his take-down, Sheila Benson, the paper's critic at large, wrote, "Please don't call it feminism." "As I understand it," she pleaded, "feminism has to do with responsibility, equality, sensitivity, understanding—not revenge, retribution or sadistic behavior."

Indignation kicked into overdrive with headlines like the *Toronto Star*'s "THELMA & LOUISE" RAISES QUESTION WHY RECENT MOVIES CAN ONLY SHOW WOMEN MAKING PROGRESS BY MAKING MEN LOOK LIKE IDIOTS. "Horrible role models," tsk-tsked Liz Smith, the gossip columnist in *Newsday*, lamenting that no one in the movie "worries about AIDS, using condoms or encountering a serial killer"—concerns that certainly never made an appearance in Tom Cruise or Sylvester Stallone movies, either. Her counterpart at the *New York Daily News*, Richard Johnson, joined the conga line of scorn by suggesting the movie be banned from theaters. "It justifies armed robbery, manslaughter and chronic drunken driving as exercises in consciousness-raising," he fulminated.

The fury reached a crescendo with TOXIC FEMINISM ON THE BIG

SCREEN in *U.S. News & World Report*, where columnist John Leo labeled *Thelma & Louise* "about as morally and intellectually screwed up as a Hollywood movie can get." It reflected the influence of "the most alienated radical feminists," he declaimed, naming the writer Andrea Dworkin, who was best known for asserting that pornography reinforced male authority over women. "With this repeated paean to transformative violence," Leo continued, "found in none of the male-buddy movies, we have left Dworkin and entered a Mussolini speech. Here we have an explicit fascist theme, wedded to the bleakest form of feminism and buried (shallowly) in a genuinely funny buddy movie. Whew! No wonder the critics worked so hard to avoid confronting what is really going on in this film."

"PEOPLE ARE OUT OF THEIR MINDS!" Callie exclaimed in a phone call with Geena. "What movie did they see?"

The actress who'd appeared in *Earth Girls Are Easy* had learned long ago that part of her job was to absorb bad reviews, but this was a level of blowback she couldn't comprehend. "I was just hoping they wouldn't hate that we killed ourselves," Geena said. She and Callie couldn't figure out what set off the rest of the vitriol.

Male bashing, for instance. "After all the shit women put up with going to see any movie?" Callie fumed. "Seriously? If you have a problem with the men in this movie, you're identifying with the wrong characters." It was a line she and Geena would both use in interviews as the controversy continued to rage.

As for poor role models and excessive violence, since when were movie characters required to be nonviolent role models? Given how frequently male action-movie killing machines mowed down anyone who got in their way, it was hard to see why anyone would be overwrought by the actions of Thelma and Louise. Those male stars didn't show remorse,

Callie and Geena knew, the way Louise did after she shot someone, wrongly, as she was the first to admit.

"My God, now the *women* have guns," Geena said in mock horror. "It's the hallmark of society being ruined!"

"Go watch a Marty Scorsese movie and get back to me," Callie snapped.

In *Thelma & Louise*, Geena Davis noted, "Three people died, and two of them were Thelma and Louise."

In contrast, movies starring men were locked in a well-armed combat for maximum body counts. Sylvester Stallone's Rambo had personally shot, strangled, incinerated, eviscerated or otherwise dispatched 137 people in three movies during the previous decade, and that was counting only clearly visible deaths, not innocent victims who no doubt cowered inside blown-up vehicles or buildings. The number of fatalities in 1990's *Die Hard 2* reached 264, including 230 in a plane crash. *Total Recall* the same year treated viewers to 74 souls meeting their ends in explicit detail, 47 of them at the hands of Arnold Schwarzenegger himself. There was no national outcry about female bashing when he blasted Sharon Stone in the head while delivering the line *Consider that a divorce*.

WITHIN A FEW WEEKS, the ruckus over *Thelma & Louise* amplified to such an extent that the only people who could tune it out must have been holed up in monasteries under mandatory vows of silence. The controversy went about as viral as possible in an era that preceded social media and the ubiquitous cable news pundits of easy outrage. Given the double standard at play, something more than repugnance toward violence or the depiction of buffoonish male characters was obviously at work.

Soon multiple forms of media put forward their theories in a more measured and thoughtful backlash to the backlash. *Newsweek* wondered where the outraged moralists had been when Eddie Murphy slept with a woman and then shot her in *Harlem Nights*, or when Brian De Palma made just about every movie he'd ever made. And as for proper role mod-els, "Well, compared with the prostitute played by Julia Roberts in last year's megahit *Pretty Woman*, who wins big by selling herself to Richard Gere," *Newsweek* said, "yes, Thelma and Louise are fabulous role models. They're modeling power, not lingerie."

New York Times critic Maslin stepped back into the fray with an anal-ysis of why this movie left a segment of the public so unhinged: "It's some-thing as simple as it is powerful," she concluded, "the fact that the men in this story don't really matter."

Soon the filmmakers themselves were called upon to defend their work. Callie had to point out that she'd written a work of fiction, not an instructional video. And she told one reporter that the movie wasn't hos-tile toward men—"it's hostile toward idiots." Ridley found himself an unlikely feminist spokesperson. "I don't believe the male species is that black," he told a British newspaper, "but because the film can only run two hours, there's a limit on what I can show." The guys were meant as archetypes, he insisted, and as for the violence, "if you want something that's violent, go and see *Terminator*."

Even Brad Pitt, in an interview about becoming a star in the making, was asked to weigh in. "I don't think the movie has some big moral the way a lot of people are making out, and I don't find it controversial," he told an interviewer. He saw the story as a slap in the face "for us guys," he said, "and we deserve it."

Susan Sarandon said to anyone who would listen, "I think people were freaked out and they didn't even know why. We had completely under-estimated how strongly the territory was held by white heterosexual men."

In retrospect, it was hard to believe that none of the filmmakers saw the controversy coming. But whether or not they intended it, a well-made movie about a couple of imperfect women breaking free from cultural norms resonated because it tapped into the powerful social forces that Hollywood had succeeded in ignoring but had been building to a flashpoint everywhere else. Feminism in the eighties had been rattling both personal relationships and public discourse with fresh debates over equality in the workplace, the recognition of date rape and other forms of sexual violence as crimes and the private power dynamics between men and women in their daily lives.

Some of this was already playing out in real time in the public arena. Just two weeks before *Thelma & Louise* opened, William Kennedy Smith, the nephew of Senator Edward Kennedy, had been arrested for raping a woman who said he had attacked her on a beach after she drove him home from a nightclub. The heavily publicized case kept so-called date rape in the news until he was acquitted in December. The Supreme Court ruled the day before the movie's release that it was constitutional to ban federally financed family-planning clinics from providing information on abortion. Later that fall, Clarence Thomas would win a contentious confirmation to the Supreme Court after Anita Hill testified that he had sexually harassed her at work. It was the first time that the widespread problem of hostile environments on the job had received such pointed public scrutiny.

It turned out that the moral ambiguity of *Thelma & Louise* made it the perfect vehicle at the perfect time to amplify the hopes and fears of people still deciding where they stood on these debates. It stirred up already messy emotions among women who might have wanted greater autonomy but were afraid of paying a price, or men who were adjusting to changing expectations but resented being portrayed as bullies or jerks, perhaps even fearing what angry females might be capable of. The movie wrapped these clashing concerns into an artistic little package that exploded on delivery. *Thelma & Louise* was a certified cultural force.

If there was one moment that stamped that certification, it was when

Time magazine put Geena Davis and Susan Sarandon on the cover of the June 24 edition with the headline WHY *THELMA & LOUISE* STRIKES A NERVE.

Although Pathé's marketing resources might have been scarce, it did have a secret weapon in Kathie Berlin, the publicist behind that coup who worked out of New York for both Pathé and MGM. Berlin had a brazen, get-the-job-done attitude sharpened over years of pulling the levers in a brash business. She got her first publicity post back in the late sixties by claiming to know the bookers at all the television shows and magazines. Assuming that the people interviewing her didn't know the real names any more than she did, Berlin tossed out those of friends and college roommates as the gatekeepers for Dick Cavett or *The Tonight Show*. Once she'd spent a few years guiding stars and directors around to appearances, she'd seen it all and knew enough not to succumb to the tawdrier expectations of publicity girls. When she had to fetch Charlton Heston from his hotel room for an interview with Mike Wallace, Heston emerged from the shower naked and tossed her a towel. "Wipe my back," he said. She kept her distance and got even by neglecting to tell him he'd left his fly open until they'd walked several blocks to the studio. Berlin knew that the men in the business weren't particularly interested in films with women, so she always invited secretaries to screenings, figuring that they would nudge their bosses if the movie was good.

When Berlin saw everyone debating in the lobby after an early screening of *Thelma & Louise*, she may have been the first person associated with the movie to fully recognize its potential as a media phenomenon. She asked prominent feminists like Gloria Steinem and Marlo Thomas to host advance screenings to jump-start the conversation. But most of all, Berlin wanted that cover of *Time*, the ultimate mark of cultural significance back then. She spoke to the magazine's intellectually oriented film critic, Richard Schickel, and his wife, Carol Rubinstein, who worked with him on documentaries about film. The movie was important, Berlin told them, a breakthrough far exceeding previous women's films in its potential for controversy. After she lured him to a screening where women in the audience yelled and clapped, he was sold.

Schickel's five-page package in *Time* declared that *Thelma & Louise* had earned a place "in the honorable line of movies whose makers, without knowing quite what they were doing, sank a drill into what appeared to be familiar American soil and found that they had somehow tapped into a wild-rushing subterranean stream of inchoate outrage and deranged violence." The occasion for all the ensuing big-think moralizing was actually a modest and very enjoyable little movie, said the article, which went on to present the thinking of all the best academics and feminist theoreticians. Another full page was dedicated to a by-now de rigueur dissent from his colleague Margaret Carlson, IS THIS WHAT FEMINISM IS ALL ABOUT? The movie didn't improve on the male-buddy genre, she wrote, exaggerating that it had "almost as many chase scenes per reel as *Smokey and the Bandit*."

Schickel let Geena Davis get in some of the last words. "Why," she asked, "because it stars women, is this suddenly a feminist treatise, given the burden of representing all women?" But that argument had long since been left behind in a billowing cloud of dust. People saw what they wanted to see. By now, no thinking person could afford to be without an opinion on *Thelma & Louise*.

THE MOVIE HELD ITS OWN on opening weekend, raking in just over $6 million, and placing fourth after *Backdraft*, a holdover Bill Murray comedy called *What About Bob?* and just behind *Hudson Hawk*, the Bruce Willis movie with four times the *Thelma & Louise* production budget. For Pathé, the news was not great, but not bad, either. Then word of mouth kicked in. The following Friday and Saturday, the take defied all movie-business gravity, actually rising 1 percent over the previous week, while *Hudson Hawk* dropped 43 percent. Greg Morrison, Pathé's head of marketing, called it "a bloody miracle."

As others flew high and then dropped by the wayside, *Thelma & Louise* kept soaring all summer. Branded a sleeper hit, naturally, it didn't catch on in the Midwest or South but added new theaters elsewhere as late as the fall, eventually earning $45 million at the box office, more than double what the opening-weekend tally would have predicted. Had Pathé been able to marshal the proper marketing resources, Laddie thought, the proceeds would have reached $20 million more. The producer-showman Harvey Weinstein once boasted to Geena that he easily would have parlayed all the publicity past the $100 million mark.

But still, *Thelma & Louise* wasn't finished. Somehow, with the passage of time, its popularity only continued to grow. The video seized the number one slot on the *Billboard* rental chart for the first eight weeks of its release, and then banked the kind of sales to the home market that were more in line with a movie that had earned twice as much in theaters. "The longevity of it was just insane," says Greg Foster of the Pathé marketing department. Or as Louise notably said to Detective Slocumb in the screenplay, *I think we got some kind of snowball effect goin' on here.*

Because, while the commentators dithered, a sizable segment of the public simply went wild for this movie. Or as an article in the *Philadelphia Inquirer* put it, "A lot of women love *Thelma & Louise*. It doesn't matter who they are or where they stand on feminism, white males or housework. They just love it." The reporter interviewed everyone from the provost at Bryn Mawr College to a lap dancer at the Fantasy Showbar, who said approvingly of the characters, "They didn't back down."

Oh sure, men loved it, too, especially in cities like New York and Los Angeles, where reviews held sway, but most men didn't take it to heart and feel it right down to their bones the way women did. *Newsweek* spotted a couple of women on a Chicago street responding to an obscene cat-call from a truck driver. They pointed imaginary pistols at his head as one yelled, "Thelma and Louise hit Chicago!" The Pennsylvania branch of the National Organization for Women did brisk business in T-shirts proclaiming GRADUATE OF THE THELMA & LOUISE FINISHING SCHOOL. Ticket sales at theaters spiked during the week because that's when women skipped out on the men in their lives and went to see the movie with their friends.

Suddenly wherever Geena or Susan went, they encountered people who would grab hold and lean in to expound on how they had experienced the movie, how it had changed their lives, how they and their friends had acted out their own versions of the trip. "I'd be like, hmm... which part?" Geena says. "Was it killing a guy? Was it picking up hitchhikers and having sex with them? Was it holding up a liquor store?"

But for the women who loved Thelma and Louise, it was not so much about what those characters did as about what they *were*: women living their lives in the movies for all to see. Women who looked like real women and talked like real women, women who had more on their minds than "Good luck, honey!" Women who could laugh in the open at the too-recognizable foibles of men—and of women, too. Who understood what it meant to become that third thing when they were together, making choices—even bad ones—on their own. The identification that viewers felt with those two desperadoes went well beyond the mere mechanics of the plot. Thelma and Louise, the audience could tell, had sprung fully formed from a real woman's perspective. However far-out their actions, the public recognized in them the texture and point of view of real women's lives.

Like its heroines, *Thelma & Louise* had taken flight from the limitations of expectation and entered the realm of myth. The choice was a deliberate one. And women in the audience felt like they finally got laid properly.

CHAPTER 29

WHO KILLED
THELMA AND LOUISE?

Gonzo ending and all, *Thelma & Louise* promised a bright new be-ginning for women in Hollywood. "Ten years from now, it will be seen as a turning point," pledged the *Boston Phoenix* in May of 1991. Fi-nally, the movie business would recognize that women liked to see them-selves on film, that women's stories were worth telling and that women had the talent to tell them. Finally, women would be heard. Yet surveying the Hollywood landscape in the years since, one might well ask: Who killed Thelma and Louise?

The extraordinary impact of the film did transform the destinies of the people who made it, some more than others. Armed with such a ster-ling credit, each participant made decisions going forward based on the options available at the time, but for the most part, the women made fewer, softer, smaller projects, often for television, often centered on feel-ings and moms. The men got slotted back into bigger-budget, big-screen vehicles, frequently featuring invincible, cold-eyed actors in bloody conflict. After creating such a genre-busting triumph, it was surprising—or perhaps not—how many of the *Thelma & Louise* collaborators steered back into the gender lanes they'd driven in before.

"It was like getting shot out of a cannon," Callie says about her sudden notoriety, which called upon her to perform as a public spokesperson for any form of feminine discontent. She won a seat on the board of the Writers Guild of America to champion the right of writers to visit the sets of their movies. And she was in such demand as the hot new talent in town that she was the flavor of the month for at least a year.

An awkward chance encounter between Steven Spielberg and James L. Brooks demonstrated how far Callie had come since she recruited the dancers for Whitesnake videos. On a weekend morning by the picnic tables at the Brentwood Country Mart, each director-producer boasted that he was about to land a deal with the industry's most in-demand screenwriter. Eventually they realized they were both talking about Callie Khouri. Brooks won the bidding war for her services, but the collaboration didn't bear fruit. Preoccupied and uninspired, Callie says, "I just never found with Jim anything where we saw eye to eye."

In truth, Callie had to admit that she was 75 to 85 percent happy with the outcome of *Thelma & Louise*—the truck driver still galled—but the commotion distracted her from other projects. Besides, *Thelma & Louise* had sprung so directly from her heart, it wasn't easy to hit on another story that lit the same fire. She got by for a while as a writer for hire doctoring other people's scripts until she was invited to write *Something to Talk About*, a 1995 southern family drama that wound up starring Julia Roberts. Once again Callie lobbied to direct, but Lasse Hallström got the nod instead. "It didn't turn out the way I would have liked," says Callie. "It got rocky after that." She didn't want to believe that there was an inherent bias against women directors, but she says, "When you spend ten years seeing guys who'd made music videos get to direct features, you start to think, *This is undeniable*."

Finally, she got a shot to write and direct an adaptation of the novel *Divine Secrets of the Ya-Ya Sisterhood*, a mother-daughter bonding saga with twelve roles for actresses, from Maggie Smith to Sandra Bullock. The film earned a solid $70 million at the box office in 2002. Callie's second and final feature-directing credit was the less successful *Mad Money*, a 2008 heist movie that brought in $21 million. After that, she circled back to the comfortable milieu of country music to create the television show *Nashville*, which premiered on ABC in 2012, running for four years until it moved to the cable channel CMT.

RIDLEY SCOTT'S REPUTATION got the boost he'd been hoping for once he demonstrated his versatility with *Thelma & Louise*. But instead of making other modest, character-driven features, he followed up with more characteristic epic and action choices like his Columbus movie, *1492: Conquest of Paradise*, a notorious flop with a take of only $7 million, and *White Squall*, a guys' sailing adventure that fared almost as poorly. He returned to a women's story in 1997 with the earnest *G.I. Jane*, starring Demi Moore as a fictional first woman in a navy training program, a moderate success. But his career from then on usually revolved around brawny men in togas, battle gear and spacesuits—action pictures, but still informed by his serious intentions.

Ridley secured his place at the pinnacle of the industry with *Gladiator*, a high-toned revival of the old swords-and-sandals formula. It was an indisputable blockbuster that won the 2001 Best Picture Oscar, although Ridley lost out in the Best Director category. Asked later if he thought he was *admired* but not really *liked* in Hollywood, he replied, "Possibly. But that puts me on the cutting edge, which is useful." His dogged work ethic propelled him through some dozen films and counting after that, from *Black Hawk Down* through *The Martian*, well into his seventies.

Mimi Polk set up her own production shop after helping Ridley pro-

duce *1492* and *White Squall*, but her solo projects didn't achieve prominence. Other women continued to hold management positions at Ridley's
company, and it produced the female-centric television smash *The Good
Wife*, but he was wise enough to decline when MGM proposed a series
derived from *Thelma & Louise*. "Guess what, they made it," the proposal
had announced. It suggested that the characters survived their fall to become itinerant do-gooders atoning for their crimes. The pitch made sure
to note that Thelma, who never seemed to wear enough clothes, would
remain a lovable "Venus Fly Trap for men." Fans of the movie were spared.

HOLLYWOOD HANDICAPPERS AGREED that playing the now-iconic
Thelma would launch the career of Geena Davis into the storied ranks of
leading ladies. "Geena Davis will go the distance in the nineties," pro-
claimed Mark Canton, the chairman of Columbia Pictures, in *Vanity
Fair*. "She represents—along with Michelle Pfeiffer and maybe Julia Roberts, and one or two others—the top of the list." Geena's own production
company, Genial Pictures, buckled down to develop projects built around
her star power. *Bigmalion* would be a takeoff on the Shavian classic, and
the company raised most of the money for Geena to play the British avia-
tor and author Beryl Markham in *West with the Night*. Neither made it to
fruition. The director Penny Marshall offered Geena her best post-Thelma
role in *A League of Their Own*, an ensemble piece about women baseball
players that scored one of the biggest hits of 1992. But her luck turned
when her new husband, the director Renny Harlin, thought she could
step into the lucrative action sector by carrying an expensive swashbuck-
ling pirate picture, *Cutthroat Island*. When it failed in 1995, as did their
collaboration in *The Long Kiss Goodnight* a year later, offers for Geena
Davis to headline a picture slowed to a trickle... and then they stopped.

Why did the business quit backing her? No one doubted Geena's talent, her beauty, her winning charisma. "Unfortunately, it was because

she was getting older," says David Eidenberg, who had left his position as Geena's agent but remained a close friend. "There aren't enough ongoing movies with parts for women. You can pick your end date—it's forty or forty-two or forty-five. It's horrible when it happens."

Geena tried two short-lived television shows, first a sitcom and then a drama called *Commander in Chief* that allowed her to play the president. "I guess I thought my career would just go on the way it had," she told a magazine. "But once I turned forty, I really did feel like I'd ceased to exist in Hollywood... it was noticeable and unmistakable. And painful." Even years later, her eyes still register bewilderment when she talks about it.

As if she needed more examples, playing the part of the adoptive mother to an animated mouse in the 1999 kids' movie *Stuart Little* drove home to Geena Davis the disparity in male and female parts. She saw an assistant director setting up young extras to compete in a race with remote-control boats. He picked out a little boy and positioned him with a remote by the side of a pond and then chose a girl to stand behind him and watch. One by one, all the boys got positioned down the line to operate the boats, and all the girls stood dutifully behind them. "Um," Geena said in her ingratiating way, "what do you think about giving half the remotes to the girls?" The assistant director looked dumbstruck and replied, "Why didn't I think of that?"

Susan Sarandon held fast to her strategy of ignoring the imperatives of stardom. She steered clear of participating in pictures with blockbuster budgets, cartoonish violence or anything that called for preening in front of a green screen until animators layered on special effects. It's impossible to imagine Susan Sarandon battling aliens in a stretchy bodysuit, although it might be amusing to try.

By choosing roles based on the quality of the material rather than conventional Hollywood notions of status, by trying not to fly too close to the sun, Susan dodged the career flameout that consumed the careers of most actresses her age. She worked steadily in the ensuing decades, not necessarily as the lead, but in smaller films of merit and a few more prominent ones as well. In the three years following *Thelma & Louise,* she earned two more Oscar nominations—for a lawyer defending a young boy in *The Client* and a mother searching for a cure for her son's rare disease in *Lorenzo's Oil.* She finally won the big prize in 1995 by playing Sister Helen Prejean in *Dead Man Walking,* a meditation on the death penalty.

When Geena appeared with Susan for the twenty-fifth anniversary of *Thelma & Louise* at the Cannes Film Festival, she remained as outspoken as ever. "I don't think the studios have had an epiphany about women in film, because after *Thelma & Louise,* it didn't happen," Susan told reporters. "And that movie made a lot of fucking money."

HARVEY KEITEL WON THE CHANCE to stretch as another sensitive man in Jane Campion's *The Piano.* Afterward, he kept busy in a variety of films, but once he inhabited one of the ultraviolent criminals in Quentin Tarantino's *Reservoir Dogs,* most of the opportunities fell into the violent, scary-guy column. The same with Michael Madsen. He toned down the menace as a normal dad in *Free Willy* two years after *Thelma & Louise,* but the genres depicting mobsters and psycho killers were where the work—and the money—was. His talent for gruff intimidation earned Michael a whopping two-hundred-plus credits. "I played some nice people," he says wistfully. "But never again did I get a romantic lead like Jimmy."

ON OPENING WEEKEND, Christopher McDonald drove a convertible down a Los Angeles street when two women pulled up next to him. "Oh my God, it's that guy from *Thelma & Louise*!" one of them squealed. The other shrieked, "Shoot him!" Fortunately, they laughed instead.

And so did the audience. The first time he saw the movie, his fear of going over the top vanished when the crowd started to roar. "I was thrilled to be a part of this thing," he says. "It was huge." But the next offer, to his chagrin, was "for the exact same kind of jerk-off guy." His performance as Darryl was widely admired in the close-knit acting community, but after playing the butt of the women's jokes, the options were narrower than might be expected for such a versatile actor who disappeared into his roles. Still, he worked constantly in a wide variety of parts, most prominently as the comic villain Shooter McGavin in the Adam Sandler movie *Happy Gilmore*.

AFTER ALL THE ACCLAIM FOR *Thelma & Louise*, Stephen Tobolowsky still didn't understand why the movie mattered so much to women. "I ask them what are their favorite movies of all time, and they say *Thelma & Louise*," he says. "Because it gave them role models, they say. *They're murderers! They've been raped!* Where are the role models? It's a great movie and a brave movie, but it is a twisted film. I think people just ironed it out in their brains to make it not be so different."

His irritating nebbish routine guaranteed him steady employment in vehicles like *Groundhog Day* and *Memento*. Stephen assumed that he'd been directed by women in some of them, but when he scrolled through his computer to check, it turned out that while he'd answered to a few women in television, he'd never worked with one on some hundred feature films. "It's shocking," he says. "I have to say, I'm relieved when I see a woman directing a television show, because I know she had to be good to get the job."

AFTER HIS NINE DAYS OF shooting wrapped on *Thelma & Louise*, Brad Pitt wrangled some day work as an extra until word of his performance leaked out. Otherwise, what can be said that hasn't already been said about his career? That he's starred in films that have earned $7 billion worldwide? Or that his production projects have topped $2 billion? Suffice it to say, it's been a while since he's had to audition. As for George Clooney and his unfortunate reading for *Thelma & Louise*, word has it that he managed to find other work.

SOME MEMBERS OF THE CREW died young: the art director Norris Spencer, the cinematographer Adrian Biddle and the costume designer Elizabeth McBride. Others cycled through the usual assortment of hits and misses, *Thelma & Louise* a source of particular pride that delivered their longest-running residual checks. Anne Ahrens gradually shifted more toward television. Kathy Nelson oversaw needle drops that pushed the limits of soundtracks on films like *Pulp Fiction*, *High Fidelity* and the Bourne movies, winding up as president of film music at Universal Pictures. Hans Zimmer became a regular fixture at award shows, having composed the scores for a long list of blockbusters, including Ridley's *Gladiator*.

Following the *Thelma & Louise* release, where Amanda Temple received "special thanks" in the end credits, she sometimes ran into people she had known in the grindhouse of music videos. "Can you believe that Callie?" they marveled. "Can you believe what she did?" Amanda would answer coolly, "Yes, asshole, of course I can."

People elsewhere in the industry met a range of fates. ICM pushed Diane Cairns out after a shake-up in 1996. She landed at Universal Pictures for a year before she left the business. Becky Pollack continued to nurture the writer Randall Wallace as he developed the battle epic *Braveheart* for Mel Gibson. But after Becky's children were born, the twenty-four-hour pace of the job and the craziness of dragging a baby around on planes overwhelmed her. She resigned to become a full-time mom. Greg

Foster, the young market researcher who collected comment cards at screenings for Pathé, eventually ascended to the post of CEO of IMAX Entertainment.

New moneymen fired Alan Ladd Jr. from the beleaguered MGM-Pathé entity in 1993. He was allowed to take one project along to produce on his own—*Braveheart,* which won Best Picture in 1996. In his modest office on Sunset, the poster for the movie hangs along with the ones for *Star Wars* and *Thelma & Louise.*

CHAPTER 30

A FILM OF THEIR OWN

It looked as if women filmmakers might finally be stepping into the spot-light the year *Thelma & Louise* lit up theaters. In 1991, Kathryn Bigelow found her way onto the commercial radar by directing the surfing-crime-caper mashup, *Point Break,* as did Barbra Streisand with *The Prince of Tides,* and Randa Haines with *The Doctor.* Martha Coolidge finally broke out of the teen-comedy ghetto to make the independent drama *Rambling Rose,* and Jodie Foster directed her first film, the mother-son story *Little Man Tate.*

A few female protagonists demonstrated real clout at the box office, too: Linda Hamilton in *Terminator 2,* Jodie Foster in *The Silence of the Lambs* and Julia Roberts in *Sleeping with the Enemy.* And Callie Khouri wasn't the only woman screenwriter to make it rain for studios. Nancy Meyers cowrote *Father of the Bride,* while Fannie Flagg created *Fried Green Tomatoes.* The screenwriter for the year's number two movie, *Beauty and the Beast,* was Linda Woolverton, who had started out in kids' television cartoons back when their male and female writers were segregated into "squishies" and "toasters"—squishies meaning cute stories for girls and toasters being boys' stories equipped with hardware like robots, ray guns and other means of destruction.

But in the end, the achievements of these women didn't signal much of a shift in the big picture. "The media narrative was that everything had changed," says Geena. "After *Thelma & Louise* came out, everyone said, 'Now we will see a flood of female-buddy movies, female road pictures, female action movies.' But nothing changed. And after *A League of Their Own*, because it was a huge hit, the press was saying, 'Well *now*, beyond a shadow of a *doubt*, there will be all these movies about women—women's sports movies!' And then nothing changed... again. It happens over and over, every two or three years."

The overall numbers don't lie. They barely budge. Of the top-fifty movies at the box office in 1991, four were directed by women. Twenty-five years later, in 2016, there were none directed by a woman alone—one woman codirected *Kung Fu Panda 3*. Four women without male partners wrote top-fifty movies in 1991, the same number as in 2016. Women as leading characters managed to move the needle a bit more. Nine movies featured them in 1991, and nine in 2016, but thirteen if you count films with men and women as equal costars.

Watching family movies with her kids, Geena Davis got so frustrated that she founded the Geena Davis Institute on Gender in Media, which lobbies the industry for more visibility for women. Ever prepared, Geena keeps studies and statistics at the ready to buttress her case that Hollywood, visible as it is, remains stuck in the dark ages when it comes to balance in the workplace. She points out that male characters have steadily outnumbered female by three to one in family films for fifty years. *Fifty years!* That women consistently make up less than a third of all speaking parts, and that in 2014 not a single woman over forty-five starred in a top-one-hundred movie—Meryl Streep played supporting roles that year. Even crowd scenes show only 17 percent women. The argument could be made that we see more *of* them—women and girls are more than three times as likely as men or boys to be shown in sexy attire, even in movies for kids. On the other hand, women working in occupations and positions of authority are rare in any kind of movie and almost unheard of in family fare.

What most impelled Geena Davis to turn activist was that she thought children rarely got to see women and girls portrayed in movies as persons of consequence and agency, limiting the choices viewers might envision for their own lives. Polls show that little girls want to be Kim Kardashian West when they grow up, Geena points out, "because that's who they see. They have to see more to aspire to more." The woman who played Thelma wields her visibility to bring attention to the issue, but the road can run uphill. Once, when she hosted a seminar on gender for Hollywood casting directors, one hundred people showed up. Ninety-nine of them were women.

Most often the blame for Hollywood's listless gender progress gets pinned on the economics of foreign markets. They are less likely to support women's films, the argument goes, and, more important, foreign entities that increasingly provide the financing for movies work off algorithms that favor male stars. (Brad Pitt—yes. Susan Sarandon—no.) It comes down to money, no surprise—projects for women can't raise it under the prevailing system.

Perversely, all this flies in the face of industry recognition that women and girls are actually driving the box office more than before. The once-reliable audience of teenage boys has turned toward other forms of entertainment on their many devices, while young women still like going to the movies with their friends. Some of the biggest blockbusters in the last couple of decades have starred women and girls and targeted that audience, earning billions along the way: *Titanic, Twilight, The Hunger Games, Maleficent, Bridesmaids, Frozen, Moana*. Their filmmakers want to tear their hair out when their triumphs get cited as anomalies or slapped with that perpetual label for breakout movies about women—sleeper hits.

"Now it's so expensive to make a movie," says Jane Fonda, who has witnessed the dance since she was a reigning star and producer back when no one talked about any of this. "There is so much riding on it, and the people who run the studios—their jobs are on the line. They don't take a risk with anything that's not familiar, and what's familiar looks like them. They are white men. So they are going with white men."

There is still no central break room or human resources department to address these matters in a sprawling entertainment complex full of freewheeling impresarios, but at least today the Tumblr blog *Shit People Say to Women Directors* lets the aggrieved share rants on the endless comments about their breasts or being asked which male subordinate is really in charge. Filmmakers finally are making noise about such affronts, and journalists are writing about them. That's why we know that the thirty-seven-year-old actress Maggie Gyllenhaal was told she was too old to play the love interest of a fifty-five-year-old actor, and that Catherine Hardwicke, after directing the $400 million–earning *Twilight*, still couldn't get her next project set up for a year and a half. When she did, her salary went down. It took the infamous Sony Pictures email hack to reveal that Jennifer Lawrence, who headlined the worldwide $3 billion *Hunger Games* franchise, still got paid less for *American Hustle* than Jeremy Renner, who filled a smaller part.

IN RETROSPECT, the new hard look at the odds against movies by and for women highlights just how remarkable it was when Callie Khouri, Ridley Scott, Geena Davis, Susan Sarandon, Becky Pollack, Alan Ladd Jr., Mimi Polk, Diane Cairns, Amanda Temple and the rest of the band pulled together to make *Thelma & Louise*. How rare it was that women got to drive the narrative, drive the car and crash the barricades. How much could have gone wrong that for once went right. Callie could have sold out and taken the sting out of her script. Ridley could have stuck with the smart money and directed a futuristic train movie instead. The stars could have pushed for more "likable" characters, and the studio could have swapped out the ending for something that wouldn't rattle the folks in the multiplex. But in a cynical business, the key players in the making of *Thelma & Louise* had just enough stars in their eyes to stay true to a story they loved.

"I think Callie didn't know what she was doing, and that's what saved her," says Hans Zimmer. The same could be said, to varying degrees, for everyone else who played a role.

Critical appreciation for *Thelma & Louise* only grew as the tenth, twentieth and twenty-fifth anniversaries passed. The *Atlantic* in 2011 called it "the last great film about women." A new selfie of Susan and Geena together went viral on Twitter in 2014, and members of show-business royalty that year named the film one of their one hundred favorites of all time in a survey by the *Hollywood Reporter*, which put the two stars on the cover. Treatises by academic and pop-culture pundits have parsed the text, subtext and ubertext, as well as a lot of other text that the filmmakers never intended.

At special screenings in theaters and intimate ones at home, the film still plays and plays. Mention of *Thelma & Louise* can still touch off a row at a dinner party, and parents debate when daughters should see it for the first time, because it still feels fresh, its critique of American culture and relations between the sexes still sharp and current. As viewers wait—and wait—for another movie like it, *Thelma & Louise* seems destined to stand alone, like Nora slamming the door in *A Doll's House* or Aretha belting out "R-E-S-P-E-C-T," a touchstone for all that follow, with a force, originality and impact that the timid will never duplicate.

EPILOGUE

There are many ways a Hollywood story can end, from a script in the waste bin of somebody's assistant to the stage of the Dorothy Chandler Pavilion. When a film becomes a classic, it simply rolls on. But as good a place as any to pause in the story of *Thelma & Louise* might be Oscar night of 1992.

It gave the filmmakers a chance to reunite, walking the red carpet as the underdogs of the occasion. Ridley, ever his mother's son, felt "bloody silly" in his starchy tux. Geena embraced the spectacle and cheerfully vamped her way onto the Worst Dressed lists in a white dress by a costume designer that made her look like a cancan dancer with the front of her skirt hitched up. Susan, serene and beaming in a simple black tunic, was eight months pregnant with her third child. Laddie had begged and scrounged for tickets so everyone on Pathé's young and giddy team could crash the party.

Callie made it an occasion. She brought her husband, her mother, her brother and her agent, and they all dressed beforehand in a snug Santa Monica house that Callie and David Warfield had bought with her earnings from *Thelma & Louise*. This was back before Oscar attendees served as walking billboards for designers, so Callie wore a vintage beaded navy blue dress that a friend had reconfigured with a different skirt. She and her little entourage didn't have far to travel in their limo, but traffic was so jammed that they barely made it to the hall in time to see the host, Billy Crystal, make an entrance trussed up as Hannibal Lecter in a spoof of the evening's favorite, the sinister thriller *The Silence of the Lambs*.

It was *Thelma & Louise* that most of Hollywood had been too spooked to make, but the community rewarded the movie with six nominations. Susan Sarandon and Geena Davis both were up for Best Actress, their performances so equally matched that they were sure to split the vote and hand the prize to Jodie Foster for *The Silence of the Lambs*, which also carried off the statue for Best Picture, as expected. Adrian Biddle was nominated for cinematography, as was Thom Noble for editing. Both lost to Oliver Stone's *JFK*. Even though *Thelma & Louise* didn't make the list of Best Picture nominees, Ridley Scott did for Best Director, but he was spared his heart-popping terror of public speaking when Jonathan Demme won for *Silence* instead. A scandal of the night was the snub of Barbra Streisand for directing *The Prince of Tides*, even though it was nominated for Best Picture. "Seven nominations on the shelf," Billy Crystal sang in his introductory medley. "Did this film direct itself?"

That left the former waitress and video producer from Paducah, Kentucky, to carry the banner for *Thelma & Louise*. Callie was thrilled, nervous and happy to share the moment with her family. But even as she settled in a forward section just behind Hollywood's biggest power brokers and stars, she didn't realize that if she did take home the Academy Award for Best Original Screenplay that night, this one would be historic. Beginner that she was, she would be the first woman working without a male partner to win in sixty years, filling the long-empty footsteps of the pioneering Frances Marion.

Callie had been borne along through some warm-up contests—the Golden Globes, the Writers Guild—oblivious to the possibility that she could prevail, and then she did. Each one took her so much by surprise that she hadn't prepared an acceptance speech and had to wing it onstage. This time, Callie had drafted some remarks, in case of an emergency. But still she couldn't wrap her head around the possibility that the stodgier Oscar voters would choose her over veterans like James Toback for *Bugsy*, Lawrence and Meg Kasdan for *Grand Canyon*, Richard LaGravenese for *The Fisher King* and another newcomer, John Singleton, who wrote the groundbreaking *Boyz n the Hood*.

Okay now, here's the big one, Callie told herself as Robert Duvall and Anjelica Huston took the stage to present her category. *This is where they give it to the real writer.*

When her name rang out, nobodies and literary renegades everywhere could delight in Callie's triumph. So could anyone who wanted to see movies that weren't easy to categorize, or hear what a woman might have to say. Even the fainthearted souls of the movie industry let out a shout that reverberated from the first parterre to the nosebleed seats of the auditorium. Laddie, Ridley, Geena, Susan, Becky Pollack, Greg Foster, Diane Cairns—all scattered throughout the hall—led the cheers, most of them thinking how fitting it was that the person who had started their whole wild ride would be the one to receive its crowning honor.

Callie bounded to the podium, steadied herself to face millions of people watching around the world, glanced down at her crumpled notes and then realized her rookie mistake: she had written the speech in pencil. It turned to invisible ink under the lights.

Her remarks were endearingly unpolished but from the heart. "Ridley, I couldn't thank you in forty-five years, let alone forty-five seconds," she began, "so I won't try now." Once again her words could be read as cryptic, but her smile in his direction was warm. She told Geena and Susan she loved them and thanked her family, assuring the crowd that her husband hadn't been the model for any of the characters. She got a laugh with the quip "In fact, my brother was—just kidding."

Then Callie Khouri withdrew to the wings, trailing all the unresolved issues her movie had raised. One line lingered in the afterglow. "For everybody that wanted to see a happy ending for *Thelma & Louise,*" Callie said, "this is it."

ACKNOWLEDGMENTS

Piecing together a story like this one depends on the extraordinary generosity and cooperation of a wide group of people. My heartfelt gratitude to everyone who shared memories and insights. I owe a special debt to those who rooted through attics and basements to find diaries, records and keepsakes, and especially to Geena Davis and Mimi Polk Gitlin, who helped me reach many of the key players.

Others who worked on *Thelma & Louise* and contributed their stories include (listed alphabetically): Anne Ahrens, Jason Beghe, Ira Belgrade, Jeff Berg, Scotty Bergstein, Kathie Berlin, Diane Cairns, Tim Carhart, Steve Danton, Tracy DeFreitas, Bonita DeHaven, David Eidenberg, Joe Everett, Greg Foster, Brett Goldstein, Ken Haber, Ross Harpold, Bonnie Blackburn Hart, Paul Hartman, Michael Hirabayashi, Lucinda Jenney, Harvey Keitel, Callie Khouri, Luca Kouimelis, Alan Ladd Jr., David Ladd, Steve La Porte, Michael Madsen, Christopher McDonald, Greg Morrison, Michael Neale, Kathy Nelson, Roland Neveu, Thom Noble, Dawna O'Brien, Rebecca Pollack Parker, Susan Sarandon, Ridley Scott, Scott Senechal, Diane Spencer, Marco St. John, Amanda Temple, Stephen Tobolowsky, Kenneth Turek, Kami Turrou, Susan Williams and Hans Zimmer.

Those who were invaluable in describing the ways of Hollywood: Candace Allen, Jeanine Basinger, Susan Braudy, Jeremiah Chechik, Martha Coolidge, Lauren Shuler Donner, Richard Donner, Lucy Fisher, Jane Fonda, Carrie Frazier, Neal Gabler, Bill Gerber, Randa Haines, Jonathan Kaplan, Sherry Lansing, Lee McCarthy, Midge Sanford, Richard Schickel, Risa Shapiro, Joan Micklin Silver, Melissa Silverstein, Penelope Spheeris, Barbra Streisand, Pam Tillis, Jim Vallely, David Warfield, Paula Weinstein and Linda Woolverton.

Those who extended themselves to help me navigate the industry: Amy Arce, Ruth Bennett, A. Scott Berg, Madeline Di Nonno, Bryan Gibbs, Debi Karolewski, John Scheinfeld, Andrea Gutierrez and Stu Zakim.

I am also indebted to everyone who assisted me with background research: The team at the Margaret Herrick Library of the Academy of Motion Picture Arts and Sciences, especially Faye Thompson, Stacey Behlmer and Jenny Romero; Edward Sykes Comstock and his coworkers at the Cinematic Arts Library at the University of Southern California; Megan Bradford and Maggie Adams at Metro-Goldwyn-Mayer; Jen Larson at the Grand Ole Opry; Walter Hickey at fivethirtyeight.com; Stephen Follows of Stephen Follows Film Data and Education; two able research assistants, David Campmeier and Andy Werle; James Madore at *Newsday*; Mary Hammond, Gayle Kaler and Bill Paxton of Paducah, Kentucky; and Ridley Scott's ace archivist, Andrea Gutíerrez.

Lindsay Maracotta and Peter Graves provided savvy advice and refuge in Los Angeles, and Glenn Kessler weighed in with an incisive reading of the manuscript. The nimble fingers of Craig Williams and Becky Schneider typed scores of hours of transcripts.

More thanks to the team at Penguin Press, especially my editor, Ann Godoff, for her unflappable demeanor and spot-on guidance, Casey Rasch for keeping it all on track and Brooke Parsons for her media savvy. My agent, the ever-sympathetic Joy Harris, supports me in ways big and small.

Lily Spitz inspired me with her foray into media work. And first, last and always, the man who shares my office and my life, my husband, Bob Spitz.

NOTES

I relied on personal interviews for most of this story, supplementing them with accounts published in newspapers, magazines and books, all cited below. Any scenes and conversations that I have reconstructed derive from interviews with one or more of the people who participated. Box-office grosses and rankings come from Box Office Mojo (boxofficemojo.com) and refer to domestic gross unless I specify worldwide gross in the text.

PROLOGUE

2 **of the top-fifty:** Rankings of top box-office movies from Box Office Mojo, cross-referenced with screenwriter credits from Internet Movie Database.

2 **that no such woman:** Records from the Academy of Motion Picture Arts and Sciences.

3 **Only seven of the top:** Rankings of top box-office movies from Box Office Mojo, cross-referenced with acting credits from Internet Movie Database.

3 *Holy mackerel*: Author interview with Diane Cairns, 1/27/15.

3 **"I don't get it":** Author interview with Ridley Scott, 4/2/15.

4 **"The phone is ringing":** Author interviews with Cairns, 1/26/15, 1/28/15 and 1/30/15, and Bonnie Blackburn Hart, 6/3/15.

4 **"You have a great movie":** Author interview with Cairns, 1/28/15.

5 **"If it was the male":** Ibid.

5 **"I think you should know":** Ibid.

6 **"the chop-chop people":** Author interview with Rebecca Pollack Parker, 11/19/14.

Named Rebecca Pollack at the time of the story, she had changed her name by the time of this interview.

6 "What can I say?": Author interviews with Cairns, 1/28/15, and Pollack Parker, 2/18/15.

7 "Everybody loves it here": Ibid.

7 *I have about a nanosecond*: Author interview with Cairns, 1/28/15.

7 "I'm really thrilled": Ibid.

CHAPTER 1: ONCE IN TEN LIFETIMES

9 was utterly at a loss: Callie Khouri's thoughts derive from author interviews with Khouri, 8/12/14, 2/5/15 and 5/12/15.

10 "There were directors": Author interview with Khouri, 8/12/14.

10 "I saw, in a flash": Sheila Weller, "The Ride of a Lifetime," *Vanity Fair*, February 10, 2012.

10 "We would get to see them": Author interview with Khouri, 8/12/14.

11 "Just to write it": Author interview with Diane Cairns, 1/26/15.

12 "A lot of really bad things": *The Dialogue: An Interview with Screenwriter Callie Khouri*, www.thedialogueseries.com, 2006. Interview conducted by Mike De Luca. Directed by Dave Modavan.

12 "All my family": Author interview with Khouri, 2/5/15.

12 "I don't think anyone": Ibid.

13 "and yet there are so many things": Ibid.

13 "Oh my God": Ibid.

13 "It's my brain": Ibid.

14 "For a good ten years": Ibid.

14 "You could have said": Ibid.

14 "College was a wasted": Ibid.

15 "You just feel hands on you": Ibid.

15 "Could somebody bring me a Coke": Author interview with Pam Tillis, 8/12/14.

15 "Hi, who are you": Conversation from joint author interview with Tillis and Khouri, 8/12/14.

15 "We had more power as a team": Weller, *Vanity Fair*.

15 "We were both ultimately ambitious": Author interview with Tillis, 8/12/14.

16 "I can play the radio": Callie Khouri, Thelma & Louise *and* Something to Talk About: *Screenplays* (New York: Grove Press, 1996), viii.

16 "*He* always goes on last": Author interview with Jim Vallely, 3/30/15.

16 "You had to have your sword": Author interview with Khouri, 5/12/15.

17 "Callie! Quit your dogheadedness": Weller, *Vanity Fair*.

17 "You guys write": Author interview with Vallely, 3/30/15.

17 "Debra Winger was having": Author interview with Khouri, 8/12/14.

18 "Those early years in her twenties": Author interview with Vallely, 3/30/15.

CHAPTER 2: PROSTITUTES AND EMPTY-HEADED BLONDES

20 "You don't *tell* a man": Susan Ware, *Notable American Women: A Biographical Dictionary* (Cambridge, MA: Belknap Press, 2005), 403.

20 "These women were the center": Author interview with Jeanine Basinger, 3/20/15.

21 "Women just disappeared": Ibid.

21 "When women do get parts": Judy Klemesrud, "Feminist Goal: Better Image at the Movies," *New York Times*, October 13, 1974.

22 Male speaking roles: Ibid.

22 top-ten list of box-office stars: Quigley Publishing Company, 2016 poll.

22 "A lot of talented people": Author interview with Martha Coolidge, 10/26/14.

22 "I was appalled": Author interview with Paula Weinstein, 2/4/14.

23 "I do really believe": Rachel Abramowitz, *Is That a Gun in Your Pocket?* (New York: Random House, 2000), 68.

24 "I had to eat shit": Chaim Potok, "The Barbra Streisand Nobody Knows," *Esquire*, October 1982.

24 "It was as if they had this very antiquated": Author interview with Barbra Streisand, 5/15/15.

25 "If you're going to do a story": Author interview with Jane Fonda, 2/16/15.

25 "A movie about Vietnam": Ibid.

25 *"Why does she have to"*: Ibid.

CHAPTER 3: "NEXT! *NEXT!*"

26 "I'm really sorry": Author interview with Callie Khouri, 8/12/14.

27 "I was literally running": Ibid.

28 "It was incredibly unsatisfying": Ibid.

28 "Everyone was snorting": Author interview with Amanda Temple, 4/13/15.

28 "For a hundred a day": Author interview with Khouri, 8/12/14.

28 "There were really talented": Ibid.

29 "Not big enough tits": Author interview with Temple, 4/13/15.

29 "We were both mortified": Ibid.

29 "You get what you settle for": Author interview with Khouri, 8/12/14.

29 "It was like having a warrior queen": Author interview with Temple, 4/13/15.

29 "She could play pool with the boys": Author interview with David Warfield, 2/14/15.

30 "It made me fall in love": Ibid.

30 "I got this": Author interview with Khouri, 8/12/14.

CHAPTER 4: WIELDING A GRACEFUL CLEAVER

33 "Look, feature films are expensive": Author interview with Joan Micklin Silver, 2/5/14.

34 "I cannot tell you": Author interview with Paula Weinstein, 12/4/14.

35 "never heard from her again": Jon Zelazny, "Gems of the 1980s: Susan Seidelman Remembers *Desperately Seeking Susan*," *The Hollywood Interview*, blogspot.com, November 22, 2009.

35 "You put two women on a poster": Author interview with Midge Sanford, 12/17/15.

36 "Don't ever send": Author interview with Martha Coolidge, 11/6/14.

36 "The girls were dressed up": Ibid.

36 "We want you to promise": Ibid.

36 "I kept trying to change": Ibid.

37 "Honey, either learn to type": Also includes anecdotes that follow. Author interview with Lauren Shuler Donner, 2/26/15.

38 "You've got three choices": This quote and the continuing anecdote: author interview with Penelope Spheeris, 1/31/15.

38 "I wanted to have hits": "An Interview with Amy Heckerling," *Charlie Rose*, November 13, 1996.

39 "It was an intersection": Manohla Dargis, "Action!!" *New York Times*, June 21, 2009.

39 "I had a good period": Author interview with Randa Haines, 11/19/14.

39 "Strange behavior": Ibid.

40 "Being part of a team": Daphne Merkin, "Can Anyone Make a Movie for Women?" *New York Times Magazine*, December 15, 2009.

40 "She was the funny, smart girl": Ibid.

40 "I'd go, 'I'm tough'": Author interview with Shuler Donner, 2/26/15.

40 "When the stakes are high": Kira Cochrane, "Why are there so few female film-makers?" *Guardian*, January 31, 2010.

40 "People want to hire a director": Author interview with Carrie Frazier, 1/23/15.

CHAPTER 5: TITS AND BULLETS

42 "I was the product": Callie Khouri, Thelma & Louise *and* Something to Talk About: *Screenplays* (New York: Grove Press, 1996), x.

43 "I had never done anything": Author interview with Callie Khouri, 8/12/14.

43 *Are you at work?* Callie Khouri, *Thelma and Louise*, First Draft, September 1988, Ridley Scott Collection, USC Cinematic Arts Library.

45 "They flew away": Khouri, Thelma & Louise *and* Something to Talk About, xiv.

45 "It required a certain": Author interview with Khouri, 8/12/14.

45 "Polyester was made for this man:" *Thelma and Louise*, First Draft.

46 "a pretty good bullshit meter": Author interview with Pam Tillis, 8/12/14.

46 *If I'd only had a gun: The Dialogue: An Interview with Screenwriter Callie Khouri*, www.thedialogueseries.com, 2006. Interview conducted by Mike De Luca. Directed by Dave Modavan.

47 "I was writing the movie": Author interview with Khouri, 8/12/14.

48 From 1985 to 1989: Walt Hickey, "The Dollar-and-Cents Case Against Hollywood's Exclusion of Women," fivethirtyeight.com, April 1, 2014, and Bechdeltest.com.

49 "the audience went crazy": Larry Rohter, "The Third Woman of 'Thelma and Louise,'" *New York Times*, June 5, 1991.

49 "bimbos, whores and nagging wives": Ibid.

49 "Right on, man": Author interview with Khouri, 8/12/14.

49 *The biggest trouble with her: Indiana Jones and the Temple of Doom*. Directed by Steven Spielberg, 1984.

49 "Oh my God!": Author interview with Amanda Temple, 4/13/15.

50 "It's *9 to 5*": Interview with Khouri, 5/12/15.

50 *If this script ever makes it*: Author interview with Khouri, 8/12/14.

CHAPTER 6: UNLIKABLE

51 "It drove me mad": Author interview with Amanda Temple, 4/13/15.

52 "There were these girls": Ibid.

52 "She was hilarious": Ibid.

52 "a little blonde behind a typewriter": Ibid.

53 "Her being from the South": Ibid.

53 "Can't they just shoot": Author interviews with Temple, 4/13/15, and Callie Khouri, 8/12/14, supplied all the quotes from the meetings.

54 "This whole issue": Author interview with Temple, 4/13/15.

54 "We were sure": Author interview with Khouri, 8/12/14.

55 "I was savvy enough": Author interview with Temple, 4/13/15.

55 "Mimi," she said as she: Ibid.

55 "I loved your script": Author interview with Khouri, 8/12/14.

55 "Is it all right": Author interview with Khouri, 8/12/14, and Mimi Polk Gitlin, 7/22/14. Named Mimi Polk at the time of this story, she later changed her name to Mimi Polk Gitlin.

56 "It had all gone so well": Author interview with Khouri, 8/12/14.

56 "Ridley loves it, too": Author interview with Polk Gitlin, 7/22/14.

56 "Callie," Amanda said: Author interview with Temple, 4/13/15.

56 "Oh my God, the Scott brothers": Ibid.

57 "Callie, it's now going": Ibid.

CHAPTER 7: THE EPIC IN RIDLEY SCOTT'S HEAD

58 "You think you're winning": Author interview with Ridley Scott, 4/2/15.

59 *Wow*, he thought: Ibid.

59 "I could see the film": Ibid.

59 *As long as a studio*: Ibid.

60 called him Mr. Macho: Author interview with Jeff Berg, 2/26/15.

60 "He hadn't been any kind": Author interview with Susan Sarandon, 10/30/15.

60 "The bottom line is": Author interview with Hans Zimmer, 11/17/14.

60 "My mom was four foot eleven": Author interview with Scott, 4/2/15.

61 "By the standards of mothers": Ibid.

61 "To me, it was a medal": Marlow Stern, "Ridley Scott on *The Martian*, his groundbreaking 1984 Apple commercial and *Prometheus 2*," *Daily Beast*, September 26, 2015.

61 "Dad was a very gentle": Stephen Galloway, Tony Scott's Unpublished Interview: "My Family Is Everything to Me," *Hollywood Reporter*, August 22, 2012.

61 "I hated school": Author interview with Scott, 4/2/15.

62 "It was just too silly": Kenneth Turan, "DGA Interviews: Man of Vision," Directors Guild of America website, Fall 2010.

62 "the world began for me": Lynn Barber, "Ridley Scott: Talking to actors was tricky—I had no idea where they were coming from," *Guardian*, January 6, 2002.

63 "You know how when you get hot": Author interview with Scott, 4/2/15.

64 "fit of total depression": Ibid.

64 "What do you think": Author interview with Alan Ladd Jr., 11/17/14.

64 "It was not for any reason": Ibid.

64 "Great idea": Author interview with Scott, 4/2/15.

64 "I never thought about it": Ibid.

64 "somebody who is physically powerful": Ibid.

65 "This giant walked in": Ibid.

65 "Who likes her": Ibid.

65 "I always felt": "Alien at 35: Sigourney Weaver Reflects on Ridley Scott's Masterpiece," *Hero Complex*, October 6, 2014.

66 "muddled yet mesmerizing": Janet Maslin, "Futuristic 'Blade Runner,'" *New York Times*, June 25, 1982.

66 "*Blade Runner* was a disaster": Author interview with Scott, 4/2/15.

66 "They would never take into account": Ibid.

67 "No—she had a great ass": Ibid.

CHAPTER 8: D-GIRLS

69 "Do you want to read it?": Author interview with Diane Cairns, 1/30/15.

69 "I had youthful ignorance": Ibid.

70 Only two women: Rankings of top box-office movies from Box Office Mojo, cross-referenced with data from Internet Movie Database.

70 "It was a no-brainer": Author interview with Cairns, 1/30/15.

70 "You're never going to be an agent": Ibid.

70 "I was this cupcake": Ibid., 1/26/15.

70 "I'll scar my face": Ibid.

71 "Everybody thinks": Ibid.

71 "It was a complete whiff": Ibid.

72 "You mean as a topless mermaid": Author interview with Mimi Polk Gitlin, 7/22/14.

72 "I found the best man for the job": Author interview with Ridley Scott, 4/2/15.

72 "One of the best ways": Author interview with Polk Gitlin, 7/22/14.

73 "Not many scripts": Ibid.

74 "Ridley is like a wizard": Author interview with Susan Sarandon, 11/17/15.

74 "He's a bull": Stephen Galloway, Tony Scott's Unpublished Interview: "My Family Is Everything to Me," *Hollywood Reporter*, August 22, 2012.

74 "It was very much not my thing": Author interview with Scott, 4/2/15.

74 "He was very good with women": Ibid.

CHAPTER 9: PLAYING A DIFFERENT GAME

76 "I was just mad for it": Geena Davis in *The Last Journey*, documentary by Charles de Lauzirika, Metro-Goldwyn-Mayer Studios video, 2002.

76 "These were two completely": Author interview with Geena Davis, 7/21/14.

77 "Has anything changed": Author interview with David Eidenberg, 12/15/15.

78 "I couldn't see spending my life": Holly Millea, "The Woman Who Fell to Earth," *Premiere*, July 1997.

78 "not rapeable enough": Author interview with Jonathan Kaplan, 3/23/15.

78 BEING DROP-DEAD GORGEOUS: Ben Steelman, *Philadelphia Inquirer*, February 23, 1989.

79 "It was lightning in a bottle": Author interview with Diane Cairns, 1/28/15.

80 "Two girls commit murder": Author interview with Mimi Polk Gitlin, 7/22/14.

80 "For guys—no problem": Ibid.

80 "It was brilliantly written": Author interview with William Gerber, 2/17/16.

80 "You've got to get in there": Author interview with Cairns, 1/28/15.

81 "*Thelma & Louise* was a magical": Author interview with Rebecca Pollack Parker, 2/18/15.

81 "Some days we had money": Ibid.
81 "The other studios": Author interview with Greg Foster, 3/24/15.
81 "the goal was to make": Author interview with Pollack Parker, 11/19/14.
82 "Some people are great movers": Ibid.
82 "He cut me loose": Ibid.
83 "The next thing I knew": Ibid.
83 "When I watched the women": Ibid.
83 "Laddie is very, very astute": Author interview with Ridley Scott, 4/2/15.
84 "I didn't think of them": Author interview with Alan Ladd Jr., 11/17/14.
84 "there were women's pictures": Ibid.
84 "It's one of the few scripts": Ibid.
85 "What can I say": Author interviews with Cairns, 1/28/15, and Pollack Parker, 2/18/15.

CHAPTER 10: THE RIGHT MAN FOR THE JOB

86 "I like it": Author interview with Ridley Scott, 4/2/15.
86 "But that's the whole point": Ibid.
87 "It was like a sponge": Author interview with Callie Khouri, 8/12/14.
87 "daily lectures": Ridley Scott, Audio Commentary, *Thelma & Louise*, DVD, MGM, 2003.
87 "Are you kidding me": Author interview with Scott, 4/2/15.
87 *A little humor, dear*: Ibid.
87 "Shit, if I walk by": Ibid.
87 "*That* happens to everybody": Author interview with Khouri, 5/12/15.
87 "I took it mainly": Scott, Audio Commentary.
88 "If you make this serious": Author interview with Scott, 4/2/15.
88 "If it's devoid of humor": Author interview with Khouri, 2/5/15.
88 "It should start out": Ibid.
88 "to see them become more": Ibid.
88 "You're supposed to be cutting": Author interview with Mimi Polk Gitlin, 7/22/14.
88 "Callie really cared about": Ibid.
88 "I liked him a lot": Author interview with Khouri, 2/5/15.
88 "I respected the fact": Author interview with Scott, 4/2/15.
89 "He didn't really get it": Ibid.
89 The newbie director admired: Author interview with Jeremiah Chechik, 3/12/15.
90 "Tony could deliver an odyssey": Author interview with Scott, 4/2/15.
90 "I was totally behind": Author interview with Jonathan Kaplan, 3/23/25.
90 "was irritated by it": Author interview with Scott, 4/2/15.
90 Harry Hook, a Brit: Pathé Memorandum, Rebecca Pollack to Alan Ladd Jr., November 9, 1989. Margaret Herrick Library, Academy of Motion Picture Arts and Sciences.
90 "I'm not sure it would have": Author interview with Scott, 4/2/15.
90 "She would have been": Ibid.
91 "Ridley is very fair-minded": Author interview with Sue Williams, 2/25/16.
91 "Because the focus": Philip Thomas, "Girls Just Wanna Have Fun…," *Empire*, August 1991.
91 "Why not me": Author interview with Khouri, 5/12/15.

91 "We're going to get the biggest": Ibid.

91 as to be "historic": Author interview with Richard Donner, 2/26/15.

91 "It was a tough time": Ibid.

92 "It would be up to the audience": Ibid.

92 proposed that his wife, **Lauren Shuler Donner**: Per author interviews with Donner and Scott. In an author interview with Shuler Donner, she does not recall.

92 "There was always a reason why": Author interview with Alan Ladd Jr., 11/17/14.

92 "If you're a producer": Ridley Scott in *The Last Journey*, documentary by Charles de Lauzirika, Metro-Goldwyn-Mayer Studios video, 2002.

CHAPTER 11: THE CURSE OF KATHERINE

94 "Every day, you'd hear different": Author interview with Jonathan Kaplan, 3/23/15.

94 "It was a free-for-all": Author interview with Diane Cairns, 1/28/15.

94 "You would have to be a complete idiot": Author interview with David Eidenberg, 12/15/15.

94 misspelled as "Gina": Various Pathé memos, including November 1, 1989, Margaret Herrick Library, Academy of Motion Picture Arts and Sciences.

94 But women captured only 29 percent: Richard Corliss and E. E. Bland, "Women on the Verge of Nervy Breakthrough," *Time*, February 18, 1991.

94 "If the trend continues": Ibid.

94 twenty-five years later: Mike McPhate, "Hollywood's Inclusion Problem Extends Far Beyond Oscars," *New York Times*, February 23, 2016.

95 With the ongoing rise of action movies: Quigley's Top-Ten Box Office Champions (1932 to Present), quigleypublishing.com.

95 "There were very few women": Author interview with Susan Sarandon, 10/21/14.

95 "By the time an actor was": Author interview with Carrie Frazier, 1/23/15.

95 "Oh, here comes Katherine again": Ibid.

96 "Katherine is sexy": Ibid.

96 They told her Cybill Shepherd: Various Pathé memos.

97 "it created a firestorm": Author interview with Rebecca Pollack Parker, 11/19//14.

97 "*He* didn't get you a hearing": Ibid.

97 "Cher could have been quite good": Author interview with Alan Ladd Jr., 11/17/14.

97 But Ridley didn't think: Author interview with Ridley Scott, 4/2/15.

97 "To sit in a meeting with Meryl Streep": Author interview with Pollack Parker, 2/18/15.

97 "I think that Meryl could": Author interview with Ladd, 11/17/14.

98 "Every actress will tell you": Bernard Weinraub, "Her Peculiar Career: Meryl Streep," *New York Times*, September 8, 1994.

98 "You just keep rejecting people": Author interview with Ladd, 11/17/14.

99 "all look and no heart": Roger Ebert, rogerebert.com, September 22, 1989.

99 "I needed to step off": Ridley Scott, Audio Commentary, *Thelma & Louise*, DVD, MGM, 2003.

99 "I'm busy and can't do it": Author interview with Scott, 5/4/15.

99 *She's bloody right:* Ibid.

CHAPTER 12: WHO'S PLAYING WHOM?

100 "Ridley's not known for humor": Author interview with Jeff Berg, 2/26/15.
100 "I knew with Ridley": Author interview with Callie Khouri, 5/12/15.
100 "But she was maybe a tad": Author interview with Ridley Scott, 4/2/15.
101 "Not that she was posh": Ibid.
101 "She's still here": Author interview with David Eidenberg, 12/15/15.
101 "I was attracted to Geena": Author interview with Scott, 4/2/15.
102 "I had read the script": Author interview with Geena Davis, 7/21/14.
102 "I need you to understand": Ibid.
102 "Geena's a tall girl": Author interview with Scott, 4/2/15.
103 "Soooo": Author interview with Davis, 7/21/14.
103 "You know, I've been listening": Ibid.
103 "We will both die": Author interview with Eidenberg, 12/15/15.
103 "Getting *Thelma & Louise*": Author interview with Davis, 2/25/15.
104 "Susan has always been": Author interview with Scott, 4/2/15.
104 "The contrast in": Author interview with Brett Goldstein, 6/25/15.
105 "Geena and Susan are so *not*": Ibid.
105 "I've always made": Author interview with Susan Sarandon, 9/29/14.
105 "I thought it would": Ibid.
105 "I never saw it": Ibid.
106 "There are a lot of questions": This and other quotes from this encounter come from author interviews with Sarandon and Scott.
107 "For a guy's guy, Ridley": Author interview with Goldstein, 6/25/15.
107 "Even though Louise": Author interview with Sarandon, 9/29/14.
107 "It fit into my needs": Ibid.
107 She was content: Author interview with Khouri, 5/12/15.
108 "Those were Ridley's choices": Author interview with Alan Ladd Jr., 11/17/14.
108 "He tended to have the most successful": Author interview with Rebecca Pollack Parker, 2/18/15.
108 "If those are the actresses": Author interview with Ladd, 11/17/14.
108 "Given the star power": Author interview with Diane Cairns, 1/28/15.

CHAPTER 13: "GOOD LUCK, HONEY!"

110 "You don't send *girls* to college": Author interview with Geena Davis, 2/25/15.
110 "Youth," she notes drily: Ibid.
110 "It never occurred to us": Ibid.
111 *Doctor Brewster kisses all the women: Tootsie.* Directed by Sydney Pollack, 1982.
112 "I got a little tired": Author interview with Davis, 2/25/15.
112 "Good luck, honey": Ibid.
112 "I didn't know how": Ibid.
112 "Not that I was the go-to gal": Author interview with Susan Sarandon, 9/29/14.
113 "I didn't know actresses": Claudia Dreifus, "The Playboy Interview: Susan Sarandon," *Playboy*, May 1989.
113 "Acting is a profession": Author interview with Sarandon, 9/29/14.
114 "Anyone who would rub lemons": Ibid.
114 "This scene should be shown": Dreifus, *Playboy*.

114 "I am very stunned and flattered": Ibid.

114 "I said something dumb": Author interview with Sarandon, 9/29/14.

114 "She's the kind of person": Author interview with Lucinda Jenney, 11/12/14.

115 "I don't think I had many problems": Author interview with Sarandon, 9/29/14.

115 "I'm just trying to find roles": Lisa Schwarzbaum, "Driving Force," *Entertainment Weekly,* May 21, 1991.

115 "The thing about having a career": Author interview with Sarandon, 9/29/14.

116 "She's always had a very strong": Schwarzbaum, *Entertainment Weekly.*

117 "I had all these girly ways": Author interview with Davis, 7/21/14.

117 "On page one": Ibid.

117 *People can be like her*: Ibid.

117 "Yeah, I have a problem": Author interview with Sarandon, 9/29/14.

117 Louise has an engagement ring: Callie Khouri, *Thelma and Louise,* First Draft, September 1988, Ridley Scott Collection, USC Cinematic Arts Library.

117 "Here's a woman": Author interview with Sarandon, 9/29/14.

118 "I see your point": Ibid.

118 "It'd be an interesting sex scene": Ibid.

118 *Are you kidding*: Author interview with Davis, 7/21/14.

CHAPTER 14: A FRESH EYE ON AMERICA

119 "She was game and brave": Author interview with Susan Sarandon, 9/29/14.

120 "European filmmakers": Author interview with Hans Zimmer, 11/17/14.

121 "I like the patina": Carl Nolte, "Obituary—John Register," *San Francisco Chronicle,* April 11, 1996.

121 "What do you think": This quote and the continuing conversation: author interview with Ken Haber, 10/20/14.

122 "It's not going to work": Ibid.

123 "In Arkansas, that's not a good idea": Author interview with Ridley Scott, 5/4/15.

123 "I wanted to show America": Ibid.

123 "I love Bakersfield": Ridley Scott, Audio Commentary, *Thelma & Louise,* DVD, MGM, 2003.

124 of top-tier stars: Budget information from Pathé memo by Mel Dellar, February 1, 1990, Margaret Herrick Library, Academy of Motion Picture Arts and Sciences.

124 "Have you ever seen Monument Valley": This quote and subsequent quotes: author interview with Haber, 10/20/14.

CHAPTER 15: REAL CHARACTERS

126 "His friends were a certain": Author interview with Brett Goldstein, 6/25/15.

127 "They didn't give a crap": Ibid.

127 "I am a very niggling caster": Author interview with Ridley Scott, 5/4/15.

127 "Surprise me": Richard Sandomir, "Seeking Ms. Right in Throngs of Ms. Wrongs," *New York Times,* November 24, 1991.

128 TV's *The Mod Squad*: Lists of actors considered for roles from 1990 audition schedules provided by Ira Belgrade.

128 "It was about women, in a real way": Author interview with Harvey Keitel, 3/6/15.

129 "The perception of Harvey": Author interview with Scott, 5/4/15.

129 "He's a very sensitive man": Ridley Scott, Audio Commentary, *Thelma & Louise*, DVD, MGM, 2003.

129 "Why don't you ever cast me": Author interview with Scott, 5/4/15.

129 "You're going to have to": Ibid.

129 "That's cool": Scott, Audio Commentary.

129 "Stop fucking about it": Sheila Weller, "The Ride of a Lifetime," *Vanity Fair*, February 10, 2012.

129 "We need to accept": Philip Thomas, "Girls Just Wanna Have Fun...," *Empire*, August 1991.

130 "Do you know how hard": Author interview with Ira Belgrade, 6/30/15.

130 "He is the funniest guy": Author interview with Geena Davis, 7/21/14.

130 *I'd have to take whatever:* Author interview with Chris McDonald, 10/28/14.

131 "I knew this woman was stuck": Ibid.

132 "I wanted somebody": Scott, Audio Commentary.

133 "Give Madsen a gun": Author interview with Michael Madsen, 11/11/14.

133 "I don't want to play Harlan": This quote and following conversation: author interview with Madsen, 11/11/14.

133 "There's a touch of Elvis Presley": Author interview with Scott, 5/4/15.

134 "If I had known how many times": Author interview with Madsen, 11/11/14.

135 "A lot of what she went on about": Ibid.

135 "He certainly was": Author interview with Susan Sarandon, 9/29/14.

135 "Susan's the kind of girl": Author interview with Madsen, 11/11/14.

CHAPTER 16: "THE *BLOND* ONE!"

136 "Dangerously sexy": Author interview with Ira Belgrade, 6/30/15.

137 "He made the biggest classic mistake": Ibid.

137 "not bad-boyish enough": Ibid.

138 "I don't know who besides Lou": Author interview with Brett Goldstein, 6/25/15.

138 "What's with the toothpick": 1990 audition tapes from the collection of Ira Belgrade.

138 "You would never in a million": Author interview with Belgrade, 6/30/15.

139 "He could play the kind of guy": Author interview with Callie Khouri, 2/5/15.

139 "It was hotter": Ibid.

140 "was the best script I've ever read": Kathryn Shattuck, "Back to the '70s to Find Relief from the '90s," *New York Times*, August 3, 2008.

141 "Hey, Ira": Author interview with Belgrade, 6/30/15.

141 "Whoever nails the hair dryer scene": Ibid.

141 "They were all handsome": Author interview with Geena Davis, 7/21/14.

142 "I want to see a real sociopath": Brad Pitt in *The Last Journey*, documentary by Charles de Lauzirika, Metro-Goldwyn-Mayer Studios video, 2002.

142 *I'm just a guy*: This and following quotes from Callie Khouri, *Thelma & Louise*, Second Draft, April 4, 1990, Ridley Scott Collection, USC Library of Cinematic Arts.

142 "Oh!" she exclaimed: This quote and the following quotes: author interview with Davis, 7/21/14.

143 "Here was this kid": Richard Sandomir, "Seeking Ms. Right in Throngs of Ms. Wrongs," *New York Times*, November 24, 1991.

143 "That Brad Pitt": This quote and subsequent anecdote: author interview with Davis, 7/21/14.

CHAPTER 17: THE GIRLS IN THE THUNDERBIRD

145 "I'll do whatever it takes": Author interview with Geena Davis, 2/25/15.
145 "It was a huge deal": Ibid.
146 *We don't need the lantern*: *Thelma & Louise*. Directed by Ridley Scott, 1991.
146 "Thelma's not silly": Author interview with Davis, 2/25/15.
146 *Careful, careful: Thelma & Louise*. Directed by Ridley Scott, 1991.
147 "You know when somebody is going": Author interview with Susan Sarandon, 10/30/15.
147 "It was a good mix": Author interview with Ridley Scott, 5/4/15.
148 "The fact that Ridley and Norris": Author interview with Michael Hirabayashi, 11/18/14.
148 "Get rid of the damn smoke": Author interview with Harvey Keitel, 3/6/15.
149 "It's hard to find somebody": Author interview with Scott, 5/4/15.
149 "We don't do anything": Author interview with Anne Ahrens, 11/6/14.
150 "The denser the look": Ibid.
150 "We wanted to show chaos": Ibid.
151 "The magic goes through": Ridley Scott, Audio Commentary, *Thelma & Louise*, DVD, MGM, 2003.
151 "She probably goes over it": Ibid.
152 *I left him a note*: *Thelma & Louise*. Directed by Ridley Scott, 1991.

CHAPTER 18: HOT AS A PISTOL

154 "Just so we'd get the taste": Author interview with Geena Davis, 7/21/14.
154 *You said you and me*: *Thelma & Louise*. Directed by Ridley Scott, 1991.
154 *There they are*: Author interview with Callie Khouri, 2/5/15.
154 "It was also so weird": Ibid.
155 "We had a lot of opportunities": Author interview with Michael Hirabayashi, 11/18/14.
155 "We were going for": Author interview with Anne Ahrens, 11/6/14.
155 *It's a good thing*: *Thelma & Louise*. Directed by Ridley Scott, 1991.
156 "The opportunities were entirely": Author interview with Lucinda Jenney, 11/12/14.
156 "It's a tough name": Ibid.
156 "At the time, I didn't have": Ibid.
156 "a Janus-faced guy": Author interview with Brett Goldstein, 6/25/15.
157 "I'm not sure you're threatening enough": Author interview with Timothy Carhart, 10/27/14.
157 "It's a Ridley Scott movie": Ibid.
157 "It's very easy to drop the ball": Ridley Scott, Audio Commentary, *Thelma & Louise*, DVD, MGM, 2003
158 "We need to go quite a way": Author interview with Ridley Scott, 5/4/15.
158 "Geena has the most insane": Author interview with Carhart, 10/27/14.
159 "Grueling, just grueling": Ibid.
159 "Doing it was upsetting": Author interview with Davis, 2/25/15.
159 "What bothers me is": Author interview with Susan Sarandon, 10/30/15.
159 "She points her finger": Author interview with Ridley Scott, 5/4/15.
160 "She's just trying": Author interview with Sarandon, 10/30/15.

160 "I have to run to the car": Betsy Sharkey, "Film: Ridley Scott Tries to Make It Personal," *New York Times,* November 18, 1990.

CHAPTER 19: BAD BOYS

162 *I want you out of here by five*: *Thelma & Louise*. Directed by Ridley Scott, 1991.
162 "That's the funniest thing": Author interview with Chris McDonald, 8/19/14.
162 "Thelma's life was out of her control": Author interview with Anne Ahrens, 11/6/14.
163 "That's how I saw": Ibid.
163 *Funny how so many people*: *Thelma & Louise*. Directed by Ridley Scott, 1991.
163 "He was on the make": Author interview with McDonald, 8/19/14.
163 "because that makes a lion": Ibid.
164 "I kept falling off the dolly": Ridley Scott, Audio Commentary, *Thelma & Louise,* DVD, MGM, 2003.
165 "He'd say, 'I love what'": Author interview with McDonald, 10/28/14.
165 "So often you": Ibid.
165 *Excuse me, you're standing*: *Thelma & Louise*. Directed by Ridley Scott, 1991.
165 "Chris's performance": Author interview with Stephen Tobolowsky, 10/20/14.
166 "It is a business": Ibid.
166 "I don't think it's bad": Ibid.
166 "I just thought that was horseshit": Ibid.
166 "So how do you see yourself": Ibid.
167 "He didn't seem to be": Ibid.
167 *This is an ugly kitchen*: Ibid.
168 "I tried to use my frustration": Ibid.
168 "What are you going to do": Ibid.
168 "You read a line in a script": Ibid.
168 "Steve talks in the film": Author interview with Ridley Scott, 5/4/15.

CHAPTER 20: THE KID ENTERS THE PICTURE

170 "If you run after him,": Subsequent anecdote also from author interview with Lucinda Jenney, 11/12/14.
171 *That's good*: Author interview with Callie Khouri, 2/5/15.
171 "Nobody knew him": Author interview with Michael Madsen, 11/11/14.
171 "Would you like to sit": Author interview with Stephen Tobolowsky, 10/20/14.
171 "I never felt so old and ugly": Stephen Tobolowsky in *The Last Journey*, documentary by Charles de Lauzirika, Metro-Goldwyn-Mayer Studios video, 2002.
171 "I dealt with staying focused": Sheila Weller, "The Ride of a Lifetime," *Vanity Fair,* February 10, 2012.
171 "not necessarily a show": Production memo, May 1, 1990, from the files of assistant director Steve Danton.
172 "By the end of the day": Weller, *Vanity Fair.*
172 *I like your wife*: *Thelma & Louise*. Directed by Ridley Scott, 1991.
172 "I was vicious": Author interview with Chris McDonald, 10/28/14.
172 "He was too strong": Author interview with Harvey Keitel, 3/6/15.

173 "He's got great taste": Ridley Scott, Audio Commentary, *Thelma & Louise*, DVD, MGM, 2003.

173 "What are you going": Subsequent anecdote also from author interview with Michael Madsen, 11/11/14.

174 "Ridley was generous": Author interview with Tobolowsky, 10/20/14.

174 "Ridley's a really masculine guy": Author interview with Madsen, 11/11/14.

CHAPTER 21: WHAT THE FUSS IS ABOUT

175 "But it's just easier to show": Richard Panek, "Some Films Need a Hand, a Hip…" *New York Times*, January 19, 1992.

175 "Very nice": Author interview with Ridley Scott, 5/4/15.

175 "Goddammit, nobody's": Ridley Scott, Audio Commentary, *Thelma & Louise*, DVD, MGM, 2003.

176 "Oh my God, this is going": Geena Davis in *The Last Journey*, documentary by Charles de Lauzirika, Metro-Goldwyn-Mayer Studios video, 2002.

177 "J.D. turns out the light": Final shooting script, *Thelma & Louise*, June 5, 1990, from the collection of Michael Hirabayashi.

177 "You go ahead": Susan Sarandon, Audio Commentary, *Thelma & Louise*, DVD, MGM, 2003.

177 "Lovemaking scenes are always": Author interview with Steve Danton, 1/13/15.

177 "It's a long day": "I didn't plan to be a star!" *Big*, July 8, 1991.

178 "I'm sweating": Brad Pitt in *The Last Journey*.

178 "One of the dilemmas": Ibid.

178 "but I flatlined": Sheila Weller, "The Ride of a Lifetime," *Vanity Fair*, February 10, 2012.

178 "Muss his hair": Ibid.; Geena Davis, Audio Commentary, *Thelma & Louise*, DVD, MGM, 2003.

178 *Ridley, hello*: Author interview with Geena Davis, 2/25/15.

179 "No, she looked pretty": Author interview with Scott, 5/4/15.

179 "What's going on": Author interview with Susan Sarandon, 10/30/15.

179 "It was truly the most incredible": Author interview with Hans Zimmer, 11/17/14.

180 "I do's": Callie Khouri, *Thelma and Louise*, First Draft, September 1988, Ridley Scott Collection, USC Cinematic Arts Library.

180 "They kind of agree": Callie Khouri, Audio Commentary, *Thelma & Louise*, DVD, MGM, 2003.

180 "It's too much of a leap": In this scene, the lines spoken by Sarandon, Madsen and Scott all derive from author interviews with each.

182 *Will you wear this*: Final shooting script, *Thelma & Louise*.

182 *Why? Why now?*: *Thelma & Louise*. Directed by Ridley Scott, 1991.

182 *You didn't see that one comin', did ya*: Ibid.

183 "I thought it was a mistake": Author interview with Callie Khouri, 2/5/15.

183 *Chalk it up to bad timing*: *Thelma & Louise*. Directed by Ridley Scott.

183 "She was particularly brilliant": Author interview with Scott, 5/4/15.

183 "a nice little scene-scene": Author interview with Sarandon, 10/30/15.

184 *I finally understand what all the fuss is about*: *Thelma & Louise*. Directed by Ridley Scott.

184 *Move!*: Ibid.

184 "If you can't get to that": Author interview with Sarandon, 10/30/15.

185 "A lot of people were saying": Author interview with Michael Madsen, 11/11/14.

CHAPTER 22: OWNING THE ROAD

186 "We're in a Ridley Scott movie": Author interviews with Geena Davis, 2/25/15, and Susan Sarandon, 10/30/15.

187 "The experience was": Author interview with Sarandon, 9/29/14.

187 "The joke was": Ibid.

187 "He brought that to it:" Ibid.

187 "Or now there's a *cattle drive*": Craig Seligman, "Settling for Sarandon," *San Francisco Chronicle*, May 27, 1991.

187 "We were shouting": Ibid.

188 "Every scene was a bloody": Ibid.

188 "All those watering machines": Ridley Scott in *The Last Journey*, documentary by Charles de Lauzirika, Metro-Goldwyn-Mayer Studios video, 2002.

189 *Darryl. Go fuck yourself*: *Thelma & Louise.* Directed by Ridley Scott, 1991.

189 "These gigantic trucks covered": Author interview with Anne Ahrens, 11/6/14.

189 "That's all just part": Author interview with Ridley Scott, 5/4/15.

189 "When the script said": Author interview with Sarandon, 9/29/14.

190 *Goddammit, Thelma*: *Thelma & Louise.*" Directed by Ridley Scott, 1991.

190 "It was the only experience": Author interview with Davis, 2/21/14.

190 *If you blow*: *Thelma & Louise.* Directed by Ridley Scott, 1991.

191 "This afternoon": This quote and subsequent anecdote until Sarandon speaks: author interview with Davis, 7/21/14.

191 "Oh, for heaven's sake": Rod Lurie, "Susan Sarandon: Sex, Drugs and Her New Role," *Manhattan Spirit*, May 28, 1991.

191 "Then that's exploitation": Ibid.

191 "Ridley, Geena is not": Author interview with Davis, 7/21/14.

191 "As it turned out": Ibid.

192 "Yeah, fine": Author interview with Scott, 5/4/15.

192 "Thanks a lot": Lurie, *Manhattan Spirit.*

192 "I wanted people to like": Author interview with Davis, 7/21/14.

192 "I hadn't really": Author interview with Sarandon, 9/29/14.

192 "Isn't it fun with girls": Author interview with Davis, 7/21/14.

193 "Look, she's more diplomatic": Lurie, *Manhattan Spirit.*

193 "Ridley pretty much listened": Author interview with Sarandon.

193 Back then, women: Estimate from author interview with Stephen Follows of Stephen Follows Film Data and Education, 1/28/16.

194 *"Thelma & Louise* had a different": Author interview with Ahrens, 11/6/14.

194 *"Thelma & Louise* was the opposite": Author interview with Ken Turek, 11/18/14.

194 "They were almost insulted": Ibid.

195 "She must be on the": Ibid.

195 "The female set": Ibid.

195 "Gentlemen": Author interview with Candace Allen, 1/17/15.

195 Kathy Nelson resolved: Author interview with Kathy Nelson, 1/21/15.

195 "guy banter and gags": Author interview with Ahrens, 11/6/14.
196 Geena without a top on: *Thelma & Louise* storyboards, from the collection of
   Michael Hirabayashi.
196 "I don't think the guys": Author interview with Steve Danton, 1/13/15.
196 "I don't think he": Author interview with Tracy DeFreitus, 11/15/14.
196 "He was mischievous": Author interview with Jason Beghe, 5/7/15.
197 "Ridley is pretty interesting": Seligman, *San Francisco Chronicle.*
197 "Part of what made": Author interview with Hans Zimmer, 11/17/14.
197 *Was this all too good*: Author interview with Scott, 5/4/15.

CHAPTER 23: SOMETHING'S CROSSED OVER

198 "dining is poor to fair": *Thelma & Louise* production memo, June 25, 1990,
   property of Michael Hirabayashi.
200 "This gave him some humanity": Author interview with Chris McDonald, 10/28/14.
200 *I don't remember ever feelin'*: *Thelma & Louise*. Directed by Ridley Scott, 1991.
201 "I knew I was": Author interview with Susan Sarandon, 10/30/15.
201 "You gotta get me": Author interview with Ken Haber, 10/20/14.
201 "We've been in the car": Author interview with Sarandon, 10/30/15.
202 "Actors offer suggestions": Ibid.
202 *Something's crossed over*: *Thelma & Louise*. Directed by Ridley Scott, 1991.
202 "I actually cried when": Author interview with Thom Noble, 5/13/15.
203 *The police radio, Louise*: *Thelma & Louise*. Directed by Ridley Scott, 1991.
203 "I have a different take": Author interview with Jason Beghe, 5/7/15.
203 "I looked rigid and vain": Ibid.
204 *Ma'am, please: Thelma & Louise*. Directed by Ridley Scott, 1991.
204 "I suppose today": Author interview with Beghe, 5/7/15.
205 "Once I've chosen a script": Author interview with Ridley Scott, 5/4/15.
205 "I don't think you can": Author interview with Callie Khouri, 5/12/15.
205 "I think she proved a certain": Author interview with Diane Cairns, 1/30/15.
206 "I think it's the perfect": Author interview with Scott, 4/2/15.
206 "Yeah, but they'll hate it": Ibid.
206 "We spent a couple hours": Author interview with Greg Foster, 3/24/15.
206 "Your traditional young": Ibid.

CHAPTER 24: READY, STEADY, BLOW

209 Harlan's hands hike up: Notes of Luca Kouimelis, script supervisor, 1/15/15.
209 "They didn't tell me": Author interview with Timothy Carhart, 10/27/14.
209 "I won't get a date": Author interview with Marco St. John, 6/19/15.
209 "Try five": Ibid.
210 "I think Ridley did": Author interview with Susan Sarandon, 10/30/15.
210 "I was mortified": Author interview with St. John, 6/19/15.
210 "My wife was very courageous": Ibid.
211 *Hey baby*: Ibid.
211 "I thought he pulled it off": Ridley Scott in *The Last Journey*, documentary by
   Charles de Lauzirika, Metro-Goldwyn-Mayer Studios video, 2002.
211 "I know guys": Author interview with St. John, 6/19/15.

211 "Yes, there is something clownish": Author interview with Brett Goldstein, 6/25/15.

211 "like there was a glass case": Author interview with St. John, 6/19/15.

211 "He was a caricature": Author interview with Callie Khouri, 8/12/14.

212 "howl at the top": Final shooting script, *Thelma & Louise*, June 5, 1990, from the collection of Michael Hirabayashi.

212 "I wanted to be somber": Author interview with Sarandon, 10/30/15.

212 *We think you have really bad manners*: Final shooting script, *Thelma & Louise*.

212 *How would you feel*: *Thelma & Louise*. Directed by Ridley Scott, 1991.

212 *Huh? What are you*: Ibid.

212 "It's not threatening": Ridley Scott, Audio Commentary, *Thelma & Louise*, DVD, MGM, 2003.

213 "You don't have to": Author interview with St. John, 6/19/15.

213 "Um, you've cleared everybody": Author interview with Sarandon, 10/30/15.

213 "It's not safe": Ibid.

213 "Well, get stunt people": Author interview with Geena Davis, 7/21/14.

213 "It had to go before": Author interview with Ridley Scott, 5/4/15.

213 "What the hell was that": Author interview with Davis, 7/21/14.

214 "It was a giant explosion": Author interview with Greg Foster, 5/1/15.

215 "It was like an": Author interview with Mimi Polk Gitlin, 7/22/14.

215 "It was something": Author interview with Sarandon, 10/30/15.

215 "Oh, you're one": Author interview with Jason Beghe, 5/7/15.

215 "I'll interact to a point": Author interview with Scott, 5/4/15.

216 "Because this was a women's film": Crew member, off the record.

216 "I'm always like that": Author interview with Sarandon, 10/30/15.

216 "Sometimes I would": Rod Lurie, "Susan Sarandon: Sex, Drugs and Her New Role," *Manhattan Spirit*, May 28, 1991.

216 "I don't remember it that way": Author interview with Sarandon, 10/30/15.

216 "Susan Sarandon is like": Author interview with Ken Turek, 11/18/14.

217 "I didn't notice her": Author interview with Michael Madsen, 11/11/14.

217 "With two very collaborative": Betsy Sharkey, "Film: Ridley Scott Tries to Make It Personal," *New York Times*, November 18, 1990.

217 "I listened, yeah": Author interview with Scott, 5/4/15.

217 "The only way": Richard Guilliatt, "Queen Bee," *Sunday Times* (London), July 6, 1991.

217 "Susan saved the picture": Author interview with Khouri, 5/12/15.

CHAPTER 25: OFF THE CLIFF

219 "Stop," Ridley ordered: Author interview with Anne Ahrens, 11/6/14.

219 *I guess I went a little crazy, huh*: *Thelma & Louise*. Directed by Ridley Scott, 1991.

220 "I wanted to be there with them": Ridley Scott, Audio Commentary, *Thelma & Louise*, DVD, MGM, 2003.

220 "It was sick how much": Author interview with Steve Danton, 1/13/15.

221 "It was physically taxing": Author interview with Stephen Tobolowsky, 10/20/14.

222 "I didn't believe": Author interview with Ridley Scott, 5/4/15.

222 "I think we had forty setups": Ibid.

222 "We are *going*": Ibid.

223 "I'll operate": Geena Davis, Audio Commentary, *Thelma & Louise*, DVD, MGM, 2003.

223 "This was it": Author interview with Geena Davis, 7/21/14.
223 "Everyone had become": Author interview with Ahrens, 11/6/14.
223 *Let's keep goin'*: *Thelma & Louise*. Directed by Ridley Scott, 1991.
223 "We did two takes": Author interview with Davis, 7/21/14.

CHAPTER 26: KEEP ON FLYING

224 "A perfect picture is rare": Author interview with Thom Noble, 5/13/15.
224 "Harvey was the most difficult": Ibid.
225 "People make fun of me": Ibid.
225 "It's a personality issue": Ibid.
226 *I'm kinda stuck here*: *Thelma & Louise*. Directed by Ridley Scott, 1991.
226 "That guy was perfect": Author interview with Noble, 5/13/15.
226 "When we first assembled": Ibid.
226 "If we had left that scene": Author interview with Hans Zimmer, 11/17/14.
227 "It was absolutely beautiful": Author interview with Noble, 5/13/15.
228 "I knew everything": Author interview with Kathy Nelson, 1/21/15.
229 "The movie dictates": Author interview with Zimmer, 11/17/14.
230 "I knew Ridley wasn't": Ibid.
230 "There's a rawness": Ibid.
230 "I'll be back on Monday": Ibid.
231 "He gave wings to the music": Ibid.
231 "I was a lot younger then": Ibid.

CHAPTER 27: MASSACRE AT THE MULTIPLEX

233 "worked, sort of": Author interview with Greg Foster, 3/24/15.
233 "Most movies were made": Ibid.
234 "The trick was not to undermine": Author interview with Rebecca Pollack Parker, 2/18/15.
234 *Okay, they're with the movie*: Author interview with Foster, 5/1/15.
234 "And you could hear it": Ibid.
235 Cries of "No": Ibid.
235 "What the fuck": Author interview with Alan Ladd Jr., 11/17/14.
235 "It changed": Author interview with Foster, 5/1/15.
235 trailed the norm at 71 percent: Results from test screenings are documented in Pathé memorandum by Greg Foster, Christine Birch, "Market Research: 'Thelma and Louise,' Recruited Production Screenings," November 2, 1990, Margaret Herrick Library, Academy of Motion Picture Arts and Sciences.
235 "It was polarizing": Author interview with Foster, 5/1/15.
235 "It was a disaster": Author interview with Ladd, 11/17/14.
235 "He was crestfallen": Ibid.
235 "The preview process": Author interview with Pollack Parker, 2/18/15.
237 "When people in the audience": Ibid.
237 "People applauded, they cheered": Author interview with Foster, 5/1/15.
237 "From that moment on": Ibid.
237 "Everything about that movie": Ibid.
238 "The center of it held": Author interview with Pollack Parker, 11/19/14.

238 "It was a nightmare": Author interview with Ladd, 11/17/14.

239 "This was a word-of-mouth movie": Author interview with Foster, 5/1/15.

239 "What a great, radical movie": This and other test screening comments are from multiple Pathé memos at the Margaret Herrick Library.

239 "Ridley really *did* get": Author interview with Diane Cairns, 1/30/15.

239 "They *cheered*": Ibid.

240 "It wouldn't have been": Author interview with Callie Khouri, 5/12/15.

240 "It was so much more heightened": Author interview with Amanda Temple, 4/13/15.

240 "I've been waiting a long time": Author interview with Khouri, 5/12/15.

240 "When she saw the cut": Author interview with Ridley Scott, 5/4/15.

240 Callie wasn't invited: Author interviews with Cairns, 1/30/15, and Khouri, 5/12/15.

CHAPTER 28: THE SNOWBALL EFFECT

242 "reckless exhilaration": "Review: 'Thelma & Louise,'" *Variety*, December 31, 1990.

243 "It reimagines the buddy film": Janet Maslin, "Review/Film; On the Run with 2 Buddies and a Gun," *New York Times*, May 24, 1991.

243 "a genuine pop myth": Jack Kroll, "Back on the Road Again," *Newsweek*, May 26, 1991.

243 "I don't know why": David Denby, "Road Warriors," *New York*, June 10, 1991.

243 "this is one chick movie": Rita Kempley, "Thelma & Louise," *Washington Post*, May 24, 1991.

243 "The movie has the look": Terrence Rafferty, "Outlaw Princesses," *New Yorker*, June 3, 1991.

244 "provocative, poignant": Kenneth Turan, "Movie Reviews: Smooth Ride for 'Thelma & Louise,'" *Los Angeles Times*, May 24, 1991.

244 "sisterhood bash-a-thon": Peter Rainer and Sheila Benson, "True or False: Thelma & Louise Just Good Ol' Boys?" *Los Angeles Times*, May 31, 1991.

244 "THELMA & LOUISE" RAISES QUESTION: Craig MacInnis, "The Real Guys: 'Thelma & Louise' raises question why recent movies can only show women making progress by making men look like idiots," *Toronto Star*, June 22, 1991.

244 "Horrible role models": Liz Smith, "'Just Say No' Gets New Shot," *Newsday*, June 4, 1991.

244 "It justifies armed robbery": Richard Johnson, *New York Daily News*, quoted in Richard Schickel, "Gender Bender," *Time*, June 24, 1991.

244 TOXIC FEMINISM: John Leo, "Toxic Feminism on the Big Screen," *U.S News & World Report*, June 10, 1991.

245 "People are out of their minds": Author interview with Callie Khouri, 8/12/14.

245 "I was just hoping": Author interview with Geena Davis, 7/21/14.

245 "After all the shit": Author interview with Khouri, 8/12/14.

246 "My God, now the *women* have guns": Author interview with Davis, 7/21/14.

246 "Go watch a Marty Scorsese": Author interview with Khouri, 8/12/14.

246 "Three people died": Author interview with Davis, 7/21/14.

246 Sylvester Stallone's Rambo: For this and other statistics from action movies: John Mueller, "Dead and Deader," *Los Angeles Times*, January 20, 2008.

246 The number of fatalities: Vincent Canby, "Critic's Notebook: Now at a Theater Near You: A Skyrocketing Body Count," *New York Times*, July 16, 1990.

247 "Well, compared with the prostitute": "Women Who Kill Too Much," *Newsweek,* June 16, 1991.

247 "It's something as simple": Janet Maslin, "Film View: Lay Off 'Thelma and Louise,'" *New York Times,* June 16, 1991.

247 "it's hostile toward idiots": Larry Rohter, "The Third Woman of 'Thelma and Louise,'" *New York Times,* June 5, 1991.

247 "I don't believe the male species": Sheila Johnston, "Hidden Gender," *Independent,* June 29, 1991.

247 "I don't think the movie": Kristine McKenna, "Up and Coming: The Bad Boy Makes Good," *New York Times,* July 7, 1991.

247 "I think people were freaked out": Author interview with Susan Sarandon, 9/29/14.

249 "Wipe my back": Author interview with Kathie Berlin, 12/21/14.

250 "in the honorable line of movies": Richard Schickel, "Gender Bender," *Time,* June 24, 1991.

250 IS THIS WHAT FEMINISM IS ALL ABOUT: Margaret Carlson, "Is This What Feminism Is All About?" *Time,* June 24, 1991.

250 "Why," she asked: Schickel, *Time.*

250 The following Friday and Saturday: Geraldine Fabrikant, "MGM-Pathé's Suprise: A Low-Cost Hit," *New York Times,* June 3, 1991.

251 "a bloody miracle": Fabrikant, *New York Times.*

251 Had Pathé been able: Ronald Grover, "Can Alan Ladd Jr. Make Leo the Lion Roar?" *BusinessWeek,* August 11, 1991.

251 The producer-showman: Author interview with Davis, 7/21/14.

251 The video seized: Dennis Hunt, "'Thelma & Louise' Sets a Speed Record," *Los Angeles Times,* May 29, 1992.

251 "The longevity of it": Author interview with Greg Foster, 5/1/15.

251 *I think we got some kind*: *Thelma & Louise.* Directed by Ridley Scott, 1991.

251 "A lot of women love": Fawn Vrazo, "Sexism or Sweet Revenge?" *Philadelphia Inquirer,* July 5, 1991.

252 "Thelma and Louise hit Chicago": "Women Who Kill Too Much," *Newsweek.*

252 "I'd be like, hmmm": Author interview with Davis, 7/21/14.

CHAPTER 29: WHO KILLED THELMA AND LOUISE?

253 "Ten years from now": Peter Keough, "Who's Bashing Who?" *Boston Phoenix,* May 24, 1991.

254 "It was like getting shot": Author interview with Callie Khouri, 5/12/15.

254 "I just never found": Ibid.

254 "It didn't turn out": Ibid.

255 "Possibly": Lynn Barber, "Ridley Scott: 'Talking to actors was tricky—I had no idea where they were coming from,'" *Guardian,* January 6, 2002.

256 "Guess what, they made it": Memo to Ridley Scott from Chris Zarpas, May 28, 1997, Ridley Scott Archive, USC Cinematic Arts Library.

256 "Geena Davis will go the distance": Kevin Sessums, "Geena's Sheen," *Vanity Fair,* September 1992.

256 "Unfortunately, it was": Author interview with David Eidenberg, 12/15/15.

257 "I guess I thought my career": Kate Coyne, "Geena Davis from Heartbreak to Happiness," *Good Housekeeping,* April 2006.

257 "Um," Geena said: Author interview with Geena Davis, 7/21/14.
258 "I don't think the studios": Nigel M. Smith, "Susan Sarandon and Geena Davis: Hollywood hasn't had an epiphany since 'Thelma & Louise,'" *Guardian,* May 16, 2016.
258 "I played some nice people": Author interview with Michael Madsen, 11/11/14.
258 "Oh my God, it's that guy": Author interview with Chris McDonald, 10/28/14.
259 "I was thrilled": Ibid.
259 "I ask them": Author interview with Stephen Tobolowsky, 10/20/14.
259 "It's shocking": Ibid.

CHAPTER 30: A FILM OF THEIR OWN

263 "squishies" and "toasters": Author interview with Linda Woolverton, 3/28/15.
263 "The media narrative": Author interview with Geena Davis, 7/21/14.
263 Of the top-fifty movies: Box-office rankings from Box Office Mojo, cross-referenced with credits from Internet Movie Database.
263 male characters have steadily outnumbered: Stacy L. Smith, Marc Choueiti and Katherine Pieper, "Gender Bias Without Borders," USC Annenberg School for Communication and Journalism, for the Geena Davis Institute on Gender in Media, 2014.
263 That women consistently make up less: Stacy L. Smith, Marc Choueiti and Katherine Pieper, "Inequality in 800 Popular Films: Examining Portrayals of Gender, Race/Ethnicity, LGBT, and Disability from 2007-2015," USC Annenberg School for Communication and Journalism, September 2016.
264 Even crowd scenes: Smith, Choueiti et al. "Gender Bias Without Borders."
264 more than three times as likely: Smith, Choueiti et al., "Inequality in 800 Popular Films."
264 rarely got to see women and girls: Martha M. Lauzen, "It's a Man's (Celluloid) World: Portrayals of Female Characters in the Top 100 Films of 2015," Center for the Study of Women in Television and Film, San Diego State University, 2015.
264 "because that's who they see": Author interview with Davis, 7/21/14.
264 Ninety-nine of them: Emily Greenhouse, "Geena Davis Is Still Locked and Loaded," Bloomberg.com, March 16, 2015.
265 "Now it's so expensive": Author interview with Jane Fonda, 2/16/15.
265 Maggie Gyllenhaal was told: Sharon Waxman, "Maggie Gyllenhaal on Hollywood Ageism: I Was Told 37 Is 'Too Old' for a 55-Year-Old Love Interest," *The Wrap,* May 20, 2015.
265 Catherine Hardwicke: Nosheen Iqbal, "*Miss You Already*'s Catherine Hardwicke: 'Only 4% of films directed by women make it. Why?'" *Guardian,* September 21, 2015.
265 It took the infamous Sony Pictures: Maureen Dowd, "The Women of Hollywood Speak Out," *New York Times Magazine,* November 20, 2015.
266 "I think Callie didn't know": Author interview with Hans Zimmer, 11/17/14.
266 The *Atlantic* in 2011: Raina Lipsitz, "'Thelma & Louise': The Last Great Film About Women," *Atlantic,* August 31, 2011.
266 members of show-business royalty: "Hollywood's 100 Favorite Films," *Hollywood Reporter,* June 25, 2014.

EPILOGUE

267 "bloody silly": Ridley Scott, Audio Commentary, *Thelma & Louise*, DVD, MGM, 2003.

268 "Seven nominations on the shelf": Billy Crystal, Academy Award Ceremony, March 30, 1992.

269 *Okay now, here's the big one*: Author interview with Callie Khouri, 5/12/15.

269 "Ridley, I couldn't thank you": Callie Khouri, Academy Award Ceremony, March 30, 1992.

270 "In fact, my brother was": Ibid.

270 "For everybody that wanted": Ibid.

INDEX